Climate, Catastrophe, and Faith

Climate, Catastrophe, and Faith

Climate, Catastrophe, and Faith

How Changes in Climate Drive Religious Upheaval

PHILIP JENKINS

OXFORD
UNIVERSITY PRESS

OXFORD
UNIVERSITY PRESS

Oxford University Press is a department of the University of Oxford. It furthers the University's objective of excellence in research, scholarship, and education by publishing worldwide. Oxford is a registered trade mark of Oxford University Press in the UK and certain other countries.

Published in the United States of America by Oxford University Press
198 Madison Avenue, New York, NY 10016, United States of America.

Library of Congress Control Number: 2021930033
ISBN 978-0-19-750621-9

DOI: 10.1093/oso/9780197506219.001.0001

1 3 5 7 9 8 6 4 2

Printed by LSC Communications, United States of America

For Diana

Contents

Note on Dates

The English calendar differed from Continental usage before 1752, when the variation amounted to eleven days. All dates here are presented according to the Continental system, or "new style," and the year is taken as beginning on January 1. That is important when I am describing periods of intense and rapid change, such as occurred between 1739 and 1742.

Acknowledgments

I am blessed with a splendid range of generous colleagues at Baylor University's Institute for Studies of Religion, including David Jeffrey, Byron Johnson, Tommy Kidd, and Gordon Melton. Special thanks to the incredibly knowledgeable Jeff Levin. Thanks also to Beth Barr and Barry Hankins, and (yet again) to the miraculous Cynthia Read of Oxford University Press. Thanks to Kathryn Hume for reading the manuscript.

Half a century ago, as an undergraduate at Cambridge University, I was supervised in social and economic history by the brilliant Roger Schofield (1937–2019), of the Cambridge Group for the History of Population and Social Structure. As it happened, these were precisely the years that the modern historical study of climate was being born, and Schofield and his colleagues were deeply conscious of the importance of that new movement for their own work in demography and social history. At the time, I had little inkling of just how cutting-edge was the work he and his friends were doing, or of how incredibly fortunate I was to share in those insights, however marginally. Nor did I realize how much those lessons would form my own thinking on historical matters, or think that they might someday find expression in a book of my own. My gratitude, then, to Roger Schofield for that early inspiration.

Thanks above all to my wife, Liz Jenkins.

1
From Disaster to Belief

Three things exercise a constant influence over the minds of men: climate, government and religion. . . . That is the only way of explaining the enigma of this world.

—Voltaire

In July 1741, Congregational minister Jonathan Edwards delivered one of the most influential sermons in American history. He warned his alarmed hearers of their utterly sinful state, of how that sin had thoroughly earned God's severe and eternal punishment. At every moment, their continued existence depended on God's extraordinary and unmerited self-restraint, which alone prevented them from falling into damnation. His hearers themselves were utterly powerless to affect their own rescue. They were "sinners in the hands of an angry God." The sermon had a transformative effect on the congregation, whose "shrieks and cries were piercing and amazing." That address is one of the most admired and studied pieces of rhetoric in American history, and it has earned the attention of scholars of history, communications, and English literature, as well as students of religion. Although it did not of itself launch the mighty revival that we call the Great Awakening, which had slowly been gathering strength for some years, it was one of its early landmarks. Observers at the time dated the movement's full flowering to the years 1740–1741.[1]

Historians place the sermon in its context, noting the underlying divisions within New England Puritanism and the theological disputes in which Edwards was involved. Rarely do they stress one fact that surely should be treated prominently: namely, that Edwards and his audience had in just the previous two years lived through a horrific period of extreme weather and glacial cold. Across Europe and North America, nations recorded some of the most alarming death rates seen in several centuries, while New England itself suffered the worst weather recorded since the time of European settlement.

Nor was it obvious that the climatic nightmares of 1740–1741 did not represent a new normal, one that would persist through coming years. Perhaps the world's end really was nigh, as the language of apocalypse became alarmingly plausible. People felt utterly powerless in the face of Nature and the God who ruled it. Such conditions could not fail to make any audience deeply attentive to the grim warnings of the Reverend Mr. Edwards.[2]

Of course, the climate-driven crisis did not of itself spark or create the Great Awakening, and Edwards's sermon made no direct reference to that background. Yet it is difficult to comprehend the movement's explosive growth at that very time without acknowledging that component. Similarly, throughout history, when other climate-related disasters have occurred, they have commonly had wide-ranging religious consequences. How could they not? As climate conditions have changed over time, they have affected human affairs and shaped attitudes. At times those conditions might have promoted prosperity, abundant food supplies, fertility, and general contentment. Quite frequently, though, we can identify periods of acute harm, either short-lived, such as that of 1739–1742, or much longer-lasting, such as the repeated hammer blows during the prolonged cooling period that has been termed the Little Ice Age.[3]

Climate and Faith

Time and again, climate convulsions have been understood in religious terms, through the language of apocalypse, millennium, and Judgment. Often too, such eras have been marked by far-reaching changes in the nature of religion and spirituality. As in the case of the Great Awakening, this does not mean that climatic conditions directly caused such outbreaks or currents; rather, they created an atmosphere in which those changes could manifest themselves, and in historical terms this happened very suddenly. Depending on the circumstances, the response to climatic visitations might include explosions in religious passion and commitment, the stirring of mystical and apocalyptic expectations, waves of religious scapegoating and persecution, or the spawning of new religious movements and revivals. In many cases, such responses have had lasting impacts, to the point of fundamentally reshaping particular faith traditions. From those eras have emerged passionate sects—some political and theocratic, some revivalistic and enthusiastic, others millenarian and subversive. The movements and ideas emerging from such conditions might last for many decades and even become a familiar part of the religious landscape, although with their origins in particular moments of crisis increasingly consigned to remote memory. By stirring conflicts and provoking persecutions that defined themselves in religious terms, such eras have redrawn the world's religious maps and created the global concentrations of believers that we know today.[4]

Throughout history, climate and climate change have been key drivers of religious development—not, of course, every innovation or movement, but many of them, and in remarkable diversity. Within Christianity, the warmth and prosperity of the High Middle Ages shaped the forms of Catholic faith and doctrine that emerged in that era and which served as a foundation for later times. Very different and much harsher climate conditions created the turbulence and polarization from which Tridentine Catholicism emerged in the 1560s. Several eras of climate stress played a role in the emergence and evolution of Protestantism, especially in its evangelical forms. Successive crises were essential to the rise and growth of the Calvinism that was such a vital force in the early modern era, as well as of Anglo-American Puritanism. Other later, transformative periods shaped evangelical and revivalist Protestantism and gave rise to many lesser-known sects, great and small. Climate factors likewise had their impact on important movements within other traditions, including Buddhism and Islam. Any historical account that ignores or underplays that climate dimension is lacking.

That history must come to mind when we contemplate the global climatic pressures that are predicted for the coming decades, and which will have their most acute effect in certain highly populated parts of the world. Based on extensive past experience, we can imagine many ways in which the response to those circumstances might take religious forms. We could foresee the rise of new apocalyptic movements, as well as the spread of bitter religiously based animosity and conflict. Although we cannot predict future events with any certainty, our historical background provides some guidance as to likely patterns. When we look at contemporary developments in both Islam and Christianity and at interfaith conflicts across Africa and Asia, it is difficult to imagine that catastrophic climatic changes might not inspire religious responses. When we trace the historical impact of climate-related change, particularly in the religious context, we see auguries of our likely futures.

Religious Revolutions

It is always tempting to write the history of religion and religious change in terms of ideas: new insights, the arguments they provoke, and the movements they inspire. When we discuss movements such as the European Reformation or the American Great Awakening, we focus on the key individuals who presented those ideas—reformers and preachers, thinkers and theologians. Such figures are portrayed in terms of individual genius, or even divine election, but leadership is a function of followership. Individuals gain a reputation for being charismatic if they appeal precisely to the needs and expectations of their audiences, who project their hopes onto a leader. Comprehending climate factors helps explain the attitudes of those popular audiences, and (often) the desperation with which they await a special spiritual messenger or prophet, even a messiah. Depending on circumstances, a prophetic claim might inspire countless thousands, or it can be ignored utterly. Institutions might flourish, or they might fail.

Scholars rightly resist the temptation to reduce religion to simple material terms, and environmental determinism has a long and sometimes controversial history. But if the material basis to social and cultural change is not everything, neither is it nothing. Throughout history, religious change has been inextricably bound up with cycles of economic prosperity and failure, of boom and catastrophe, which manifest themselves in political and cultural terms no less than economic ones. Such cycles have diverse origins, which may or may not be linked to climate. In many cases, though, eras of transformation leave little alternative to a climate-based interpretation.[5]

That particularly applies to those periods in religious life and thought that can be termed revolutionary. By this, I mean the fast-paced moments of transformation and innovation, concentrated within a few years or a decade, that have so often proved critical to the development of religions—to so many of the great revivals, conflicts, persecutions, awakenings, and reformations. At such times, ideas and currents that have gradually been developing in society suddenly and swiftly gain very wide influence as the process of gaining adherents accelerates startlingly. During such periods, conditions and expectations change so much, and so abruptly, that after the event it is difficult even to recall how things were in the old world. Some of these eras are well known and easily labeled: the sixteenth-century Reformation is one such time. But other eras too play a quite disproportionate role in the process of religious change and development, and commonly these are also moments of worldly catastrophe. The years around 1740 fit in this category.[6]

We might apply the biological notion of punctuated equilibrium, which is so central to theories of evolution. According to this theory, changes occur over extended periods, but at very unequal rates. For long stretches of time, biological changes are slight and gradual, to the extent that conditions appear almost static. That seeming stability masks the gradual changes that are accumulating powerfully below the surface. Under various external forces, perhaps driven by climate, the pace of change then accelerates intensely, with rapid and obvious development and diversification. As the crisis fades, conditions once more resume something approaching stasis or equilibrium. However short-lived those transformative eras might appear in the full span of historical time, their influence is profound and enduring. If we make appropriate adjustments for the behavior of human societies, something like that pattern marks the story of religious change and development. Movements arise and develop slowly and gradually, but short eras of revolutionary change produce breakneck acceleration, and the resulting forms in turn serve as the foundation for later growth.[7]

Sometimes a crisis or revival is largely confined to one region or country, and it must be understood in terms of local conditions and circumstances. We might look for a purely local series of conflicts and grievances, such as a response to a singularly inept or malicious regime. But commonly, such events coincide with similar upsurges in other regions and even other faiths, although there is no sign of direct influence from one to the other. These moments are often characterized by larger trends that did not necessarily have anything directly to do with religion at all but rather with crop failures and famines, plagues, and natural disasters. Such eras are richly productive of wars and rebellions, of demographic crises and hunger riots, of pogroms and witchcraft panics, and of apocalyptic and millenarian outbreaks. Such dreadful times of social turmoil, starvation, and mass mortality simultaneously affect societies that are geographically widely separated and unconnected. Of necessity, a widespread concatenation of disasters must make us consider the role of factors and influences beyond the merely local and specific, and that must include a climate dimension.

To make this point is in no sense to trivialize the content or message of a religious event or revolution, but rather to supply its essential context. We need to understand why people in particular eras felt such stress, fear, and anxiety, which is expressed in religious forms.

Climate and Catastrophe

As I will suggest in Chapter 2, we can identify multiple mechanisms that cause major climatic shocks, which might or might not be truly global in scale: some might affect the whole planet, others just particular regions, such as the North Atlantic world or East Asia.

Volcanoes have often had such effects. In 43 BCE, a formidable eruption (probably in the Aleutian Islands) darkened the skies worldwide, alarming observers in China, Egypt, and the Roman Mediterranean. In Rome itself, still reeling from the assassination of Julius Caesar, the event was felt to be a dreadful omen of judgment, which contributed to the destabilization and collapse of the Republic. In the 530s CE, a terrifying pair of eruptions caused crises in many parts of the world. The event at Ilopango in Central America in 536 had a global impact. In the words of one observer in the eastern Mediterranean:

> The sun gave forth its light without brightness, like the moon, during this whole year, and it seemed exceedingly like the sun in eclipse, for the beams it shed were not clear nor such as it is accustomed to shed. And from the time when this thing happened men were free neither from war, nor pestilence, nor any other thing leading to death.

That event provoked global cooling, a full-scale volcanic winter, which was followed within four years or so by another massive explosion at some other presently unknown point. The result was a dire famine in large parts of the world, and enormous social dislocation. Some scholars describe the following century or so as a "Late Antique Little Ice Age." We can trace the ruin wrought by the dark skies of the 530s in Central America, of course, but also as far away as India and China. In 541, humanity's woes increased still further with the onset of a deadly plague, named for the then-ruling Roman emperor Justinian. The Plague of Justinian, perhaps the worst global pandemic before the Black Death of the 1340s, would not vanish entirely for two centuries, and it killed many millions. Another catastrophe was the 1815 eruption of Mount Tambora in what is now Indonesia, which literally cast a shadow around the globe, causing agricultural crises and political unrest for several years throughout Europe and North America.[8]

Such eruptions might be one-off events, black swans in the broad course of human affairs, but in other instances we are looking at long-term climatic cycles. One such was the global cooling phenomenon that occurred from the thirteenth century through the mid-nineteenth, the Little Ice Age, to which I will often have cause to return in the course of the present book. To be sure, this "ice age" was anything but monolithic or universal, and it saw nothing like consistently cold temperatures over that half millennium. It is better to imagine the period in terms of a series of frigid spells, interspersed with eras of relative normality or even unusual warmth. But some of those cold patches stand out as particularly severe, and at their worst, climate conditions could threaten the existence of states and societies. In the 1640s, climate-driven famines created what is termed the General Crisis of governments and social structures in many different parts of the globe. The causes of such cycles are not fully understood, but one key factor is the El Niño cycle in the Pacific Ocean, and extreme El Niño events shape climate over much of the globe. In ways that are still not fully understood, those long cycles are related to volcanic action, and the centuries of the Little Ice Age were associated with intense and frequent volcanism, chiefly in and around the Pacific.[9]

As I will stress, such episodes were qualitatively different from the global warming menace that has emerged in recent decades as a consequence of carbon emissions. But they were nevertheless very severe, and their known consequences offer a terrifying portent of the possible impact of the modern-day crisis.

Four Horsemen

To understand the broad consequences of such climatic phenomena, we can usefully deploy the biblical language of the Four Horsemen of the book of Revelation, the original apocalypse. Famine, plague, death, and war all rode closely together, and all were shaped by climatic forces.

The connection between climate and food supplies is obvious enough, but just how bad things could become, and how rapidly, has to be emphasized for people in the modern West. It is sobering to realize how close Euro-Americans in quite recent times were to what we today might call Third World conditions of undernourishment and precarious survival. Not until well into the nineteenth century, and initially in western Europe and North America, do we see the emergence of societies in which city dwellers outnumbered rural people. Only gradually, with the rise of industry, were societies able to create enough buffers against failures in the food supply, through global trading networks and effective methods of storage and preservation. The concept of food security is an unnervingly modern development.[10]

Through most of human history, the great majority of people in any community have been directly engaged in various forms of food production, and they have naturally depended on favorable weather conditions and natural cycles. Whether or not people openly admitted the fact, all other professions and activities ultimately relied on the success of those productive activities. Ultimately, the farmer fed all. The whole glittering superstructure of towns and cities, royal courts and aristocratic houses, monasteries and temples existed and flourished only so long as crops grew and rents and taxes were paid. When the climate changed, often with little warning, the whole system could falter and fail, and precipitously. A climate shock—such as the effects of a major volcanic eruption or the larger cooling trend—inflicted multiple harms. Meanwhile, spectacular weather events such as torrential rain destroyed crops outright. Droughts were no less lethal.

In normal circumstances in the premodern West, a single bad harvest was not a catastrophe, as some food reserves usually existed. Two or three bad years wreaked real havoc, but it was when four or five bad years succeeded one another that things moved into the realm of catastrophe. The effects reverberated through the whole of society and ultimately affected all classes. Bad harvests meant food shortages, nonpayment of rents, defaults and debt crises, and sharply declining trade. If food was available at all, it became wildly expensive or dear—hence the term "dearth." People starved and died, the children and elderly being the first to perish. Miscarriages became more common. It was at that point that we begin to talk of subsistence crisis or years of crisis mortality, outright famine, and social breakdown. Poverty rates soared, as did crime and vagrancy, and food riots or tax revolts could easily explode. Such disasters betokened bad times for everyone, landowners and merchants as well as peasants.[11]

In the longer term, the new conditions shortened growing seasons by a month or more, and reduced the areas in which crops could be grown. Higher-altitude areas suffered particularly. Such changes were especially damaging for marginal areas into which people had expanded during the favorable periods. As life in such areas ceased to be viable, inhabitants faced grave dilemmas about possible movement to more fruitful areas, at a time when even the best land was under heavy pressure. Climate's impact even affected matters of physical development, and some scientists seek to trace climate shifts through the shape of skulls found in graves. According to this view, people shifted shape over generations, to the extent that we see the effects of prolonged warm or cold eras on human remains.[12]

Plague and Tempest

Simple starvation was only one peril that afflicted populations, as eras of climate crisis are almost invariably marked by the onslaught of epidemic or pandemic diseases. To invoke the language of apocalypse once again, the link between famine and plague—broadly defined—was, and remains, very strong.[13]

When studying such diseases, scholars use the concept of the epidemiological triad or triangle, which gives due attention not just to the *agent* directly causing the disease but also to the *host* carrying that agent and the *environment* in which it spreads. Sudden climate changes transform all three components of that equation. They cause the emergence of agents of infection by assisting the evolution of new pathogens or by spreading others that had previously existed only in very limited geographical regions. They also alter the behavior or distribution of hosts. New diseases often arise in animals before crossing over to human beings by various mechanisms of transmission; such diseases are called zoonotic, and the COVID-19 pandemic (SARS-CoV-2) offers a notorious recent example. As climatic changes around the world transform ecologies and habitats, they have their impact on the flora and fauna with which humans come into contact. The El Niño cycle illustrates the processes at work. Depending on the region, El Niño events are particularly linked to higher rainfall and floods, or to severe heatwaves and drought. Any or all of those changes can profoundly affect the spread of disease vectors, notably insects. In warmer climates, that especially means mosquitos, but a wide variety of pests can benefit from such changes. Not surprisingly, then, El Niño cycles often correlate with disease outbreaks. Long-term studies of Chinese history, for example, suggest a strong connection between climate and epidemic cycles. Whether through changes in agents or hosts, successive climate phenomena of various kinds have caused the emergence and spread of such new or newly mutated diseases. The best known example is bubonic plague in the 1330s, but similar trajectories can be traced for typhus in the 1480s, influenza around 1560, and cholera after 1815.[14]

Dramatic climate changes radically alter the environment in which diseases spread, as weakened and malnourished populations become highly vulnerable. Food crises had medical consequences, as populations succumbed to typhus and dysentery, but poor nutrition plays a part in many diseases, including smallpox, typhoid, and even bubonic plague. Poor hygiene and sanitation made matters worse. Extreme weather increases the time that people have to spend indoors, in close confinement, and in overly close proximity to others. This increases vulnerability to lice and the diseases they carry. Typhus is especially linked to the human body louse, and in the early modern era, outbreaks of typhus were a reliable indicator of famine years. Famine-induced migrations and population movements further raised the risk of spreading diseases. Taken together, these events might be so ruinous as to cause a steep and lasting decline in population. Climatic change is inextricably linked to demographic history, which is a critical factor in the development of any society.[15]

Epidemics and pandemics affect human beings, hence the words' origin in the Greek *demos*, "people." But other conditions attack animals, *zoion*, and when they are widespread they are known by the parallel terms "epizootics" and "panzootics." Although the words are not in common use, those curses have had immense consequences through human history, destroying economies and agricultural systems, and detonating political upheavals. As we will see, a history of panzootics demonstrates a close correlation with climate spasms. One of the worst cattle plagues, or murrains, struck immediately following the climate disaster of the mid-1310s. A successor pestilence in eighteenth-century Europe began in the frigid year of 1709 and received a new impetus in 1740—those two years being among the very coldest of the past millennium in the Atlantic world.[16]

Weather must not be confused with climate, which represents a long-term trend measured by averaging out conditions as they existed over lengthy periods. But eras of sudden and dramatic climate change were often characterized by unforgettably violent episodes of extreme weather, with storms or floods far worse than anything known in historical record—the sort of events recalled for generations afterward. Such spectacularly dreadful events were exceptional, but they could occur with some frequency. As they observe the growth of global warming today, climate experts warn of such a normalization of extremes, of the growing frequency of superstorms and other sudden natural onslaughts. The Little Ice Age likewise witnessed several cataclysmic assaults. In 1362, a tremendous cyclone swept across northern and western Europe in what was remembered as the Grote Mandrenke (Great Drowning). Deaths ran at least into the tens of thousands, thousands of buildings were brought down, fleets of ships were sunk, and some once-great ports were wrecked so badly that they never recovered. Other epic disasters followed, and commonly during the most acute periods of climate transition. In 1562, central Europe was harried by thunderstorms so severe as to lead contemporaries to seek out supernatural causes, likely directed by sorcerers. In 1703, England suffered the catastrophic Great Storm, which uprooted thousands of trees and brought down countless chimneys. Storms and floods at Christmas 1717 killed some fourteen thousand around the North Sea, and called forth religious alarms about "God's Judgments on the Earth."[17]

War and Revolution

Three of the appalling horsemen, famine, plague, and death, rarely traveled without a further companion, war—or rather, rebellion, civil conflict, and wars both domestic and foreign.

The causes of outright violence were many. Starving people rioted to seize food or plundered the wealthy. Miserable and frightened people resisted taxes, and in Christian societies, obligatory tithe payments to the institutional church proved a source of special bitterness. But elites were affected. A collapsing economy spreads misery among all classes, including merchants and traders, who depended on commerce, and landlords of any size, who struggled to collect rents. Those classes too sought relief from distress and put severe pressure on king or central government, resulting in constitutional crises, rebellions, or civil wars. Nor were such conditions confined to Christian Europe. In the 1590s, climate change caused a thoroughgoing crisis in the Ottoman Empire, which was duly manifested in economic, social, and political turmoil. Sam White's history of that era is titled *The Climate of Rebellion in the Early Modern Ottoman Empire*. "The climate of rebellion" is an evocative phrase that deserves wider application.[18]

In such conditions, people framed their sufferings according to whatever ideologies lay close at hand, which might be nationalist or localist, religious or political, populist or anti-elite. Often too, grievances were manifested in paranoia, conspiracy theories, and scapegoating. Depending on the particular society, such eras were very fruitful in producing witchcraft panics and (as I will discuss shortly) purges or pogroms directed at particular minorities. Such assaults on minorities often had international ramifications. Attacks on minorities in one land drew the attention of other states, which took advantage of their enemies' weakness. A revolt in one country easily turned into full-scale interstate warfare, which in its turn escalated suffering. Beyond the damage caused by warfare and battles, wars disrupt agriculture and trade. Pirates and privateers plunder sea travel, and armies and bandits steal merchants' goods on land. Labor shortages and disruptions of trade wreck the economy and often bring hunger to communities that always existed on the verge of subsistence. Meanwhile, movements of masses of soldiers and sailors further spread diseases, which can kill far more victims than do swords or rifles. Wars aggravate social and economic crisis by escalating tax levels and disrupting credit systems. The resulting sequence of interventions and wars might shape political life for decades, long after the immediate social and economic conditions have passed.[19]

Just how extensive the effects of such a crisis were depended on its length and severity, and most societies eventually recovered, even after suffering unnerving population losses. When Britain suffered calamitous defeats in its war in the American colonies, one observer lamented that the nation was ruined, only to have the legendary economist Adam Smith reassure him "that there is a great deal of ruin in a nation." But in extreme cases, societies could be so affected by sudden and sweeping climate change as to suffer disintegration, with the obliteration of a familiar social system with its institutions and hierarchies, and even the loss of literacy. The question of how societies collapse, and the role of environmental and climate factors, has been a topic of lively scholarly interest and debate in recent years.[20]

Although medievalists detest the term "Dark Age" for Europe's post-Roman centuries, that term can reasonably be used for a lengthy era in which state mechanisms fragment, when knowledge, science, and literacy suffer massive declines, all against a social context of sharply contracting populations and the loss of economic complexity. Even if societies do stagger on in something like their older form, losses can take generations to make up. One of the best-studied examples of such a collapse involved the Bronze Age Mediterranean world of the twelfth century BCE, which is variously attributed to volcanic eruptions or a megadrought.[21]

God's Anger

Societies endure through catastrophes, and in most cases they survive them. Indeed, the question of how societies cope with calamities of various kinds now occupies a sizable body of academic writing. Those same studies leave no doubt that disasters of various kinds can be powerful drivers of social and cultural change, and often of progress in human affairs. But any possible long-term benefits are small comfort to the sufferers at the time. Historically, as communities struggled to explain what exactly had happened to them, they often did so by drawing on religious or spiritual resources. Religious ideas dominated popular discourse and formed public agendas. Religion is by no means the only aspect of human affairs that is transformed during climate-driven disasters, but it is a very significant one, especially because this has so often been the primary means through which human beings have interpreted the world they see around them. Religious resources come to the fore when those worlds are crumbling, and the Maya lands of Central America offer a clear example of such a response to catastrophic climate change. A calamitous drought in the ninth century CE provoked the collapse of that society's Classic civilization and the ruin of its cities. Those Maya regions have a very high concentration of caves, which were regarded as gateways to the underworld, Xibalba, the "place of fear," and these were moreover sacred to the rain god Chac. During the ninth century, those caves became the setting for extensive ritual deposits of cherished goods and ceramics, and also witnessed large-scale sacrifices, of human beings as well as animals. In the vast majority of those instances, the sacrificial remains date to the era of drought, suggesting a mass collective ritual and even a sweeping new religious movement.[22]

With few exceptions, premodern societies accepted broadly providential worldviews, based on the idea that worldly affairs are controlled by the divine and that human conduct induces God or gods to show their pleasure or displeasure. Until recent times, many languages drew no distinction between Heaven and "the heavens"—between the supernatural realm of the divine and the natural world of skies and seasons. We might here employ the familiar Chinese concept of the Mandate of Heaven, the supernaturally grounded authority that sustains the earthly power of successive empires and regimes. When worldly matters are going well, it is evident that the empire can rest secure, and enemy nations or internal rebellions are struggling uselessly against Heaven as well as the emperor. But as worldly difficulties swell—as crops fail, droughts afflict, plagues rage—the regime's power fragments. It is clear that the spiritual mandate has been lost and is available to be grasped by a new successor. This-worldly failures or disasters reflect and advertise the loss of supernatural support.[23]

Such an idea forms the basis of one of the foundational texts of Western literature, the *Oedipus Tyrannus* of Sophocles, first performed around 429 BCE. The city of Thebes has fallen prey to epidemics and blights: "A blight has fallen on the fruitful blossoms of the land, the herds among the pastures, the barren pangs of women. And the flaming god, the malign plague, has swooped upon us, and ravages the town: he lays waste to the house of Cadmus, but enriches Hades with groans and tears." The king, Oedipus, learns from an oracle that this is the result of a heinous act of religious pollution, and it can be resolved only by purging that defilement through bloodshed or the expulsion of the offender. The offender is of course Oedipus himself, who has murdered his father and unwittingly married his mother.[24]

Such a worldview is explicit in the Abrahamic faiths and is deeply inlaid in their respective scriptures. A cascading series of disasters and spectacular events evidently implies that God is punishing the world for some evil or misbehavior, and that only some major change or reform can appease divine anger. Yet nothing purges as effectively as blood. Among a great many scriptural examples, we find the ugly story of Phinehas in the Old Testament book of Numbers. God's anger is stirred when the Children of Israel form sexual liaisons with the women of pagan peoples. In response, the Almighty sends a plague that slaughters tens of thousands of his people, and it ends only when Phinehas murders an Israelite man and his foreign wife. This zealous act turns God's anger away from the Israelite people and stops the plague in its tracks. From this perspective, famines or plagues are no mere natural phenomena: they are portents, signs, and auguries. That interpretation might imply a new direction in moral or spiritual behavior, perhaps some form of public penitence, or even a moral reformation. Medieval and early modern Christian societies were very familiar with the concept of national sinfulness.[25]

A crisis might demand a campaign against perceived social and political injustice, and perhaps a scapegoating of those offenders against the moral order who hitherto have been tolerated. The task then is to determine which groups or individuals have so provoked the Lord of Hosts that they must be visited with bloodshed or banishment. Hungry and frightened people needed to know why God was so angry with his people. Scapegoating, persecution, and vigilantism found solid theological justification, as intergroup tensions manifested themselves in religious terms. One quantitative study of long-term patterns in Europe's Jewish history found that "a fall in average temperatures of only a third of a degree increased the probability of a pogrom or expulsion by 50 percent over the next five years."[26] Depending on circumstances, the scapegoats could be other Christian groups or sects rather than Jews. In other parts of the world, Christians themselves served as ideal scapegoats.

This situation provides rich opportunities for factions to direct public anger and fear against rivals and enemies. At such moments, governments have a powerful vested interest in attributing the lamentable events to minority groups or sinister individuals, to deflect blame from themselves. Crisis eras of famine and epidemic are very likely to produce persecution or pogrom, which are commonly justified by florid conspiracy theories.

Catastrophe and God's Power

But crises generate other religious consequences, which can transform attitudes and beliefs for generations to come.

Religious responses to crisis could be quite negative in their impact, above all in times of pandemic or epidemic disease. In premodern societies, religious activities often provided the opportunity for the largest gatherings known to society, with the exception of major military mobilizations. At times when diseases were spreading, those assemblies provided uniquely productive environments for the rapid growth and dissemination of pestilence. That was true of teeming pilgrimages, such as the Muslim hajj, the Hindu Kumbh Mela, or their many Christian counterparts. Pilgrims from different parts of the world gathered, shared pathogens, and then returned to their homelands to continue the process. In a Christian context, a normal response to the menace of disease involved calling special processions of pilgrimages to plead that God would lift his wrath from the community. Depending on the particular church tradition, such events might mean thousands of devotees successively kissing a crucifix or sacred image, with predictable biomedical outcomes.[27]

Sometimes religions and religious institutions actively benefited from crises. In premodern times, climate-related disasters forced even tepid believers to learn the lessons that were being offered about God's power and his ability to intervene in the world. In 1703, journalist Daniel Defoe reported the catastrophic weather event of that year in his book *The Storm*, and duly addressed the religious consequences. As he noted:

> I cannot believe any man so rooted in atheistical opinions, as not to find some cause to doubt whether he was not in the wrong, and a little to apprehend the possibility of a Supreme Being, when he felt the terrible blasts of this tempest. I cannot doubt but the atheist's hardened soul trembled a little as well as his house, and he felt some nature asking him some little questions; as these—*Am not I mistaken? Certainly there is some such thing as a God—What can all this be? What is the matter in the world?*[28]

A quick resort to scripture readily produces weather-related texts. The word "storm" occurs more than fifty times in the English Bible, not counting many cognate terms or all the references to rain, drought, famine, thirst, and fierce heat, often framed in a context of divine action or displeasure. Such words abound throughout both Old and New Testaments, as do waters and floods, and by no means only in the context of Noah. When Increase Mather preached on these themes in the aftermath of that same storm of 1703, he drew his text from the Psalms: "Fire, and hail; snow, and vapors; stormy wind fulfilling his word." From that, he deduced that "there is a Providence of the God of Heaven, in whatsoever storms fall upon men on the Earth." The connection between heavenly signs and worldly religious transformation was amply illustrated by another event that occurred in New England in May 1780, when a combination of fogs and distant forest fires blackened the skies, creating the legendary Dark Day. People openly talked of Judgment Day. The event stirred apocalyptic sentiment, launching regional religious revivals, and sparking enthusiastic sects.[29]

Living in the End Times

If such isolated incidents could overwhelm individuals or local communities, larger crises transformed whole societies, and those emergencies too were viewed through religious lenses. At such times, churches and religious institutions drew on their abundant repertoire of images and explanations to account for such happenings, and they cited certain key texts to interpret the signs they saw around them. Often, both persecuted and persecutors turn to exactly the same texts, although they draw radically different conclusions. Repeatedly, communities drew on the apocalyptic literature available to them. In Christian Europe, this meant above all the book of Revelation, which was written in the 90s CE during a time of dearth, famine, and plague.

Wars and catastrophes form the subject of widely cited passages in the book of Daniel, in the thirteenth chapter of Mark's gospel, and other texts, which reinforced the lesson that the world genuinely might be experiencing the end times. In each given era, whole new apocalyptic texts and prophecies could arise, and regularly did so.[30]

I have repeatedly used the word "apocalyptic," which has entered the language as a characterization of extreme disaster or calamity. But beyond that meaning, the term describes a world that is facing terminal stress and likely is in the hands of evil forces, which are numerous and powerful. An apocalyptic framework assumes that God will shortly intervene in his creation to institute a radically new and different order. As that end approaches, the righteous form a remnant increasingly at enmity with the powers ruling the world, and awaiting divine vindication. Such a setting assumes and demands the separation of the righteous from the world. In various ways, that idea of exclusion and separation has often guided responses to worldly scourges, and by no means only for Christians.

Such extremities naturally produce apocalyptic and millenarian rhetoric, which is often declared and promoted by established religious institutions themselves. But the atmosphere of crisis drives religious innovation, in the form of charismatic leaders or upstart sects and cults. A nation laid low by disease is open to claims of healing in both body and soul. A traumatized people willingly gives ear to messianic or prophetic expectations, to charismatic leaders and new spiritual movements. The existence of such upstart movements in turn provokes orthodox preachers to portray the emerging leaders as false messiahs, as warning signs of coming Judgment. Again, such polemic exactly fits the rhetorical world of the book of Revelation, which becomes a practical textbook of political science.

Apocalyptic enthusiasm has a dynamic quality of its own. If in theory the end times should be a singular, once-and-for-all event, in practice the associated ideologies have a strongly cumulative aspect. Through the early modern period, several epochs produced climate-related crises in Europe, each of which left a stunning impact on mortality records. The 1640s are a famous example, but others are easily found. Each period produced its share of apocalyptic writing, preaching, and theorizing, and in a literate age, each of those eras left its mark in print. Those new interpretations and insights were then ready to influence the next generation of thinkers when they in turn had to face crises, whether these occurred decades or centuries later. Through the centuries, constantly reinforced by new eras of agony, apocalyptic writing became ever more elaborate, drawing on an ever-expanding mythological system. Apocalypses grew and expanded as needed.[31]

New Faiths for Old

For traditional religious structures and institutions, such times of worldly crisis are ambiguous affairs, offering many opportunities but also highly dangerous. In some cases, religious groups take the lead in offering charity and relief to desperate populations, a function for which the state is usually quite inadequate. That can allow those institutions to win rich long-term rewards in the form of new recruits and supporters. But in the truly threatening crises, when no institution can realistically offer any serious relief, those mainstream institutions are severely undermined, with established groups left discredited or in disfavor. That opens the way to new sects and alternative religious movements. One celebrated example of such a transition occurred during the so-called Plague of Cyprian that laid waste the Roman Empire during the mid-third century. The then small Christian movement earned enormous credit for the work believers did tending to the sick and maintaining support networks. Pagans conspicuously behaved less bravely and less altruistically. When the plague threat eventually faded, Christian numbers had grown enormously, making the church a potent presence in society and a plausible contender for cultural dominance. When we describe the Cyprianic event today, the name we give it is that of the Christian bishop of the time who described it, and whose writings survived when those of the privileged elites had perished.[32]

In the sixth century CE, the volcano-induced catastrophes of famine and plague inflamed the Roman Empire's ongoing religious crises, which focused on theological interpretations of the nature of Christ. The resulting schisms and conflicts provoked widespread violence between Orthodox/Catholic believers and rival movements, the Monophysites and Nestorians. Those struggles persisted into the seventh century, when they fatally subverted the Christian empire in the face of emerging Islam.

A new climate onslaught in the 620s provided the coup de grâce. A still understudied global occurrence—presumably an epically large volcanic eruption in 626—left its unmistakable scar in tree ring records as far afield as North America. That event sparked renewed crises across Eurasia over the next five years. The sudden cooling and darkening wiped out livestock herds, precipitating the collapse of the Eastern Turkic Empire, then the most powerful state in northeast Asia. The southward migration of other Turkic peoples led to overwhelming assaults on the already stumbling Persian Empire, where Mesopotamia now suffered a plague that reportedly killed half its population. In neighboring Arabia, this was just the time when the Prophet Muhammad was struggling against the wealthy trading elites, preaching a message of divine Judgment that suddenly sounded all the more relevant. Although the sequence of events is uncertain, the calamity undermined those traditional leaders, wrecking their food supplies and trade networks, and opened the way to the revolutionary new Islamic order. Muhammad's forces initially suffered repeated setbacks but suddenly recovered to capture Medina in 627 and Mecca in 630, and they had conquered most of Arabia by 632. As Muslim forces expanded out of Arabia, they easily conquered the older states and empires that were now fatally weakened. The succession of climate catastrophes smashed long-established transcontinental churches and institutional structures and opened the door to altogether new entities.[33]

The religious consequences extended still further. As often in successive eras, influential minorities responded to crisis by withdrawing from a failed world, commonly as monks or hermits. In the sixth-century case, the era of famine and darkness contributed powerfully to the rise of the vibrant and deeply influential monastic movement in Ireland and the other Celtic realms. The disasters of the sixth century effectively ended the Roman Empire as it had been known for half a millennium, and ushered in a new and grimmer early medieval reality.[34]

Other examples abound. The 1640s were a time of multiple catastrophes around the globe, not just in Europe. When natural scourges such as hunger, plagues and subsistence crises were accompanied by intense warfare, heavy taxation, and economic disruption, the pressures provoking resistance and revolt multiplied. The religious consequences in Europe were varied and abundant, including savage fighting and persecutions that pitted Protestants against Catholics, Catholics against Orthodox, and Christians of all shades against Jews. The same years were decisive in the formation and definition of numerous religious groups that would later become global forces in their own right, including Baptists, Presbyterians, Quakers, and others. In the longer term, the savagery of religious conflict and persecution in these years provoked a reaction that laid the foundation for the Enlightenment, and ultimately for the emergence of secular politics and philosophies. Climate change created the religious world that we know in modern history.[35]

Failure to Launch

We are not dealing here with simple determinism. Some vital moments of religious transformation did not have an obvious climate context, or at least climate's role was nothing like sufficient to produce such outcomes. As we will see in Chapter 5, it is not easy to locate a direct climate or economic explanation for the outbreak of the original Reformation movement of the 1510s—although we do find a powerful context for the later evolution of the Protestant movement, and indeed its survival.

In other cases, some eras of truly extreme climate stress produced little in the way of enduring religious consequences such as influential revivals, reformations, or mass movements. That does not mean that religious responses were absent, but for whatever reasons, the political and social alignments of the time did not offer the foundations for more sweeping change. In climate terms, one of the most traumatic periods of recorded history was the 1430s. Temperatures plunged to unheard-of depths in the coldest decade of the past millennium; predictably, it was a time of famine and epidemic, with obscenely high mortality rates. The years 1437–1438 saw the worst European famines of the whole century. Those historically parlous conditions might have been expected to produce a proportionately large and even sweeping religious response or interpretation, but they did not. What manifestations did occur are found in the form of healing cults, with their appropriate saint and shrines, while the scapegoating of evil or conspiratorial minorities found a sharp new focus in the Roma, or Gypsies. As we will see in Chapter 4, the decade produced a steep escalation in the perceived scale and lethality of witchcraft. But even such responses were confined to specific regions, and the 1430s produced neither a Reformation nor a Great Awakening, still less the creation of an apocalyptic new faith. Nor did the years following a titanic volcanic eruption in 1465, which for several years caused economic ruin across Europe and farther afield. Catastrophic rains and flooding were followed by a severe accentuation of the Little Ice Age, with deep snow, failed crops, and stunted trees. Yet explicitly religious consequences were few and not lasting.[36]

The equation between climate crisis and religious revolution is neither neat nor straightforward. As I will suggest, so much depends on the larger contexts—political, social, and cultural. But in multiple critical instances, the path of causation from climate to religious revolution is evident.

The Missing Dimension

Understanding that climate dimension is a critical contribution to our knowledge of pivotal movements of religious history, but it raises a larger issue for historical writing. If the role of climate seems so obvious to us today, why has it taken so long for it to become a standard part of the historical narrative? In fact, we are dealing with quite a recent set of insights. Historians had long known about particular spells of severe weather and recognized their impact on social or political change, but only in the 1950s and 1960s did such observations find a sound scientific basis. Reinforcing the lessons of climatological research was the contemporary work of historical demographers, who used European church records to identify periods that were particularly genial or severe, reflected in low or high mortality.[37]

One landmark scholar who integrated various kinds of scientific evidence was Emmanuel Le Roy Ladurie, who in 1967 published his *Histoire du climat depuis l'an mil* (History of climate since the year 1000), which in 1971 appeared in English as *Times of Feast, Times of Famine*. In retrospect, Ladurie was surprisingly reluctant to attribute political or religious consequences to the various crises that he identified, even that of the 1640s, but he stands as a critical pioneer of a new discipline. From 1972, Hubert Lamb headed the innovative Climate Research Unit at the University of East Anglia. The first academic conference devoted to the theme of climate and history was held in 1976, and Continental Europe produced such pioneers in the discipline as Christian Pfister. Climate history has since become a flourishing field of research and writing.[38]

Even as demographers and economic historians were discovering the impact of climate change through the millennia, those technical-seeming insights were slow to impinge on mainstream historians who applied themselves to political or religious affairs. Referring to global climate issues seemed neither necessary nor appropriate. Until quite recently, we might semi-seriously summarize the attitude of many historians as: What has the climate got to do with the real world? Contributing to the lack of awareness was the parochial nature of much historical writing, and not just in religious matters. Historians who focus on particular nations or geographical areas sometimes fail to recognize a broad cross-cultural or transnational dimension. But as I have suggested, when we do apply such a global perspective, we recognize the appearance of very similar conditions and trends emerging in very different societies and regions at exactly the same time—in France and Japan, Germany and Peru.

Recently, matters have changed substantially, as global and transnational history has become much more familiar. Also, climate issues have entered the popular consciousness and political debate, and this has had an enormous impact on academic study. As we become conscious of the likely scale of present and future impacts of these global changes, we naturally apply those insights to the historic past.

The past decade has seen a remarkable flowering of scholarship about the impact of climate in various eras. Just to take some landmark studies from the past few years: Geoffrey Parker produced the magisterial *Global Crisis: War, Climate Change and Catastrophe in the Seventeenth Century* (2013); Kyle Harper studied the crises of late antiquity in his ambitious work *The Fate of Rome: Climate, Disease, and the End of an Empire* (2017); Brian Fagan's several important contributions include *The Little Ice Age: How Climate Made History, 1300–1850* (2000); and Philipp Blom published *Nature's Mutiny: How the Little Ice Age of the Long Seventeenth Century Transformed the West and Shaped the Present.* Such approaches have fundamentally rewritten our accounts of crucial historical eras and themes. A noteworthy example is Dagomar Degroot's sweeping *The Frigid Golden Age: Climate Change, the Little Ice Age, and the Dutch Republic, 1560–1720.* Climate history has inspired historians of the American colonies, notably in Sam White's *A Cold Welcome: The Little Ice Age and Europe's Encounter with North America* (2017). The volcano-related disasters following 1815 have attracted several authors. Besides those major books, articles and focused studies now abound in the scholarly literature.[39]

In contrast to the earlier neglect, contemporary scholars now strive to take full account of climate factors, much as an earlier generation of historians suddenly awoke to the crucial significance of gender issues. Besides mainstream history, literary scholars now apply climate themes to the work of celebrated authors. Taken together, this new perception constitutes a real paradigm shift in our ways of looking at the past.[40]

Yet for all the current outpouring of climate-related history, one area in particular stands out as a very significant gap, and that is religion, broadly defined. Of course scholars such as Parker and Harper have much to say on religious matters—inevitably, given the central importance of religious institutions and ideologies in the particular worlds they are describing. But the role of climate issues in making and remaking religion really has not been prominent in the literature, whether we are looking at major book publications or the copious resources now available in scholarly journals. Whatever the reason, the fact remains that those momentous times of religious transformation have rarely been studied or expounded in terms of global conditions, above all the climate context. Climate remains the missing dimension in the history of religions.

The Book

Crises differ in their exact effects on religion, and by no means all of the consequences I have suggested will occur in any one era. If the religious impulses are broadly similar in different times, then how they are expressed depends on the constraints and opportunities applying in different settings; witness my remarks about the lack of revivals or reformations in fifteenth-century Europe. Critical to any process of explanation are the social and political arrangements of a particular time and what we can loosely call its degree of modernity: the sophistication of its governments and economic structures, its technology and media. Viewed over a long historical span, we trace the growing capacity of states and societies to withstand short-term disruption and shortages. More advanced states generally have little time for internecine religious riots or persecutions, but they provide very rich opportunities for the emergence and spread of revivals and new denominations. Literacy and education obviously play their part in these developments. Our story can only be told by choosing a number of periods and episodes for description, to show the range of possible effects and responses, and thus to create a model for explanation and prediction.

One way to appreciate the potential role of climate in human affairs is to observe what happens when—at least from a human-centric perspective—matters are going very well and the heavens appear to be smiling. Despite the emphasis so far on eras of disaster and deprivation, some historical epochs were wonderfully benevolent times when the sun's warmth evidently manifested God's bounty. One such era was the High Middle Ages, which coincided with a period of warming over large parts of the globe. Trade and commerce flourished, abundant harvests produced generous food supplies, and prosperity was conspicuously manifested in religious experiment and innovation. Such eras are often recalled through legendary and even exalted figures, such as St. Francis or Thomas Aquinas in the medieval European context. Whatever we term them, cultural golden ages have existed, and they have their foundations in climate conditions.

Other eras were far more hostile to human endeavor, or even to survival. The number of possible candidates for such times of trouble is large, and several eras stand out as extremely significant, the most dramatic of their kind for centuries before or afterward. These include the years pivoting around 1320, 1570, 1680, and 1740, and these four successive epochs form the main subject of the book. Each period tells a very different story. In the case of 1740, we see the impact of a specific short-term crisis, while the other periods represent a phase in a much longer-term transition. The 1680 instance represents a combination of those two patterns, an especially acute situation within a longer-term cooling trend. By tracing the very different effects of climate-caused disturbance or disaster in each era, we see how the growing sophistication of states, societies, and technology affected the degree of damage and the extent of transformation. Each of the four eras offers a distinctive model of the impact of catastrophe on religious thought and life. Each also left substantial legacies for later generations.

The first of these is the early fourteenth century, especially the years between 1310 and 1325. This bears the closest resemblance to modern circumstances in that it involved a broad and lasting era of climatic change, a time of global cooling that marked the onset of the Little Ice Age. Societies around the world suffered times of shocking paranoia and conspiracy-mongering. They responded with persecutions of minorities and dissidents, leading to purges and expulsions on an appalling scale. Whole populations suffered bitter times of exile and diaspora, and those changes did much to create our familiar maps of the great faiths and their geographical concentrations. In describing the consequences of that series of disasters, I centrally emphasize the role of religiously based violence and hostility, of hating others.

About 1560, the Little Ice Age entered a new and brutally cold era, when social strains threatened the survival of social and political orders. The resulting unrest and disaffection took multiple forms, but it especially manifested in one notorious form of social paranoia: the witch-hunts, which now reached their peak in Europe. At the same time, the 1560s witnessed a dramatic religious transformation within Christianity, affecting both its Catholic and Protestant dimensions. The fast-growing Calvinist movement represented a revolutionary current that threatened the near-overnight razing of ancient religious ways. On the other side, reformed and restructured Catholicism became equally hard-edged and confrontational—a comparable faith of crisis. The Christian world entered a new and much harsher period of polarization as revolutionary religious change detonated savage wars.

The third era stretches from 1675 through the end of the century, which constituted one of the very coldest and most ruinous periods of the Little Ice Age. Curiously, it is far less well known or studied than other crisis years such as the 1640s, and it represents something of an orphan period in modern writing. Most books on the General Crisis focus sharply on the parlous midcentury decades of the 1640s and 1650s and say little about that later era. Yet the religious consequences of those latter years were just as far-reaching, not least in redrawing frontiers between faiths. Unlike the fourteenth century, Europeans now lived in a world of sea travel and far-flung colonial possessions, and persecuted populations amply exploited these opportunities to seek safe haven. If the years around 1320 were characterized by hating, then themes of fleeing and flight emerge powerfully in this later era, in a time of religious globalization. Settlements in foreign lands far from the motherland offered the prospect of new concepts of religious liberty, opening a dramatic new phase in attitudes to religious freedom and spiritual experimentation.

I have already mentioned the baleful conditions of 1739–1742, which produced responses rather different from those of earlier eras. The enormous growth of state power arising from war and imperial expansion severely limited expressions of popular religious violence or hatred. State mechanisms were better-developed, while forms of media and communication were much more sophisticated than in earlier centuries. This new world allowed the circulation of ideas and beliefs on an international and intercontinental scale. Popular fears were channeled into radical new forms of enthusiastic revivalist religion. New denominations and sects emerged within particular faiths, and many became globally significant in their own right.

As the Western economy grew and industrialized, society came to rely less directly on agriculture and the vagaries of the seasons. I will illustrate that by tracing a series of major climatic disturbances from the late eighteenth century onward and showing how those natural factors lost much of their impact. In the early part of that era, from the 1780s onward, volcanic eruptions contributed to an alarming era of climate disruption, and the Tambora blast in particular sparked new churches and denominations teaching apocalyptic and millenarian doctrines and highlighting dreams of the end times. But as we proceed deeper into the nineteenth century, much of Western humanity, at least, felt ever more detached from the direct impact of climate. Even so, if climate factors ceased to shape religion in some parts of the world, the situation was very different in the poorer areas that would come to be called the global South.

Years to Come

We presently hear a great deal about global climate change and the disasters it threatens in the imminent future. Although detailed projections vary, it is virtually certain that within a few decades, large sections of the human race, chiefly in nations of the global South, will regularly be suffering calamities not unlike those familiar to the world of 1320 or 1680. Of course, the responses will not be identical to what took place in those earlier times. State systems are better developed globally, as are international aid mechanisms, and modes of communication are utterly different. Nevertheless, this will unquestionably be a time of widespread hunger, acute water shortages, and dramatic environmental changes, which could well threaten the survival of state mechanisms in many nations. Together, these changes could drive mass migrations and provoke conflict between groups and nations, peoples and faiths.

In terms of religious consequences, only a truly rash would-be prophet would venture to speculate which of the different historical approaches laid out here would come to the fore in that near future. But what we can say is that those historical precedents establish a framework for understanding the coming era of crisis.

2
Forcing Climate

> He looks on the earth, and it trembles; He touches the mountains, and they smoke.
>
> —Psalm 104:32

The European winter of 1683–1684 was so harsh as to defy superlatives. England suffered the coldest winter in its recorded history. The Thames froze solid for two months, allowing the creation of the Frost Fair markets and stalls on the foot-thick ice. Diarist John Evelyn recorded that by early January, entrepreneurs had set up whole streets of booths on the river, "in which they roasted meat, and had divers shops of wares, quite across as in a town, but coaches, carts, and horses passed over." On January 11, a priest at the venerable Swiss monastery of Einsiedeln recorded that he had never before known the sacrament literally to freeze in the chalice. "But on January 13 it got even worse, and one could say it has never been so cold in human memory."[1]

Historians have long known about such extreme episodes, which were once treated as picturesque oddities of a "believe it or not" quality. Only in the late twentieth century were they contextualized not as isolated moments but as integral parts of long-term cycles of warming or cooling. The frigid 1680s are now commonly recognized as a particularly cold moment of the Little Ice Age. Few scholars today would deny that climatic conditions have varied enormously, both globally and within particular regions. Yet despite that broad consensus, much remains uncertain, and it is important at the outset to outline some of those areas of continuing controversy. Fraught contemporary debates over global warming and the "climate crisis" have often led to serious disagreements about how those past phenomena should properly be interpreted. We have to understand

and confront those controversies before we can make any worthwhile comments about cultural or religious transformations.

We are far from any consensus about the exact reasons for such historical changes in climate or about the relative importance of the different forces credited as makers and shapers of climate. So multifaceted are the forces driving change, and so diverse, that we must sympathize with older generations that saw the Earth as a living being, tormented and capricious. We should respect the attention that ancient and medieval sages paid to the close interaction of the four elements: fire, earth, air, and water. When early modern people blamed catastrophic weather on prodigious cosmic forces driving the winds and rains, we might give them credit for their intuition. Even today, it is often difficult to write about such climatic transformations without deploying mythological metaphors.[2]

Warming and Freezing

The scientific foundations for modern climate history were laid in the 1950s and 1960s, and one cutting-edge figure was Hubert Lamb, who was based at the University of East Anglia. In the 1950s, most scientists agreed that large-scale changes in global climate were confined to the distant past and had more or less ended with the conclusion of the last great ice ages, around 10,000 years ago. The very term "ice age" conjured images of cave people and mammoths. Drawing on various disciplines, especially from the record of pollen found in sediment cores, Lamb argued to the contrary that sweeping changes had occurred much more recently, in eras well known from the documented historical record. In a seminal paper published in 1965, titled "The Early Medieval Warm Epoch and Its Sequel," Lamb described the growing evidence for

> a notably warm climate in many parts of the world, that lasted a few centuries around A.D. 1000–1200, and was followed by a decline of temperature levels till between 1500 and 1700 the coldest phase since the last ice age occurred. . . . Changes of prevailing temperature and rainfall in England between periods of 50–150 years duration around 1200 and around 1600 are found which, on all the evidence at present available, probably amounted to 1.2–1.4°C and 10% respectively. Changes in some seasons of the year may have exceeded these ranges of the annual mean.

As he remarked, such temperature fluctuations might not sound too impressive, but they were startling in terms of previous assumptions about climate, and they were "undoubtedly upsetting for the human economies of those times (and perhaps of *any* time)."[3] That last comment was important, suggesting just how much impact even a fluctuation of a degree or two might have.

Lamb's general model was widely accepted. Researchers came to accept the reality of the Medieval Warm Period, which was originally dated from roughly 1000 to 1200 CE, although more recent estimates expand the period somewhat, from the mid-tenth century through the mid- or late thirteenth. That was then followed by a plunge in temperatures during the Little Ice Age, which lasted through the mid-nineteenth century. That period has come to play such a standard part in the literature that it has acquired its own familiar acronym, the LIA. (As I will explain, the reality of both those eras, warm and cold, has been challenged.) Scholars of many disciplines have applied that framework, stressing the critical role that climate may have played in their particular areas.[4]

I offer one general caution about dating these events. When we read accounts of the various eras, we soon notice how flexible their dates appear to be, reflecting the predilections of particular authors and the events that they seek to include in given eras. According to taste, the Medieval Warm Period lasted from 1000 to 1200, or from 800 to 1300, or from the mid-tenth century to around 1260; other permutations are easily found. The Little Ice Age is even more flexible in its limits, and the undeniably worst and most frigid core of that period is variously dated as beginning in 1560, or 1580, or 1590, with an ending in 1685, or 1700, or 1720; it thus lasted either around 90 years, or 160 years, or something in between. Such variations are, and must be, of enormous concern to historians, for whom a decade or two might be a crucial period of transformation in a given society. Throughout this book, I have made my best efforts to date those transition points as precisely and consistently as feasible.[5]

Debate and Denial

In recent times, growing awareness of global warming has been a landmark event, for politics and culture as well as science, and it is natural to refer to historical precedents. But for climate scientists and activists, that historical focus is a perilously double-edged sword. As climate history reaches a mass audience, many nonspecialists have come to realize how thoroughly climate shapes their world, and in previously unsuspected areas of social life and politics. At the same time, describing bygone eras of dramatic climate change or crisis raises potentially troubling questions about what, if anything, is distinctive about the present age.

The question of human intervention in making or distorting the climate—about anthropogenic (human-caused) climate change—has been uniquely sensitive. Since the early 1990s, skeptics have attacked the evidence for global warming, and more particularly have rejected claims that any observable warming results from human actions. One rhetorical tactic has been to note that the world's climate goes through cycles quite naturally, for reasons not entirely understood, but mainly not of human shaping. If in fact the world had warmed so sharply during recorded history and then cooled so suddenly, the contention goes, then surely that discredited claims about the role of human intervention. One potent piece of evidence for this argument has been the Medieval Warm Period and the ensuing ice age. That argument found a memorable symbol in the vineyards that flourished in England through the Middle Ages into the early sixteenth century, suggesting that much warmer conditions extended far north in those centuries. In the same centuries, fig trees grew in Germany. Yet that period duly ended of its own accord, to be followed by a Little Ice Age that had a catastrophic impact across Asia as well as in Europe—which among other things killed off British vineyards and German figs. Yet that crisis too passed, as the climate improved. It was all part of the circle of life.[6]

Reading contemporary alerts about global warming, a lay public might well ask why things should be different this time around. If the world naturally gets hotter or cooler, regardless of human action, why should we start worrying about any present signs of warming? Scarcely less provocative: if the Medieval Warm Period was a time of general prosperity and expansion, then is it reasonable to ask whether warming is something to welcome rather than to fear? To that extent, a concept as academic and even as cheery-sounding as the Medieval Warm Period was weaponized. That warmth became the focus of an ugly political debate in 2009–2010, when a large cache of leaked emails allegedly showed some of the world's prominent scholars of climate history conspiring to manipulate or suppress data on various topics, including evidence of that warm period. Climate skeptics crowed about the revelations of "Climategate," which supposedly overthrew modern claims of climate change as fraudulent. Of course, it did nothing of the sort, and the critics were systematically misinterpreting the internal documents. But the affair did show the extreme sensitivity of the issue.[7]

Aware of the power of the medieval warmth argument, scientists who accepted the climate consensus emphasized how fundamentally different those historical eras were from present conditions. That has meant stressing the local and regional nature of changes once thought to be global, or nearly so. It has also involved minimizing and on occasion underplaying the scale of earlier temperature changes. According to this view, and contrary to what climate skeptics might argue, those early phases of warming and cooling simply offered no reasonable analogy to modern trends. That critique initially focused on the so-called Medieval Warm Period, which is now known more neutrally as the Medieval Climate Anomaly—although the existence of some kind of anomaly is not disputed.[8]

One controversial chart published in 1998 suggested that *global* climate fluctuations over the past thousand years were quite minor when compared with the steep and truly worldwide temperature climb of the late twentieth century. To oversimplify, the resulting graph was a "hockey stick" that was generally flat along most of the time scale, but with a sharp upward curve at the end. At first sight, that seems to eliminate both the Medieval Warm Period and the Little Ice Age, but that influential graph must be interpreted with some care. For one thing, its presentation properly takes full account of the large uncertainty range in its claims, especially for periods before 1600 or so. That qualification is significant because virtually all observers, believers and skeptics alike, accept a definite temperature rise from the mid-nineteenth century onward. If we trace conditions from the early modern period—say, from 1600—then the hockey stick model broadly applies. Disagreement centers on much earlier eras, and especially on what is still widely recognized as the late medieval shift from warm to cold.[9]

A global perspective is essential. Much of the early work that identified those earlier epochs of temperature shifts drew largely on European records, mainly because materials from that region were so readily available, while non-Western sources were more difficult to access. But when we do view things globally, such trends were nothing like so evident or universal. The issue is not whether warming or cooling occurred in particular times or places (as it assuredly did) but whether it can properly earn the title of "global." Over the past decade, various types of evidence have been deployed to challenge claims about earlier fluctuations, and we now know much more than we did about paleoclimates. In the case of the Medieval Climate Anomaly, evidence from glacier ice cores, corals, and tree rings indicates that while some regions were warming during the relevant periods, others were cooling. In the words of one study, those patterns were not "globally coherent." Arguably, such "incoherence" can even be found within the larger Mediterranean region, on Europe's margins. Similar arguments apply to the Little Ice Age, as modern debates have questioned the scale of any temperature drop and (again) the global impact.[10]

So venomous have debates over these issues been that even discussing those historical eras can arouse suspicion of so-called denialism—of rejecting the current consensus about global warming. Reading the different academic literatures from the historians and the climate scientists can produce a real dissonance. Are they really describing the same centuries? Even the same planet? Fortunately, for present purposes, it is not necessary to engage those debates in detail, and certainly not to resolve them.

What can be said uncontroversially is that some regions of the world definitely did experience prolonged periods of warming or cooling in the years claimed, and certainly in the North Atlantic world. Because of the nature of our archival evidence, this story can be traced strongly in Europe, and often but not always in the larger world. Changes can be transcontinental, if not fully global. Yes, there really were vineyards in the unusually warm environment of medieval England, and Europe's rivers froze in the 1560s and the 1680s in ways they could not have done several centuries before. Something can be very widespread without being totally global. To that extent, it is permissible to use a term like "Little Ice Age," while recognizing all the appropriate caveats and constraints. We can legitimately talk about historical eras of quite radical climate change and their very broad effects.

Climate Makers

In modern times, discussion of climate change focuses almost entirely on human-driven emissions, chiefly of carbon by-products. But other natural factors or "forcings" can indeed shape the climate, including solar activity, volcanic eruptions, and the cycles of El Niño, and their interactions are complex and often surprising. Scholarship on climate emphasizes the concept of Earth systems, in which such seemingly distinct components as the Sun, water, air, and the Earth's magnetic field all interact. Understanding these different forces and facts shows how climatic changes can affect some parts of the world but not others, and why particular regions can indeed experience dramatic waves of heat or cold. They also point to the qualitative difference that separates present-day climate change from its apparent predecessors. In describing these forcings, I am in a sense presenting the essential vocabulary for the stories and case studies that will occur throughout this book, and particularly for the religious dimensions.[11]

The Sun itself has been a major culprit in terrestrial change, and fluctuations in solar activity can be measured through the relatively cooler or darker areas known as sunspots. The exact mechanisms driving these phenomena are not well understood, but their impact is apparent. Scientific observations of sunspots became possible with Galileo's development of the telescope in the early seventeenth century, and the growing body of records allowed trends to be mapped. For over a century, scholars have been aware of major changes in the number of sunspots at given times, and fewer sunspots indicate lower solar activity. Periods of very low sunspot activity correlate well with notably cold eras on Earth. In the 1890s, solar astronomers Edward and Annie Maunder were researching historical observations of the frequency of sunspots, which in a normal modern year run to a couple of thousand. But in the later seventeenth century, they found, sunspots all but vanished, with just one or two recorded each year, and that at a time when scientists were making and keeping detailed observations. We now speak of the Maunder Minimum, which lasted from 1645 through 1715, and particularly the latter years of that strange phenomenon, the Late Maunder Minimum, the years after 1675. The sunspot cycle coincided neatly with a period of spectacular earthly cooling, which we recall through events such as the Thames Frost Fairs—and which also left its mark in eras of starvation, epidemic, and political turbulence. Sunspots were rare or close to nonexistent during the Spörer Minimum (circa 1450–1530/1550), another time of troubled climate conditions, and the Dalton Minimum (1780–1820). We will return to those mysterious epochs.[12]

Low solar activity was closely related to water supplies. A particularly cold era meant that more of the world's water was locked in ice, at the polar ice caps or in advancing glaciers. Cooling of this kind often coincided with droughts in tropical or semitropical climates, and even with ruinous megadroughts.[13]

Volcanoes

Volcanic activity also emerges as a critical factor shaping or forcing global climate, with all that implies for human affairs. The immediate impact of such volcanoes is obvious enough. Volcanoes throw ash and solid particles (tephra) into the atmosphere, together with gases such as sulfur dioxide and carbon dioxide, and together these circulate around the Earth. The 1991 eruption of Mount Pinatubo produced some 20 million tons of sulfur dioxide and ash particles, which were thrown as much as twelve miles into the atmosphere. By shading the planet from solar radiation, such events can cause widespread cooling, often on a dramatic scale. An impact of only a degree or so Celsius can inflict massive damage on agriculture, and on many aspects of human society. The effects can last for lengthy periods, depending on the power of the eruption, but major events can have their impact over several years. One celebrated such event was the Tambora eruption of 1815 in what we would today call Indonesia. That played havoc with the seasons around the world, giving North America its "year without a summer," and it inflicted famine and disorder across Europe through the end of the decade. (I will discuss this era in Chapter 8.) When we find reports of a sudden and catastrophic change of climate with consequences over a relatively short period, we should often look for the role of a volcano, conceivably on the other side of the world.[14]

The power of eruptions is measured through the Volcanic Explosivity Index (VEI), which is similar to the better-known Richter scale for earthquakes. Like the Richter scale, the index is logarithmic, so each point on the scale is ten times larger in terms of ejecta than the preceding: a VEI of 6 is ten times larger than a 5, which in turn is ten times more than a 4. A grade 5 produces a cubic kilometer of ejecta; a 6 produces ten cubic kilometers, and a 7 more than a hundred cubic kilometers. By this standard, the eruption of Vesuvius that destroyed Pompeii in 79 CE was a 5, and the famous Krakatoa blast of 1883 was a 6, a "colossal." So was Pinatubo. (Estimates of the exact power of historical volcanoes are open to some debate.) To find 7s (supercolossals) we would look to Tambora, or the less well-known eruption at Samalas, on the Indonesian island of Lombok, in 1257. Apart from those two, only one volcano in the past 1,500 years indisputably scored a 7: the Paektu eruption in northeastern China, which occurred in the mid- or late tenth century (estimated dates vary widely, but 946 is a common estimate).

Thankfully, it has been a very long time indeed since the Earth experienced a "megacolossal" grade 8 eruption, with a thousand cubic kilometers of ejecta. One of the last such events, 74,000 years ago, came close to driving humanity to extinction.[15]

Our records of eruptions are far from perfect, but traces in tree ring and ice core data in various parts of the world prove that some kind of volcanic event happened somewhere around the world at or around a particular time, even if we cannot say exactly where the blast occurred. Only as recently as 2013 was Samalas definitively identified as the source of the 1257 supercolossal that left such obvious traces around the world. We are still seeking the whereabouts of some giant blasts that had an enormous impact around the world in historical times, including eruptions that left significant traces worldwide in 1465 and 1808–1809.[16]

Of Sixes and Sevens

When we describe the impact of particular volcanoes, we sometimes fail to appreciate how such activity operates in cycles. Volcanoes do not just happen randomly; eruptions can be more or less frequent in given eras. Waves of repeated eruptions can prove shattering, but we can also identify long and seemingly unnatural periods of volcanic calm. Those respective waves of vigor or torpor correlate well with the occurrence of dramatic and disturbing climatic patterns around the world. Understanding such waves or cycles depends on the available evidence. At first sight, it is odd that major volcanic activity was apparently so little in evidence during large parts of the Middle Ages and, coincidentally or not, during the Medieval Climate Anomaly. After the eruption of Paektu in the mid- or late tenth century, thereafter we find no comparable examples until Samalas three centuries later. Blasts on the 6 or 7 level are not easily recognized in the three centuries between roughly 950 and 1250. In sharp contrast, we find at least eleven examples at this level between 1450 and 1850, or one every thirty-five years or so.[17]

To some extent, this contrast might be an artifact of research and recording, rather than marking a real phenomenon. Some climatic episodes during the warm period bear a fair resemblance to later calamities that certainly were a result of a major eruption, even if no specific volcano can currently be blamed. Recent research has identified a cluster of eruptions in 1108–1110 that were responsible for terrifying dust clouds over Europe and for mass starvation. Another likely instance occurred around 1229, a ghastly period marked by famine and bizarre weather conditions in so many parts of the globe. A lethal famine killed around a third of Japan's population, Russia was almost as hard hit, and the rest of Europe suffered appallingly. Even so, the relative scarcity of major *recorded* volcanic episodes in the Middle Ages—when compared to the sixteenth and seventeenth centuries—is suggestive. Was the Earth really so quiet between 1110 and 1229? If we are indeed seeing a genuine phenomenon, then that period of relative volcanic tranquility contributed to the benevolent climate conditions of the medieval years.[18]

Volcanoes likewise contributed to the conditions of the Little Ice Age, the start of which is generally dated to the mid- or late thirteenth century. Samalas itself had disastrous effects on human societies around the world, and it marked the beginning of a frightening new historical era. Although the direct results of that blast passed within a few years, similar patterns now became frequent, even standard. A grade 6 eruption in the Andes followed in 1280. Multiple later eruptions then contributed to maintaining the world in a frozen state. Several struck in the mid- and late fifteenth century, driving what is termed the second pulse, or wave, of the Little Ice Age. Between 1450 and 1482, there were at least seven eruptions that were a grade 5 or larger. Around 1452, a level 6 eruption struck the Pacific island of Vanuatu, and a similar-size blast at Bárðarbunga in 1477 was the largest eruption ever known in Iceland. Another still unlocated event in 1465 may have been a 7, conceivably larger than Tambora. Large eruptions were also strikingly frequent in the frigid depths of the Little Ice Age. Just in the century after 1580, there were no fewer than eleven known events in the 5 to 6 index range. Most were in the western and southwestern Pacific, on the western side of the so-called Ring of Fire, in Japan, Indonesia, the Philippines, and New Guinea. Their effects spanned much of the globe, and the combined consequences of multiple eruptions within a few years proved devastating.[19]

Focusing on volcanoes helps explain why some climate shifts should be regional rather than global phenomena. For one thing, volcanoes in tropical latitudes can have their impact on both hemispheres, while eruptions in high latitudes—for instance, in Iceland—will only affect that particular hemisphere. As we will see, volcanoes have a massive impact on oceanic systems that shape climates in some parts of the world rather than others.

The Holy Child

Large volcanoes have a direct and immediate impact on climate, but there are also wider and more insidious consequences. To appreciate these, we must understand the changes in the seas that do so much to affect the prosperity of human populations.

One factor involves the El Niño–Southern Oscillation (ENSO), a Pacific phenomenon that affects climate conditions over a sizable share of the globe (and to which I will often return in the course of this book). First described scientifically in the 1890s, El Niño has in recent years become one of the most studied aspects of climate, and some reputable scholars argue that it has had far-reaching effects on human history and the rise and fall of civilizations. As a concept, El Niño has enjoyed a triumphant imperial expansion comparable to those of the greatest human realms.[20]

At their simplest, El Niño events involve a periodic warming of surface temperatures in parts of the Pacific Ocean, as warmer oceanic currents supplant colder ones on the Latin American side of the ocean. That change is accompanied by heavy rain, high humidity, and flooding. The results are particularly in evidence around Christmastime, which to Catholic societies of the Pacific coast of Latin America is the time of the holy Child, El Niño. Every few years, the scale of the change is enough to reverse the normal westward flow of water across the Pacific, as high-pressure systems affect the Asian side. Strong El Niño conditions are followed and reversed within a year or two by La Niña, the cool phase of the cycle, which gives dry conditions in the Americas while soaking Asia. El Niños normally last for a year, but they can be substantially longer, even running to three or four years. El Niño events occur with some frequency. Since 1900 alone, there have been around thirty occurrences, an average of one every four years. Warming can last anywhere between seven months and two years.[21]

Current research has raised several questions about the conventional interpretation of El Niño, suggesting that the simple label might comprehend several distinct but related events. One intriguing theory suggests the existence of long cycles lasting decades or centuries, during which one of the two models—El Niño or La Niña—might have predominated. It is also open to question whether other El Niño–type phenomena might occur elsewhere in the world. Further west, we find the Indian Ocean Dipole, or the Indian Niño, which likewise fluctuates in strength depending on larger climate conditions.[22]

El Niño and the Wider World

When Peruvian scholars first described El Niño, they assumed that they were dealing with a local phenomenon that was mainly relevant to the coasts of their own country. Over the past century, the scope of its impact has become ever more clearly understood, particularly with the full implications of ENSO, with the atmospheric changes that accompany the oceanic transitions. We trace the effects of El Niño cycles through the Indian Ocean into the Atlantic, into the Amazon and the Nile Valley. Severe El Niños are associated with higher rainfall in higher latitudes and droughts in lower ones, and those conditions can be extremely damaging. El Niño–related droughts lasting years or decades have plausibly been blamed for the crisis or collapse of several great societies, including the eastern Mediterranean world of Bronze Age times, and the Classic Maya civilization of Central America (although other factors may well have played their part).[23]

Adding to the global impact of El Niño cycles is their intimate connection with the monsoon system. The Asian monsoon is arguably "the Earth's largest and most important climate phenomenon," in that it presently influences the livelihood of over 60 percent of the human population. If the exact share of population differed somewhat several centuries ago, it was always very substantial. Across much of Asia, rice-based agriculture was critically dependent on irrigation systems and on water regulation, so periods of very high or low rainfall were uniquely perilous. From the end of the nineteenth century, observers were realizing the linkages between droughts around the larger region, affecting eastern and southeastern Asia and coinciding closely in India and Australia, and they found explanations in the Pacific oceanic systems. The iciest portion of Europe's Little Ice Age in the seventeenth century coincided with repeated monsoon failures in South Asia. At its most damaging, El Niño could threaten famines on a frightful scale.[24]

The Burning Child

The relationship between El Niño and volcanoes has startling implications. Few dispute that volcanoes can affect El Niños, raising both their frequency and intensity and sizably enhancing their effects. Taken together, that can potentially cause perilous climatic disruption in different parts of the globe. Some scientists, however, suggest a contrary chain of causation whereby oceanic cycles can actually trigger volcanoes. The theory begins with solar activity. Lower levels of solar radiation raise the risk of more and larger El Niño events. Depending on oceanic conditions, sea levels can stand far higher on the Asian side of the Pacific, or on the American side, and at times of transition unimaginably weighty bodies of water are in movement from one side to the other. Such shifts place immense pressure on tectonic plates, and hypothetically can trigger volcanic eruptions. As volcanic eruptions throw up material that blots out the sun, that in turn lowers temperatures, further encouraging strong and lengthy El Niños.[25]

Such a sequence of interactions fits well with the long-term climatic changes that I have already described. Through the warming period of the Middle Ages, we have already seen that major volcanic activity was relatively sparse. Whatever the nature of the linkage, El Niño events in those centuries were also fewer, less frequent, and weaker than before or since. Conditions changed quite suddenly from the late thirteenth century, when the Child stirred from slumber, and again strong El Niños coincided with renewed volcanism. Other factors became evident in the decades after 1450, when the onset of the Spörer Minimum in sunspot activity coincided with some very large eruptions on the Pacific Rim. Those eruptions had global effects.

Even describing such a possible linkage between phenomena runs the risk of sounding like the recitation of a fanciful ancient mythology: The sun warms the sea; the sea shakes the land; the mountains give forth fire; and the Holy Child is over all. But we can properly say that the connections between volcanism and climate are complex, if still debatable.

Does the Child also make the earth shake? A growing academic literature suggests that extremely heavy storms, particularly typhoons or cyclones, correlate closely with earthquakes. The mechanisms are unclear. Perhaps the atmospheric disturbance created by storms increases stress on the earth's crust, detonating quakes on faults that were already close to releasing pressure. Perhaps torrential rains and heavy flooding lubricate faults, or else they cause erosion that reduces the amount of soil pressing down on faults. But for whatever reason, we might have to add earthquakes to the consequences of El Niño systems. In some eras, such quakes could add immeasurably to the human suffering caused by chaotic climate change.[26]

Atlantic Realms

Although great movements in the Pacific had their influence worldwide, other oceanic cycles help explain why quite sudden climatic shifts could occur in a way that affected some parts of the globe and not others. One very potent feature is the North Atlantic Oscillation (NAO), which involves fluctuations in atmospheric pressure between the cold regions of the Icelandic low and the warm Azores high. The oscillation involves a shift in which each specific region experiences higher or lower than normal air pressure. When both the Iceland low and the Azores high are weaker than usual, we speak of a negative phase. When both are stronger than usual, that is a positive phase. The more positive the NAO, the warmer the air blowing over Europe. A change in the NAO affects climatic conditions in Europe and North America, but not necessarily farther afield. As with its Pacific equivalents, the NAO can be affected by such factors as solar activity and volcanoes.[27]

Because the oscillations involve changes in the atmosphere rather than the seas, this is not a precise equivalent of the Pacific system, and the Atlantic has no exact counterpart to El Niño. The closest parallel is the Atlantic Multidecadal Oscillation (AMO), a long-term pattern of sea surface temperature, which customarily operates on a cycle of sixty to seventy years. When the AMO is negative and the ocean is cooler, that is followed by drier summers in western Europe and ferocious heat or droughts in northern Africa. Volcanic action can also affect the AMO.[28]

Yet if the Atlantic has its own climate systems, those are not isolated from the larger oceanic realities, which operate together in a common global system. On occasion, different Atlantic and Pacific trends converge, as both the NAO and ENSO contribute to sharply colder weather. The two are linked by what is known as thermohaline (literally, "heat/salt") circulation, which drives what has been described as a worldwide ocean conveyor belt. As recently as 2009–2010, Europe experienced a historically cold winter, although unaccompanied by the famine that might have occurred in earlier centuries. This resulted from a combination of low solar activity, an extremely negative phase of the NAO, and a warm El Niño event. Looking at any such event, we are not forced to choose between volcanoes, oceanic currents, and a weakened sun. It is not a question of either/or. The gods of fire and water might be collaborating to reward or punish their ungrateful human subjects.[29]

That interconnectedness is crucial to understanding the historical eras that I will be discussing. Europe and North America are of course the regions that have produced so many of our documentary sources and most shaped our periodization of centuries as the Medieval Warm Period or the Little Ice Age. Looking at events that have had a disproportionate effect on those parts of the world, climate scientists often emphasize the workings of the NAO. Researchers have argued convincingly that a positive phase of that oscillation was responsible for medieval warmth, and a strong negative for the later freezing, and there is no reason to challenge those conclusions. But as I will suggest, such trends found parallels far from the shores of the Atlantic, and we see a powerful correlation between climate-driven trends on opposite sides of the world. To take one example, the ice age years around 1630 were as abominable for China as for Italy, for India as for Britain. The NAO alone cannot have been responsible for those widely separated outcomes. One or two such examples might be coincidental, but repeatedly, eras of smiling prosperity or crushing gloom very often do echo across continents. What such instances indicate, irrefutably, is that the world and its oceans constitute an interlocking and interdependent system.[30]

Then and Now

I have described the appropriation of climate history in strictly contemporary debates over emissions and global warming. Yet the better we understand the very diverse forces driving climate changes through the centuries, the harder it is to relate those former times of feast and famine to the conditions that affect the world today and in the near future. We are dealing with quite different worlds.

Historically, multiple forces could trigger periods of unusual warmth or cold, either in some regions or across a large part of the globe, and such conditions arise entirely free of human intervention. Yet such changes need not have any relevance to contemporary climate issues. In each of the cases mentioned, conditions indeed arose from transient circumstances, which (from a human perspective) might be better or worse in some periods than others. That is utterly different from the present-day reality, in which warming can indisputably be linked to ever rising levels of emissions, which promise a substantial and ever-growing transformation of climate. Moreover, those present trends emphatically are not going to vanish of their own accord. That is what separates historical climate changes over the past millennium or so from their present-day counterparts. It is quite possible to believe that the Medieval Warm Period (say) was an observable reality without casting doubt on contemporary climate science.[31]

3
Ages of Gold

The Thirteenth: Greatest of Centuries
—Title of book by James J. Walsh, 1907

In the 1130s, the abbot Suger began rebuilding his abbey church of St. Denis, near Paris. He used a daring new style that did not fit well with known architectural approaches, and it was generally termed *opus modernum*, from the word *modo*, meaning "of the current manner." What he termed "modern" art, later generations would call Gothic. That style dominated Latin European building and design for centuries to come, awing generations of admiring observers. Samuel Taylor Coleridge proclaimed that "the principle of the Gothic architecture is infinity made imaginable."[1]

Gothic architecture was the most recognizable symbol of an age of breathtaking cultural achievement, which was at its height between the late eleventh and late thirteenth centuries. In Europe alone, besides the awe-inspiring cathedrals, this "modern" cultural explosion was the age of the schools and universities that made so many breakthroughs in philosophy, learning, and theology. The religious efflorescence would be recalled as an age of faith, a golden age of spirituality that later eras would idealize and exalt. Among many other luminaries, the saints Francis, Dominic, and Thomas Aquinas all lived in the century after 1170. In these same years too, secular culture achieved flamboyant heights in romance and literature, represented, for instance, by the Arthurian cycle. Historians speak of a twelfth-century renaissance. Obviously, there were terrible misdeeds and atrocities, especially with respect to the persecution and massacre of Jews, heretics, and unbelievers, but this genuinely was a time of material progress and intellectual endeavor, which was expressed above all in the realm of religion. For Latin Europe at least, these accomplishments were unparalleled since the fall of the Roman Empire in the West in the fifth century.[2]

But why then? Why should that great age—that proto-modern age—have occurred when it did? Why were the 700s, say, not vaunted as the greatest of centuries? Neither the cultural growth nor the spiritual achievement of the High Middle Ages is explicable except in terms of its material foundations, the wealth that was generated before it could be invested in churches and monasteries, schools and universities. This era laid the essential economic foundations of the Europe we know in recent times, in terms of its towns, its commerce, and its financial structures. In turn, that underlying prosperity is incomprehensible except in terms of the climatic conditions of the time. Europe and much of the world basked in warmer weather than had been known for centuries, and the effects of that Medieval Warm Period reverberated through society, the economy, and the worlds of culture and religion. Climate begat this first modern age, and its religious consciousness.[3]

The effects of that warmer environment are evident in the context of Europe and Christianity, which I will explore in some detail. The trend was not truly global, in that other parts of the world, including regions of the Pacific, ran counter to the warming pattern. But Europe was not quite alone, as we can find signs of similar patterns in areas of North and South America and of East Asia. The resulting parallels, across otherwise unconnected cultures and faiths, are remarkably close. Beyond Europe too, later generations recalled the greatest of centuries.

The Medieval Sun

In Europe, that climate anomaly involved a temperature rise of around one or one and a half degrees Celsius over the earlier era. The reasons for the change are much debated, but the relative lack of major volcanic activity played its part. More important was the intensity of solar activity, as measured through the occurrence of sunspots: the height of activity, the Medieval Maximum, lasted from 1100 through 1250. Current theories also cite a persistent positive and warming effect from the North Atlantic Oscillation, working together in a kind of feedback loop with the Pacific La Niña. For my present purposes, the exact sequence of causation scarcely matters: warming still happened, and we can trace its impact, especially on cultural and religious life.[4]

Within the European world, that temperature rise was enough to drive substantial growth. If the scale of the increase sounds small, the cumulative impact of such a change spread over three centuries—ten or twelve human generations—was powerful. The overwhelming majority of people worked directly on the land, and those who did not depended entirely for their survival on the farmers and peasants. A warmer world meant longer growing seasons, which improved agricultural productivity. By expanding the areas in which crops could be grown and livestock raised, these conditions significantly increased food supply. More food allowed the expansion of settlements and encouraged the settling of new lands that not long before would have been marginal or undesirable, including uplands and former wastelands. Some of those reclaimed lands became pasture, as the proliferation of sheep herds laid the foundation for a booming textile industry. The people of the Low Countries pushed steadily ahead with the long process of reclaiming land from the sea. New villages sprang up across Europe. In turn, these new opportunities allowed the establishment of homes and families. The greater availability of food allowed Europe's population to swell from perhaps 35–40 million in the tenth century to over 80 million by the end of the thirteenth. Between 1000 and 1250, France's population alone grew from 9 to 15 million.[5]

Of course, growth was neither uniform nor untrammeled, and there were periods of dreadful conditions, of droughts, heatwaves, or floods, on a local or continental scale. Such were the mid-1090s and the 1108–1110 period, the years around 1200, and the several years following 1229. At such times, famines continued to occur, and some were disastrous. As in modern times, some of the absolute worst actually resulted from human intervention, such as the Norman destruction of food supplies in northern England in the 1060s, which resulted in hundreds of thousands of fatalities. But even apart from such atrocities, famine remained a factor in human affairs, and it is powerful testimony to the influence of the generally warm climate that overall population numbers continued to surge as they did.[6]

Contributing to this sustained growth, medieval Europeans suffered less from disastrous plagues than in previous or later eras. Modern stereotypes of medieval life rightly imagine widespread ill health, but also incessant epidemic diseases. Epidemics did strike in particular times and places, but between the seventh century and the fourteenth, Europe did not experience a pandemic catastrophe on anything like the scale of Justinian's Plague or the later Black Death. The latter centuries of the warm period, between 1090 and 1270, were relatively benign in that regard. The main exception to this statement was leprosy, or Hansen's Disease, which became much more widespread in exactly these years. This was a disease most closely associated with warm climates, and coincidentally or not, the worst years of that scourge in Britain at least corresponded closely with that anomalous climatic period, from the eleventh century through the fourteenth. One dreadful consequence of warming was to expand the range of the climate conditions in which the disease flourished, along with the animal hosts that carried it.[7]

Trade and Towns

Favorable weather improved life in many ways, as warmer conditions on land and sea opened trade routes. Iceland was settled in the 870s, Greenland a century later, and around 1000 the Norse established a foothold in North America. Both the Baltic and the North Sea remained free of significant ice dangers. Greater access to the seas increased opportunities for fishing, and those in turn augmented European protein supplies. But other appetites also drove geographical expansion, above all the elite taste for high-value items like spices. By far the most significant of the world's trade connections was the Silk Route, which connected the Middle East to Central Asia and China, allowing the growth of great trading entrepôts that for some years flourished astonishingly. By 1200, the now forgotten center of Merv in Turkmenistan might briefly have been the world's most populous city. In these teeming trading emporia, Christians, Muslims, Buddhists, and Manicheans coexisted and interacted.[8]

Within Europe, increased trade—both long and short range—combined with higher production to boost urban development on a far greater scale than anything seen since the later Roman Empire. Urban and industrial activity were at their height in the Rhineland, northern France, northern Italy, and the Low Countries. In 900, we would be hard pressed to find many cities in Christian Europe with populations exceeding 30,000. Constantinople at that point might have had 150,000 people, Rome and Venice around 40,000 apiece. By 1200, Constantinople was still a massive center for the time, with 200,000 people, but it no longer stood in such splendid isolation. By this point, perhaps twenty-five European cities had populations of between 30,000 and 60,000. Paris and Palermo each exceeded 100,000, with Genoa and Venice approaching that size. As I will describe later, Europe's Islamic-ruled regions followed a rather different trajectory, but still produced significant urban development.[9]

New networks of towns, trade, and commerce demanded a new commercial sophistication. From the eleventh century, merchant banks emerged, initially in the Lombard cities of Italy, which benefited immeasurably from the dependable wealth of local cereal crops. Financial innovation was inextricably bound up with agricultural wealth, and finance grew from the benches—or *bancae*, banks—erected in the midst of grain markets. From the 1150s, we find the earliest foreign exchange contracts (Genoa) and the first state-guaranteed bank (Venice). Lombard bankers and Florentine merchants grew rich on the profits of distant trade routes. Meanwhile, the transnational world that developed out of the Crusades demanded secure deposits and new means to transfer money safely over long distances, which the knights of the Templar Order offered reliable service through letters of credit. Systems of insurance and underwriting emerged at just this time to safeguard trade. Most such innovations involved violating the church's strict laws against usury, but entrepreneurs creatively devised legal fictions to get around those restraints. In the Low Countries, thirteenth-century merchants met at the sign of the purse or moneybag, the *bourse*, which in various forms (*borsa, Börse*) is still the word for "stock exchange" or "trading exchange" in many languages. By the start of the thirteenth century, Europe's financial systems were beginning to take on a recognizably modern shape.[10]

Growth acquired a harshly political dimension. Population pressures encouraged states to annex and settle new lands, either from pagan or newly Christianized areas in eastern Europe or from Muslim territories in the Mediterranean and the Levant. Obviously, the Crusades have left a controversial historical reputation, with such hideous manifestations as the slaughter of European Jews in the 1090s, the brutal capture of Jerusalem, and the disastrous sack of Constantinople in 1204. But the movement serves to illustrate the extraordinary demographic changes of the time. Although the famous Crusades to the Holy Land began in the 1090s, this was only part of a larger expansion in those same years into Spain, Sicily, and the Baltic lands. Latin Europeans succeeded as long as they did because they had the population numbers to build and consolidate settlements. This was the time of the German *Ostsiedlung*, or Eastern Settlement, the steady drive of population east of the Elbe into what had been Slavic lands. That colonization was at its height between the tenth and thirteenth centuries. Besides introducing new forms of agriculture and cultivation, the movement also spread a wide network of German towns and cities deep into what we today call Poland, as well as parts of Hungary, the Czech Republic, and Romania. They created a dense landscape of German place and family names that remained vibrant until the ethnic cleansing and mass expulsions of the 1940s.[11]

Courts and Learning

This "modern" world was a very good time for institutions and structures of all kinds, both secular and religious, which developed mightily in sophistication and ambition. Rural prosperity echoed through the whole social and political system. As tenants paid rents, lords were more prosperous and less inclined to seek violent solutions for their economic crises. Thriving cities and towns enriched states with their tax payments, and their elites supported stronger states as a means of ensuring orderly trade. Traditional Marxist theory made much of these emerging towns and the challenges that their "bourgeois" residents posed to the feudal aristocratic order. But if that was an overly simple characterization, towns did indeed form a natural alliance with ambitious kings. In some countries, especially England and France, royal authority grew dramatically during the twelfth and thirteenth centuries, creating a need for more and better-educated bureaucrats. That in turn drove the founding of schools and universities. Centralized monarchies fared more poorly in other realms, especially the Empire that was centered in the German-speaking lands. But even in those territories, many lesser kings and aristocrats formed their own flourishing courts. Taken together, these materially based changes made possible the efflorescence of the medieval culture that so entranced later generations. Those wealthy courts, whether royal or aristocratic, offered the patronage that supported the poets and artists who catered to their enthusiasms. Variously, that meant epic works set in ancient Troy or the courts of Arthur or Charlemagne, or the brilliant world of visual arts that now emerged in gold, enamels, and textiles.[12]

The cities and towns supported a different form of cultural explosion in the form of the universities. Already in the late eleventh century, a guild of students at Bologna formed a new institution of comprehensive learning for which they invented a new word, *universitas*; the date usually cited is 1088. The University of Paris dates from the mid-twelfth century. That example inspired other envious cities and states, and universities proliferated in the thirteenth century, including such famous examples as Oxford, Cambridge, Padua, and Salamanca. By 1300, at least twenty universities were in operation across Europe, and any self-respecting kingdom felt the need to develop its own example. That substantial network laid the essential foundation for the development of scholarship across the continent, which among other things produced the legal and political thought on which emerging state systems were based. From the nature of the educated world at the time, that scholarship inevitably meant religious and theological exploration.[13]

Making Medieval Faith

Rural prosperity and flourishing trade created an economic surplus that was channeled into public displays of wealth, and that in turn gave a whole new material basis to religious life. In a Christian world based on the compulsory payment of tithes, surging agriculture and thriving towns gave enormous capacity for building, as people thanked God for their evident and abundant blessings. The consequence was the landscape of cathedrals and churches that we think of today as the epitome of medieval culture and art. Although those edifices took decades or even generations to complete, the chronology of construction fits precisely with the height of the warm period, especially the years between 1150 and 1260. Climatic conditions equipped communities with the motive, means, and opportunity to undertake an epic building boom.[14]

Among the most celebrated monuments was the cathedral of Chartres (1194–1220). In France, the century after 1150 also saw the main phases of building at Notre Dame de Paris, Laon, Reims, Beauvais, Bourges, and Amiens; English counterparts were Canterbury, York, Wells, Salisbury, Lincoln, and Westminster Abbey; Spain produced Toledo, León, and Burgos. There were also many spectacular monastic houses. Any such list is subjective in the architectural treasures it highlights, and that list could be expanded much further. Over and above such a catalogue would be the thousands of parish churches built or rebuilt in this era, usually in the most fashionable styles of the time, whether Romanesque or Gothic. Besides the physical fabric of the buildings themselves, the construction boom created a flourishing market for craftspeople of every kind: masons and sculptors, painters and engravers, embroiderers and textile workers, jewelers and the creators of stained glass. The sheer scale of the economic investment is almost inconceivable.[15] Church builders quickly learned the lesson that spending money so lavishly was also an ideal way to make money, or rather, to siphon off some of the surplus that society was generating. In 1125, the influential monastic leader Bernard of Clairvaux complained about the incredible wealth of newly built churches, marked by "the enormous height, extravagant length and unnecessary width of the churches, of their costly polishings and curious paintings which catch the worshipper's eye and dry up his devotion . . . Thus riches attract riches and money produces more money. I don't know why, but the wealthier a place, the readier people are to contribute to it."[16]

Religious orders transformed the Latin church and left their imprint in the physical landscape. From the late eleventh century, the roster of orders expanded and diversified enormously, and so did their numerical strength. This was the age of such long-famous orders as the Cistercians, Premonstratensians, and Carthusians. The Crusades produced their share of new religious orders as well, such as the Templars and Hospitallers, and this proliferation in itself suggests the contemporary population surplus. But these new orders also contributed to the emerging society, filling important social niches, and sometimes becoming critical drivers of the medieval economy. Monasteries were in the forefront of technological innovation, particularly as they had the resources to invest in new machinery and techniques. They were active in building and popularizing watermills and windmills and in extending their use to agriculture and even industry, especially in textiles.[17]

The Cistercian story demonstrates the complex relationship between monastic experience and the wealth of the era. In the late eleventh century, the Benedictine religious order centered at the French house of Cluny was suffering acutely from the problems of success. Cluniac houses had simply become too prosperous, and the motherhouse was flourishing on the strength of a boom in pilgrimage. Monks had abandoned primitive austerities and were employing serfs to perform much of the manual labor. In 1098, a dissident abbot named Robert of Molesme led a secession of monks who shared his distaste for prosperity, worldliness, and comfort. The new community settled at a place called Cîteaux (in Latin, Cistercium). The piety and severe discipline of the new order attracted widespread popular enthusiasm, and recruits joined in large numbers. One early member was Bernard, who headed a new house at Clairvaux, and who from the 1120s through the 1150s was arguably the most influential thinker in Latin Europe.[18]

By the mid-twelfth century, Cistercian houses could be found across much of western and central Europe. The burgeoning Cistercian communities sought new lands far removed from the busy and heavily populated secular world. Thus they expanded into undesirable waste territories, which they cleared and developed for pastoral agriculture. This in turn promoted the ongoing expansion into new rural settlements, and generated a boom in livestock and associated products. Almost by accident, this escape into the wilderness gave religious houses inordinate wealth and political power, and further escalated the building boom in churches and monasteries. Soon the Cistercian houses were constructing large and magnificent churches on exactly the lines that Bernard himself had condemned.

Other religious movements targeted the cities and towns for evangelization. From the start of the thirteenth century, Franciscan and Dominican friars represented a whole new phase in Christian life, one that would have been inconceivable except in the context of the underlying prosperity and economic expansion. Dominicans specifically directed their activities at urban audiences. Francis himself neatly symbolizes the larger story. Born in 1182, he was the son of a prosperous silk merchant, a type of occupation barely imaginable two centuries earlier. Francis himself was very much a product of the new economy of the time. His call for the absolute rejection of material goods spoke loudly to a growing and urbanizing society conscious of its material wealth and increasingly nervous about reconciling that with faith. Calls for apostolic poverty appeal best to societies that are far removed from that ideal. Francis's successors faced the perpetual problem that the faithful gave them so much of their abundance, constantly tempting the brothers to accept worldly ways. (As we will see, the resulting debates over poverty generated a vicious and enduring church crisis in the bleaker century that followed.)[19]

Remaking Doctrine

Between them, universities, monasteries, and friaries provided the setting for new learning and debate, for new theologies, new forms of spirituality. From the late eleventh century through the late thirteenth, we see the emergence and maturing of several ideas and beliefs that have been at the heart of Catholic doctrine ever since, and some of which—by no means all—have been inherited by later Protestant churches. It is startling to realize that so many key ideas and beliefs emerged or became far more central to church teaching at roughly the same time. They occurred when they did because prosperity allowed states and the social order to become more stable, while an unprecedented institutional foundation permitted the expansion of learning and speculation.

Those ideas include something as basic as the theory of Christ's Atonement. From earliest times, Christians had believed that Christ had in some sense died for the sins of the world, but the interpretations of that statement varied greatly. The dominant Western idea was formulated by Anselm of Canterbury in the 1090s, when he argued that Christ's death satisfied the offense against God that humanity had committed through the Fall. By paying the debt, this sacrificial act redeemed humanity. That era, at the end of the eleventh century, also saw the growth of other foundational Catholic ideas, including the exalted doctrine of the Papacy as the monarchical head of the church, independent of secular control. Again, those ideas had been discussed in earlier times, but they were now declared openly and aggressively, generating decades of bitter church-state conflict, to the point of open warfare.[20]

The Pope who was most closely associated with those claims, Gregory VII (1073–1085), also pressed another seemingly radical doctrine, demanding clerical celibacy. That practice was not new to the church and had been required several centuries before, but it had fallen into disuse. By reasserting that discipline, the church was seeking to demarcate clergy as a distinct caste or class, with all the privileges that entailed, and subject to internal discipline. About 1150, the monk Gratian compiled the work entitled *The Concordance of Discordant Canons*, or the *Decretum*, the first systematic effort to organize the church's canon law. That system grew dramatically over the following century, again largely through the universities. Adding to the prestige of the priestly order was a radical new emphasis on the transformation of bread and wine that occurred at the Eucharist, when those worldly materials literally become Christ's body and blood. That idea had existed for centuries, but it was at the end of the eleventh century that it achieved a newly formal and elaborate status, and the word "transubstantiation" was invented to explain the philosophical underpinnings.[21]

Many of these ideas were asserted and defended by Pope Innocent III (1198–1216), who is widely regarded as the greatest Pope of the Middle Ages, and perhaps of all time. His most visible memorial was the Fourth Lateran Council, in 1215, which offered a comprehensive survey of Catholic thought as it had emerged in recent centuries. That centrally included such ideas as transubstantiation, papal primacy, and clerical celibacy. In the mid-thirteenth century, the towering figure of Dominican friar Thomas Aquinas was systematizing Catholic theology and belief, supplying a foundation for all later generations.[22]

Throughout the period, the key focus of piety was the Virgin Mary. The Virgin inspired multiple new forms of devotion: her image was widely reproduced in all forms of visual art and design, and she was commemorated in poetry and prose. Although Marian devotion had a long history before this era, it was above all in the High Middle Ages that it became so central. This was the era when the rosary became a beloved part of Catholic piety. In 1223, St. Francis created the world's first Nativity scene in a cave in the city of Greccio, an innovative cultural symbol that spread triumphantly across all forms of Christianity and beyond.[23]

Catholicism looks like it does largely because of developments in these High Middle Ages. To that extent, it is a product of a warm sun and warm seas.

Beyond the Boundaries

Many of those religious impulses remained within the framework of church orthodoxy, while others did not. From the start of the eleventh century, we see an upsurge of movements that were designated as heretical, a development that reached a climax in the century after 1150. Again, these all have to be understood in terms of underlying social trends that had been made possible by the warming sun.

Not coincidentally, the efflorescence of heretical movements tracks very closely with the enormous building boom that transformed the material landscape of the Catholic Church. The expansion of towns and trades coupled with new educational opportunities to raise standards and expectations among a pious laity. Some of those aspiring laypeople hoped to use expanded literacy to access truths found in scripture. Others demanded that clergy live up to the highest standards of behavior and moral purity, or be expelled or penalized if they failed. Beyond the call for purity, some people were even in contact with daring alternative theological ideas emanating from southeast Europe or the Levant. Widespread religious dissidence was a direct outcome of prosperity, which included international contacts and early forms of globalization.[24]

The church hierarchy confronted a hydra of critical currents and ideas, some of which reached the stage of constituting full-scale alternative churches and sects, some with their own hierarchies. Campaigns to suppress heresy grew during the twelfth century and reached a fearsome crescendo in the early thirteenth, with a full-fledged military crusade against the Albigensian heretics of southern France. Those campaigns introduced the terrifying judicial innovation of the Inquisition. Such horrors throw an essential and troubling light on any idea of the "greatest of centuries." But however bitter their consequences, the struggles over heresy demonstrate a new world of aspirations and dreams that simply could not have happened without the impressive prosperity that Europe experienced in these centuries. These too were the problems of prosperity.[25]

Beyond Europe

Europe was not alone in experiencing such conditions. If varying somewhat on the chronology, other regions of the world readily concur with the loving memories left by the warm period as the greatest of eras. The Islamic golden age is normally dated from the mid-ninth century through the mid-thirteenth, the era of the Abbasid Caliphate based in Baghdad. The great age of Islamic Spain began somewhat later, in the early tenth century, and continued through the mid-thirteenth.[26]

This was by no means a time of universal or unrelieved success, and greater warmth in one area might be harmful in another. The Islamic-ruled Levant suffered severe droughts, famines, and insect plagues during what happened to be Europe's best years.[27] In Spain, in contrast, the cultural golden age reflected highly favorable climatic conditions. Warmth allowed more food production, and that was enhanced still further by technological skills imported into the country, especially in the form of irrigation. The population boomed, and by the eleventh century Córdoba was either the largest city in Europe or else the largest apart from Constantinople (population estimates vary widely). Palermo, in Sicily, was another thriving metropolis. Spanish kings collected multiple taxes and tithes from their prospering subjects, with extra charges levied on non-Muslim minorities. Those funds made them extremely wealthy and able to undertake the building boom that found its finest monument in the Great Mosque of Córdoba.[28]

Beyond its material remains, the faith of Islam enjoyed a spectacular era of intellectual achievement, notably in theology and philosophy. Besides this, the cultural achievement had many facets, with significant advances in fields as diverse as mathematics, architecture, medicine, astronomy, and engineering, but scholars freely integrated sacred and secular learning. Among the most celebrated figures were Ibn Sina (Avicenna, 980–1037) and the Spanish-born Ibn Rushd (Averroes, 1126–1198); the latter was a dazzling polymath. Such thinkers placed the faith of Islam on a whole new intellectual foundation, which took full account of the insights of Classical Greek philosophy and tried to reconcile human and divine knowledge. Their philosophical insights would later revolutionize learning in Christian Europe and thoroughly shape the studies of the emerging universities. In the fourteenth century, Dante would commemorate both Avicenna and Averroes as among the greatest of all non-Christian scholars, to be counted along the mightiest figures of Classical Greece and Rome.[29]

The Islamic golden age suffered dreadful blows in the mid-thirteenth century, and that chronology helps explain why we do not usually place these accomplishments in a climate context. As we know from Christian Europe, climatic conditions go far to explaining the great prosperity before about 1260 and the mounting difficulties thereafter. For the Islamic world too, the mid-thirteenth century marked a period of crisis and decline, but one that is most obviously explained in terms of political events and warfare. In Spain, Christian forces took Córdoba in 1236, and in 1258 the Mongols sacked Baghdad in one of the most traumatic disasters in the history of culture and civilization worldwide. Other wars, meanwhile, ruined large sections of the Middle East. But however important that political context unquestionably was, in a sense it disguises the larger climate context: as we will see, climate shifts would have gravely altered circumstances around the Islamic world even if those brutal conquests had never occurred.[30]

In other ways too, climate offers an essential context for the overthrow of the older Islamic order. In the early thirteenth century, the Mongol steppes of Central Asia enjoyed particularly benevolent conditions, with heavy rains and mild temperatures combining to produce rich grasslands for the feeding of livestock. That included the horses on which warriors depended, and this cavalry launched the campaigns that founded the Mongol Empire from 1206 onward. The Mongol invasions that ravaged the Islamic Middle East in midcentury were a product of medieval warmth. The states and empires they founded began a new and very different phase of Islamic history across Asia.[31]

East Asia

Almost exactly coinciding with Europe's climate anomaly, China was from 960 through 1279 ruled by the Song dynasty, which is commonly regarded as the greatest era of the country's imperial past. Here too, benevolent climate conditions played their part. Significant warming affected the whole empire, most dramatically during the twelfth and early thirteenth centuries. If Europe has its Medieval Warm Period, China has its Song-Yuan Warm Period.[32]

Like Europe, Song China experienced a great population expansion, though on a still greater scale. The country's population probably doubled during the dynasty's rule, to perhaps 140 million by the thirteenth century. This growth owed something to the shrewd cultivation of new forms of rice, but climate conditions allowed the expansion of rice cultivation into many new regions. Booming harvests and food surpluses allowed the maintenance of strong and numerous armed forces. They also provided the basis for legendary prosperity, broad social diversification, and incredible urban growth. By 1250, China had a dozen cities with populations running into the hundreds of thousands, and the capital, Kaifeng, had between half a million and a million residents. The Song state presided over some innovations that dwarfed progress in contemporary Europe. Among the most famous, China now developed gunpowder and deployed the maritime compass, and the state issued banknotes. Movable-type printing also became commonplace. Culture, art, and literature all thrived, creating some of the most esteemed achievements in the nation's whole history.[33]

Korea and Japan

That century after 1150 repeatedly emerges as a pivotal period, in which China's neighbors likewise flourished. From the eleventh century through the thirteenth, Korea enjoyed a political and cultural golden age, its Goryeo period, which was marked by the creation of many universities. Buddhist learning and scholarship prospered, with many figures who earned reputations as saints and scholars, notably Jinul, a near-contemporary of Europe's Dominic. As in Europe, new religious orders proliferated. Korean Buddhism found its greatest monument in the so-called Korean Tripitaka, a comprehensive collection of scriptures carved onto more than 80,000 wooden printing blocks. An earlier version was destroyed during warfare, and the present collection mainly dates from the 1240s. The scholarship is no less impressive than the technological accomplishment and the degree of innovation. Europe has Gothic cathedrals; Korea has its Tripitaka. Each in its way is a key monument to civilization, and to faith.[34]

Japan offers still closer parallels to the European experience. Indeed, the number of resemblances is remarkable, and the synchronicity has often been noted. That is striking because of the total lack of connection between the two regions: at most, a handful of travelers might have created tenuous connections between Europe and Eastern Asia, but nothing sufficient to explain the parallels. In 1185, Japan entered its Kamakura period, so named from the city that was the capital of its shoguns, its feudal/military elite. Japanese society clearly differed in so many ways from the West, but as in Europe, the Kamakura era was a time of blossoming rural prosperity, with growth and diversification of agriculture and commercial activity. While government reforms played some role in this improvement, Japan benefited fundamentally from underlying climate changes.[35]

In terms of religious history, Japan over the next century experienced what Europeans might term at once a time of renaissance and of religious reformation, an astonishingly fertile period of creativity. By the Kamakura era, Japanese Buddhism already had several centuries of history, with a widespread monastic network. A wealthier society poured resources into temples and monasteries, allowing more monks and priests to pursue their activities, to imagine and enact sweeping reforms. The word "faith" carries different connotations in Buddhism than in Christianity, but the Kamakura years certainly look like an age of faith, the height of which coincided neatly with European developments. As in Europe too, an age of ebullient religious expansion has left many remains in the form of artistic treasures. Kamakura-era Buddhism is associated with some of the most awe-inspiring treasures of Japanese culture, above all in painting and sculpture, as well as calligraphy. As Suger of St. Denis might have said, each in its way was a triumph of the modern.

This was the time of New Buddhism, Shin Bukkyo, which is remembered for several key strands of reform and innovation. As in Europe, those developments shaped the major faith—in this case, Buddhism—up to the present day. And as in Europe, the story is marked by several wildly creative individuals who are among the best known in the history of the respective faiths. The most successful Buddhist schools emphasized outreach to a mass public, in a way that would have made instant sense to Europe's Catholic reformers, as well as to its heretical sects.[36] From the end of the twelfth century, several critical movements developed almost simultaneously. In terms of numerical influence, the greatest was Pure Land Buddhism, which taught that ordinary people could achieve salvation by faith in the bodhisattva Amitabha, and by reciting his name. The great figure here was the monk Honen (1133–1212), who led what he saw as a total reform of the religion. He was in turn followed by his disciple Shinran, founder of the Shin Buddhist tradition. Today, Pure Land Buddhism has by far the largest number of followers of any Buddhist school, not just in Japan but in the world. Also very influential to this day is the tradition founded by the priest Nichiren (1222–1282), a tempestuous reformer who is often compared to Europe's Martin Luther. Nichiren's faith centered on devotion to one scripture, the Lotus Sutra, but he offered many new and radical ideas, including the abandonment of clerical celibacy.[37]

Best known in the West was the school of Zen Buddhism, which in its Japanese form was founded by two key reformers of the century after 1170, Eisai and Dogen. (Zen has much older Chinese roots, but its implanting and cultivation in Japan belongs to these years.) Dogen (1200–1253) in particular was one of the central figures of Japanese history, a mystic, philosopher, poet, and religious reformer of incalculable influence on later generations. To portray his importance in Western terms, we would have to combine the figures of his three close contemporaries, Francis, Dominic, and (especially) Thomas Aquinas.[38]

China and Japan

The Japanese flowering is so evident as to raise questions about why China should have produced so little on similar lines, and especially nothing comparable in terms of religious diversity. The very different nature of state power in the two societies goes far toward supplying an explanation.

Religion shared in the general prosperity of Song China. There was some innovation at elite levels, with the development of neo-Confucianism, while Daoism enjoyed a revival under imperial patronage. Meanwhile, easier international communications allowed many foreigners to travel to and from China, and to take with them scriptures and beliefs, especially in the Buddhist tradition. But in contrast to Japan, or indeed to Europe, we do not find anything like the upsurge of new movements and currents, the obvious stirrings among grassroots believers. The European contrast was largely because of fundamental differences between the nature of religion (and, indeed, its very definition) in the two societies. While religious beliefs and behavior were pervasive in China, most of those actions were conducted within a state-approved mechanism, and new movements were most likely during a period of governmental weakness or anarchy. The Song state was usually very strong, and bureaucratic control actually became far tighter and more comprehensive during these years. In this case at least, a country experienced a true golden age, but without the religious responses we have seen in Europe.

That same explanation underlies the contrast with Japan. In China, prosperity buttressed central state control, reinforcing the power and prestige of the emperor and his bureaucratic servants, who tightly regulated the religious environment. Japan offered nothing similar: warlords and samurai exercised much independence, and with it the ability to patronize whatever religious currents appealed to them. Whatever the shoguns may have wished, there was always a great deal of de facto decentralization, recalling the Europe of this same period. In Japan, as in Europe, local aristocrats and their courts offered rich patronage to religious innovators and entrepreneurs. The wealth of their lands gave those lords the resources to do so.[39]

Prosperity drove religious growth and expansion; but political structures conditioned and constrained the opportunities available to religious impulses.

Conclusion

Whether in Eastern or Western worlds, accounts of the High Middle Ages—especially the century or so after 1150—tend to invite superlatives, and that is nowhere more true than in matters of religion. Such an era simply could not have occurred without the material foundations made possible by the changing climate. Warmth allowed growth and complexity, in effect creating religious systems that in large measure survive today. Just how thoroughly the climate shaped religious life can best be appreciated when we see the opposite reality, when a sudden shift to colder and wetter conditions began an era of hunger and disease, of conflict and resentment.

4
God's Anger and the Demons Within

> Those killed by the sword are better off
> than those who die of famine;
> racked with hunger, they waste away
> for lack of food from the field.
>
> —Lamentations 4:9

Warmth and prosperity shaped cultures, and called forth particular kinds of religious response. But if we reverse those factors, the religious manifestations appear utterly different. Expansion, creativity, and hope give place to contraction, paranoia, and outright violence. However we define or explain the Medieval Warm Period, it was followed by the troubled era of the Little Ice Age, which endured for centuries.

I will focus here on one uniquely dreadful time of climate-based crisis, one with far-reaching effects. Over time, governments and subjects alike would learn to cope with the new climatic regime and its constraints, adjusting food production techniques where possible, and withdrawing from overexposed settlements. But matters were deeply stressed in the early phases of the new era, when expectations were still conditioned by the warmer years gone by. In Europe and the Middle East, the years between 1310 and 1325 were among the very worst in recorded history, as Europe suffered its horrific Great Famine.[1] Particularly in the years around 1320, both Christian and Muslim worlds experienced a hideous outbreak of ill-focused paranoia and scapegoating. Large sections of the population imagined a series of insidious dangers and projected them onto various minorities, real and imaginary. Christians dreaded Jews, lepers, and that newly defined menace, witches. The definitions of heresy expanded broadly, as did the willingness to root out dissent through bloodshed. Muslims, meanwhile, stigmatized Christians. Within both Islam and Christianity, rigorists sought to exclude believers from the respective faiths, condemning them as apostates and false believers. Violence and persecution mounted, culminating in the Black Death years of the 1340s. Among Christians, apocalyptic belief became so pervasive that the Book of Revelation became at once a critical source of comfort and of lethal controversy.[2]

The result of the climate-driven catastrophe was a religious world that we find familiar today. Christians were reduced to the status of a small minority in the Islamic world, while many of Europe's Jews relocated to the eastern parts of the continent, where they remained until the new massacres of the Holocaust. Europe's witch panic endured for four more centuries. The crisis also affected Asian societies, and the rise of a robustly nationalist and xenophobic regime in China resulted in the obliteration of what had until then been a thriving and expanding Christian church. In numerical terms, Christianity decisively became a European religion, in a way it had never been previously. For Christians as for Jews, a climate crisis destroyed one religious world and created another.

The Little Ice Age

The Little Ice Age is usually dated from the late thirteenth century through the mid-nineteenth. As often in such matters, debates about the exact limits of the era differ substantially, but a fair consensus would locate a starting point between 1260 and 1300. Severe and repeated El Niño events certainly played a role, while the North Atlantic Oscillation shifted decisively into negative (colder) mode. I have also noted the proliferation of really major volcanic eruptions through a large portion of this era, far more than in the High Middle Ages. Beyond the effects of any one eruption, on several occasions the world had to cope with the cumulative impact of two or three within a period of a few years. That steady bombardment could not fail to reshape climate in many ways, especially through the fluctuation of oceanic cycles. Declining amounts of solar radiation reaching the planetary surface caused cooling, and as we have seen, it might have contributed to volcanic activity. The Wolf Minimum in sunspot activity is dated from 1280 through the 1340s, with its nadir around 1315.[3]

Within the larger ice age, we can differentiate some particularly horrible eras, such as the winter of 1407–1408, a time of extraordinary cold that was among the very worst winters of the millennium. Most of Europe's rivers froze, including the whole lower Danube, as icebergs menaced the North Sea and even the English Channel. Temperatures again plummeted through the decade of the 1430s, described earlier. The cold era went through a number of successive pulses or waves, and the one beginning about 1560 began a singularly harsh era that endured until around 1720. I will return to those years in the next chapter. Conditions did not change fundamentally until the mid-nineteenth century, coinciding with the sudden rise of polluting industries.[4]

Reconstructions of older climates point to sizable temperature variations worldwide, challenging ideas of a single global ice age event. But the cumulative evidence of some kind of cooling is strong, above all in Eurasia and the Middle East. And as we will see, evidence from China and East Asia show temperature fluctuations closely parallel to those of western Eurasia. We are dealing with very expansive, if not completely global, effects.[5]

The First Crisis

In 1257, the enormous (and highly sulfurous) Samalas eruption offered an ugly foretaste of future centuries. Through 1258 and 1259, many societies around the world reported dark skies, with extremely cold and rainy weather, which together ruined harvests and drove famine and epidemic. This was a dark year, a year of fog. Over the past thousand years, the summer of 1259 was the third-coldest, and 1258 and 1259 were the coldest two consecutive summers in that era. Effects are reported in chronicles and official records across Europe, the Islamic world, and East Asia, and are hypothesized for other regions, including North America and the Pacific. In England,

> the north wind prevailed for several months. . . . scarcely a small rare flower or shooting germ appeared, whence the hope of harvest was uncertain. . . . Innumerable multitudes of poor people died, and their bodies were found lying all about swollen from want. . . . Nor did those who had homes dare to harbor the sick and dying, for fear of infection. . . . The pestilence was immense—insufferable; it attacked the poor particularly.

Perhaps a third of Londoners died.[6]

Rebellions and riots toppled regimes. In England, 1258 is celebrated as the year when the country's first Parliament was established, and thus as a breakthrough in representative government. In the context of the time, this was an extreme concession by the monarchy, which confronted furious and fearful barons driven to desperation by economic circumstances.

The transcontinental crisis drove religious responses. Japan suffered its severe Shoga famine between 1257 and 1260, creating a terrifying mood of national calamity. That in turn inspired the prophetic religious reformer Nichiren to escalate his activity from seeking to convert individuals to launching a movement for national salvation, attacking religious and secular authorities. Although he somehow kept his life, that crisis around 1260 marked the decisive turning point in his very influential career.[7]

In Europe, one notorious aspect of medieval faith was the Flagellant movement, in which hundreds or thousands of believers would march in procession in a kind of pilgrimage, mortifying their flesh by whipping themselves, often with great severity. The first recorded instances of this behavior occurred in Italy in 1259–1260, in response to calamitous food shortages. The movement found its charter in a letter that an angel reputedly delivered directly from Heaven, which explained that human failure to observe the Sabbath had so enraged God that he was close to destroying the world altogether. Only the penance of the Flagellants could save humanity. Flagellant movements regularly reappeared over the next century, in response to new famines and plagues and successive new threats of the imminent end times.[8]

As so often, volcanoes coincided with damaging El Niños, and conditions deteriorated sharply in the later thirteenth century. The mid-1290s were parlous across Europe, with vicious droughts, and many rivers and seaways frozen hard. The waterways that normally separate the Scandinavian lands all became passable on foot or sled, with the Kattegat and Baltic under thick ice. England in 1294 suffered a dire famine, and the following year "produced no grain or fruits, so that the poor died of hunger." The worst years of hunger persisted through 1298, as Flagellants were once more in evidence across Europe. Famines became commonplace events in the Europe of the opening decade of the new century. The years between 1287 and 1317 witnessed extraordinarily damaging droughts from the Mediterranean across to South Asia. From 1312 through 1329, the Mediterranean suffered one of its worst droughts of the millennium, with a reprise from 1351 through 1366. Large sections of the Americas suffered comparably from the late thirteenth century. Such an intense and lasting drought was responsible for the collapse of the thriving civilization in the US Southwest that was traditionally known as the Anasazi, with all its awe-inspiring monuments. The societies that emerged from that crash developed a revolutionary new religious movement, the kachina cult, with its central emphases on water supply and rainfall.[9]

The Hungriest Years

Although European conditions were deteriorating from the later thirteenth century, the full scale of disaster did not become evident until after 1310. The onslaught of climate-driven changes was magnified because it followed so shortly on the warmth and prosperity of the previous two centuries, when population pressures had forced settlers to swarm onto new and marginal lands. In the new conditions, Europe and the Middle East faced a harsh new world, as pack ice grew in the oceans and both land and sea trade routes became more difficult. In 1306 and 1323, the Baltic Sea was completely icebound. Besides crippling trade, those changes ruined fishing activities and severely reduced supplies of protein. Even if other food production had held steady, that would have had a special impact on a Christian Europe that enforced lengthy fast periods when meat was prohibited and people relied on fish.[10]

From 1315, Europe suffered horrendous cold and rain that ruined successive summers, and for several years farming became all but impossible. The origins of this event are unclear, but volcanism just might have played a role. Conditions at this time resembled those following the supercolossal Tambora eruption of a half millennium later. No such volcanic event in or near 1314 features in presently known lists of the most destructive eruptions, although New Zealand's Mount Tarawera is a possible candidate. Future research might fill that gap.[11]

Whatever the causes, incessant torrential rains resulted in catastrophic flooding. Wood became so waterlogged that it could not serve as fuel, and that in turn eliminated production of salt, the main food preservative. No preservative meant removing the food on which people depended for survival through the winter months, especially fish. Meanwhile, livestock suffered their own disasters. Hungry people were forced to eat the animals that should have been plowing fields, further hitting the possibility of revived production. If that was not bad enough, animal diseases then eliminated a very large share of livestock. The rinderpest panzootic that began in 1318 was ruinous on a scale never before seen in large parts of Europe.[12] Here is a contemporary English account of the great dearth:

> The summer rains were so heavy that grain could not ripen. It could hardly be gathered and used to bake bread down to the said feast day unless it was first put in vessels to dry. Around the end of autumn the dearth was

> mitigated in part, but toward Christmas it became as bad as before. . . . There can be no doubt that the poor wasted away when even the rich were constantly hungry. . . . The usual kinds of meat, suitable for eating, were too scarce; horse meat was precious; plump dogs were stolen. And, according to many reports, men and women in many places secretly ate their own children.[13]

As in any era, the phrase "even the rich were constantly hungry" is arresting.

Between 1315 and 1322, much of Europe suffered the worst famine of the whole Middle Ages, and not until 1325 did food supplies return to anything like a normal level. Even so, underlying trends continued unabated, and the prospects for food production remained difficult at best. Disease followed hunger. In 1316,

> an universal dearth prevailed, and such a mortality, particularly of the poor, followed, that the living could scarce bury the dead; for a dysentery, generated by corrupted food, infected nearly all, and this was accompanied by an acute fever, which reduced many to extremity. Cattle as well as men were affected. The wisdom of medical men availed not, as the herbs had lost their medicinal virtues.

This prolonged crisis left a poisonous memory in European minds for centuries afterward.[14]

Famine and Plague

Starved populations were exposed to diseases, and the coming of the Black Death pandemic proved the coup de grâce. That plague began in China in 1331 and struck Europe during the following decade. It wreaked havoc on an incalculable scale. In Europe alone, it eliminated between a third and a half of the population, and the global toll might have approached 200 million. Some two-thirds of China's population perished. In 1377, the Arab polymath scholar Ibn Khaldun recorded how the plague had

> devastated nations and caused populations to vanish. . . . Cities and buildings were laid waste, roads and way signs were obliterated, settlements and mansions became empty, dynasties and tribes grew weak. The entire

> inhabited world changed. It was as if the voice of existence in the world had called out for oblivion and restriction. And the world had responded to its call.[15]

The exact relationship between the earlier famine and the later plague is open to some debate, especially if a significant length of time—two decades or more—separated the two crises. Recent scholarship, however, supports the strong continuity of conditions between the early 1320s and the mid-1340s. Studies of ice core evidence show that the cold and wet weather affected a much wider area than hitherto believed, and for longer periods. Europe suffered severe droughts in 1325, while terrible rains and floods returned in 1330–1331 and 1338. Even in Italy, many rivers were frozen in 1334. Endemic food shortages of varying severity persisted long after the most notorious years of the Great Famine. Indeed, they endured for much for the period between 1325 and the arrival of the plague in the mid-1340s, resulting in a steep population decline across Eurasia even before the plague itself. That evidence gives climate a much more plausible role in causing the cataclysm of the Black Death and aggravating its effects.[16]

Climate played its part in initiating the original outbreak of plague, which probably began in Tibet or Qinghai. The same catastrophe that drenched Europe manifested elsewhere in a lengthy drought, which killed off wild rodents in huge numbers. That in turn left their fleas to seek new hosts in the form of rats, which proved far more successful than their predecessors in incubating and spreading disease.[17]

A World in Crisis

Economic and social collapse naturally produced political crises. Historians have long been familiar with turmoil and breakdowns in particular countries in the early fourteenth century, but when we map them together, they form a strikingly consistent pattern.

Even if the rich could somehow find food for themselves, their tenants were in no position to pay rents, and bitterly resented landlords' efforts to enforce their rights. Desperation and anger trickled upward, threatening monarchies. Revolts and conspiracies proliferated, and the English king Edward II faced extensive baronial risings in 1321–1322. Edward's government collapsed in 1327, when he died mysteriously, presumably murdered. Scotland took the opportunity to assert its national independence, and in 1320 the Declaration of Arbroath represented a fiery assertion of national autonomy.[18]

Internecine struggles in the eastern Mediterranean laid the foundations for the emergence of the mighty Ottoman Empire. From 1321 to 1328, civil war rent the reduced but still powerful Byzantine Empire. The beneficiaries were the eastern Turkish people who followed the family of Osman, from which we get the term "Ottoman." Those Muslim forces took advantage of Byzantine divisions to advance their power decisively in Asia Minor, setting up their capital at Bursa, just sixty miles from Constantinople. From the 1350s, the next generation of Ottomans began the military push that would give them control over much of southeastern Europe by the end of the century. That expansion would have been inconceivable if not for the extreme weakening of the Christian powers by plague and famine, and specifically from the crisis around 1320.[19]

Violence was by no means confined to the world of kings and aristocrats. From the start of the century, generalized suffering spawned waves of paranoia and conspiracy theory, which affected widely disparate societies throughout Europe and far beyond. It was in 1290 that England expelled all its Jews, followed by France in 1306. In 1298, the Rintfleisch massacres began a new and large-scale series of pogroms directed against Jews in the German lands. Perhaps 20,000 were slaughtered. In several of the worst outbreaks, mobs were reacting to blood libel charges, allegations that Jews murdered Christian children for ritual purposes. Such charges originated in the twelfth century but became more common, and much more widespread geographically, from the 1250s onward.[20]

Other groups besides Jews were demonized, including some who had very recently been regarded as Christians of exemplary holiness. In 1307, the French king arrested the members of the Knights Templar on trumped-up charges of devil worship, heresy, and conspiracy, eradicating what had been the greatest crusading order. Among other sins, the knights were accused of denying Christ and spitting on the cross. Those horrible allegations received wide publicity when they were reported at length in the great Council of Vienne held by the church in 1311–1312. The exact nature of the Templars' misdeeds has been the source of florid speculation through the centuries, and it remains open to question whether the charges had any core of truth, however exaggerated or misinterpreted. The confessions in the case were certainly brought forth under torture. But the fact of those charges would prove immensely influential in offering a readily available repertoire of nightmares on which later inquisitors and persecutors could draw as needed. Such opportunities often arose during the famine years after 1314.[21]

Plotters and Poisoners

The sheer range of such conspiracy theories suggests an urgent quest for dangerous outsiders of any and all kinds. We see something like a natural progression in terms of the reality of the menaces imagined. It began with targeting people who assuredly did exist and were to some extent organized through social and family networks, notably Jews, whose threat potential was ferociously enhanced. It then moved to people who existed as a category, such as lepers, who were now presented as a sinister organized movement. It progressed to people who had been accepted and tolerated within the church, but who were now stigmatized as deadly enemies of faith. Particularly at risk were those Christians who strove most arduously for personal piety and even perfection, initially the Templars and then other groups. And most tellingly, the catalogue of evils included people who did not exist in the form that was alleged—namely, witches. Campaigns now targeted a bewilderingly large array of plotters and poisoners, many of whom supposedly concealed their evil intentions behind a mask of innocuous decency. An ordinary believer could never be sure whether friends or neighbors were what they seemed or were part of the various inchoate conspiracies.

I emphasize the novelty of some aspects of this atmosphere of paranoia. The persecution of Jews was anything but new, and the massacres in the 1090s had been on a horrific scale. So, likewise, was the bloodshed directed against heretics in the early thirteenth century. With this said, the persecution of Jews after 1320 was not only much more systematic but also grounded in detailed theories and mythologies of Jewish misdeeds. Equally, the crusade against heretics in the age of the Albigensians had targeted a genuine alternative current of belief and practice, with a distinctive hierarchy. After 1310, in contrast, the church was freely applying the heretical label on an ever more expansive scale to believers who were critical of the church but had nothing like the subversive theologies of earlier groups.[22]

Time and again, the years around 1320 mark a pivotal moment in this process of general scapegoating and stigmatization. In 1321, France suffered various outbreaks of hysterical violence, including the so-called Lepers' Plot. In the words of the inquisitor Bernard Gui:

> There was detected and prevented an evil plan of the lepers against the healthy persons in the kingdom of France. Indeed, plotting against the safety of the people, these persons, unhealthy in body and insane in mind, had arranged to infect the waters of the rivers and fountains and wells everywhere, by placing poison and infected matter in them and by mixing (into the water) prepared powders, so that healthy men drinking from them or using the water thus infected, would become lepers, or die, or almost die, and thus the numbers of the lepers would be increased and the healthy decreased.[23]

In an age of appalling sanitation, any suggestion that water supplies could lead to disease was likely to find near-instant confirmation, regardless of any actual malfeasance by lepers or any other group. As the investigation widened, the supposed malefactors were accused of working on behalf of Jewish manipulators, who in turn were in the pay of Spain's Muslim regimes, as part of a general scheme to subvert Christianity.

Witches

The European witch persecutions have their roots in precisely these years. Hitherto, witchcraft commonly had been interpreted as supernatural malice directed against neighbors, which might be carried out on an individual or collective basis. When people died suddenly, as they so often did, it was common to seek some kind of supernatural agency. In the famous words of a modern anthropological study, "Death evokes the notion of witchcraft; oracles are consulted to determine the course of vengeance; magic is made to attain it; oracles decide when magic has executed vengeance; and its magical task being ended, the medicine is destroyed." But such activities had no necessary connections with devil worship or religious unorthodoxy. Nor, initially, was there yet any sign of the pact with the Devil that became so standard a component of later prosecutions. All that now changed very rapidly—in historical terms, almost overnight.[24]

We get a sense of shifting attitudes from the visions of the otherworld offered by Dante Alighieri and his *Divine Comedy*, which was published before his death in 1321. His *Inferno*, probably written in 1314–1315, gives a magnificent survey of concepts of the diabolical at exactly this time, and of the demonic role as tempters. Given his encyclopedic awareness of types of sins, we might be surprised that he says so little about conscious human alliances with the demonic, in the form of witchcraft. The issue receives passing references in Canto 20, as a minor topic alongside the larger themes of divination, soothsaying, and astrology, but commonplace witches feature only as those who "do harm with herbs and effigies": *fecer malie con erbe e con imago*. But that lack of reference is important in its own right. Dante was writing immediately before the radical transformation of concepts of witchcraft and a critical escalation of the danger it posed to society and to salvation.[25]

Inquisitors had repeatedly asked the Papacy for permission to investigate such occult crimes, together with divination, but such requests were not approved. Matters changed with the arrival of Pope John XXII (1316–1334), who in his attitudes toward the supernatural was a perfect microcosm of his times. He became Pope at one of the darkest moments in the era, an age of despair and paranoia. He lived in personal dread of supernatural assaults, just as other Renaissance potentates might fear assassination, and in 1317 he had the bishop of Cahors arrested on a hair-raising series of charges involving sorcery and demonic invocation. Other similar supernaturally oriented charges against political enemies followed over the next few years.[26]

In 1320, Pope John allowed the Inquisition at Carcassonne and Toulouse to investigate and punish sorcerers and witches, *sortilegiis et maleficis*. He referred specifically to "those who make sacrifice to demons or adore them, or do homage unto them by giving them as a sign a written pact or other token; or who make certain binding pacts with them." However conventional this language may sound from what we know of later witch trials, it was very innovative at the time in suggesting that witches were members of a whole alternative diabolical religion, and that they enrolled in this sinister and fanatically anti-Christian faith by signing a formal pact or contract. That such charges appeared only a decade or so after the similar allegations made against the Templars suggests that prosecutors were drawing on that earlier case and its attendant mythologies. Templars too had been accused of using bizarre rites to initiate members into a diabolical clandestine religion. Such ideas fitted well with the apocalyptic framework, in which righteous believers find themselves increasingly under siege from the godless as the end times approach.[27] John further developed his interpretation of witchcraft in his 1326 decretal *Super illius specula* (Upon his watchtower), which became a key part of the developing legal arsenal. The Pope denounced those who

> sacrifice to demons and adore them, they make or cause to be made images, rings, mirrors, phials or some such things in which by the art of magic evil spirits are to be enclosed. From them they seek and receive replies, and ask aid in satisfying their evil desires. For a foul purpose they submit to the foulest slavery. Alas! this deadly malady is increasing more than usual in the world and inflicting greater and greater ravages on the flock of Christ.

Such people were Christians only in name. Abandoning the light, they "allow their minds to be so clouded with the darkness of error as to enter into a league with death and a compact with hell [*cum morte fœdus ineunt et pactum faciunt cum inferno*]."[28]

That last phrase is significant. It is a quote from Isaiah 28:15, and it is often used metaphorically to suggest that someone has strayed badly. But in the context of church thought as it was developing at this time, it meant that witches signed a literal *pactus* with the Devil or demons, that they were apostasizing from the Christian faith. However normal or conventional an individual might appear, they might be part of a rival faith as sinister and diabolical as—well, as Judaism. The very term "Sabbat" is adapted from the Jewish Sabbath. John, in effect, was inventing a whole new religion, the religion of diabolical witchcraft, and he was doing so precisely around 1320. Also novel in this era was the movement to contextualize witchcraft together with heresy as part of a common, and deeply sinister, phenomenon. Even if a group was deemed heretical for beliefs that do not seem too extravagant in retrospect—such as demanding access to the vernacular scriptures—they increasingly found themselves lumped together with the darkest deeds attributed to witches.[29]

In witchcraft cases, John commanded that investigators should proceed as they did against heresy, deploying the same techniques of torture. As with heresy, investigation of this kind could not fail to call forth confessions on the lines suggested by inquisitors, so that suspects would admit to ever more damning charges involving supernatural crimes and alliances with demons. They would also be forced to name other individuals as conspirators, and these would be investigated in their turn, creating a network effect that in theory could expand almost infinitely. In turn, future investigators would incorporate those charges into their own interrogatories, beginning a pattern of narrative escalation that would culminate with tales of mass Sabbats where hundreds or even thousands of witches worshipped the Devil.[30]

Women in particular were soon being accused of the familiar package of crimes, including devil worship, poisoning, and black magic. In 1324, the Irish case of Dame Alice Kyteler was the first of the internationally notorious witch trials, with a soon-to-be-familiar roster of charges that included sacrificing to demons and having sexual relations with demons. At the time, the charges were innovative and startling, but they would soon become commonplace. The repertoire of the classic witch trial era was already firmly established.[31]

The ideas expressed by John did not immediately spread across Europe, but they remained in place for a new generation. In terms of concepts of witchcraft, Europe's next great leap forward in paranoia had to wait until the next great frozen decade, the 1430s, which reached its worst point during the crop failures and starvation of 1437–1438. This was exactly the time that a group of highly visible church leaders appropriated Pope John's theories of the alternative religion, systematized and expanded them, and expressed them through such sensational and long-influential texts as the *Formicarius* (Anthill) of German theologian Johannes Nider. Nider and several like-minded witch-hunters found an ideal venue for their theories in the church council then meeting at Basel in Switzerland, which has been aptly described as "a Sabbat of demonologists." It was in 1437 that Nider distributed his explosive book to the assembled leaders. Those ideas became the foundation for the European witchcraft nightmares of the next quarter millennium. In all crucial respects, those ideas and theories were the product of two distinct periods of extraordinary climate turmoil, with the social misery each inflicted.[32]

Jews

Witches did not exist, and while lepers did, they were not organized into any kind of movement, political or otherwise. Jews, on the other hand, assuredly did exist, and they maintained their congregations and larger international networks. For Christians, they became the most frequent targets of conspiratorial charges and were regularly blamed for disasters of all kinds, especially for disease outbreaks and epidemics.[33]

Pogroms and massacres surged, particularly around 1320. Illustrating the mood of the time was the Shepherds' Crusade of that year, as France's poor and humble mobilized spontaneously to march against the Muslims in Spain. As they gathered strength, they targeted an illustrative variety of foes and scapegoats, including royal officials, landlords, and lepers, but most of the murderous violence was directed against Jews. More than a hundred communities were obliterated, and thousands of Jews were slaughtered. But this was no mere mob outbreak or riot. Rather, it swiftly evolved into a mass popular revolution that threatened the stability of the state. In their tens of thousands, these "shepherds," the *pastoureaux*, marched on Paris, where they forced the king to take fortified refuge. The insurgents wandered over much of France, spreading chaos. Often local citizens joined enthusiastically in the pogroms they inflicted on local Jews. At Carcassonne, the shepherds were ultimately defeated, and in turn they were massacred in the thousands. In Spain, the forces of royal order killed many thousands more.[34]

The chronology of anti-Semitism suggested here demands emphasis. As with lepers and witches, the main allegations in these years involved the poisoning of wells and the deliberate spread of disease. That image of well-poisoning as the rationale for anti-Semitic violence is familiar in many different eras, but recent research stresses how slim the evidence is for such a linkage before the pivotal year of 1321. After that, the charges proliferate mightily, culminating in the pogroms following the Black Death. Also in 1321, the king of Castile forced Jews to wear a yellow badge, and the following year the king of France ordered Jews expelled from his realm, an order not revoked until 1359. According to the standards of the time, Pope John XXII was not particularly harsh in his policies to Jews, partly because he drew on them for loans and revenue. From 1319, however, even he considered and partly implemented some draconian measures, including expulsions from church lands.[35]

One deeply sensitive issue was Jewish access to the Talmud. Christian kings and prelates had repeatedly called for the work's suppression, not because it was evidently the basis of Jewish faith and life but because of its allegedly blasphemous and scurrilously anti-Christian content. Besides the actual Talmud, the minds of church authorities imagined a clandestine alternative tract filled with explicit and obscene attacks on Christianity, a grotesque parody of the actual book that served almost as a kind of anti-Bible. Calls for action proliferated from the 1280s, and in 1319, the ever-active Bernard Gui ordered the burnings of Talmuds in Toulouse, together with the work of other learned Jewish commentators. In 1322, Pope John commanded a public burning.[36]

The conspiracies and terrors that emerged around 1320 reached full fruition with the coming of the Black Death, and the years between 1348 and 1351 were among the worst in European Jewish history before the twentieth century. Jewish communities were attacked and destroyed across France, Spain, Flanders, and the Rhineland, and several hundred communities were altogether uprooted. Particularly active in inciting anti-Jewish violence were Flagellant movements, or the so-called Brethren of the Cross. They now gained unprecedented public respect and visibility amidst hopes that their penitential activities would avert plague. Confessions extracted under torture supposedly revealed Jewish plots to poison water supplies. Such charges provoked the mass murder of the community in Toulon in 1348, and in the following year 600 Jews were burned at the stake in Basel. Jews were relatively mobile, and they were alleged to use these opportunities to travel to foreign lands to import poisons. Among the worst of the mass killings was that in Strasbourg on St. Valentine's Day of 1349, when "they burnt the Jews on a wooden platform in their cemetery. There were about two thousand people of them." Some accepted baptism as the price of their lives, and some children were forcibly taken from their parents to be baptized. But at least several hundred Jews were burned alive. March brought a similar atrocity in Erfurt. Here and elsewhere, Jews often killed themselves and their families in order to escape murder and torture. Such massacres remained an endemic fact of European life through the 1380s.[37]

Across western Europe, Jewish communities were uprooted. That in turn led to mass migrations eastward, to lands then controlled by Poland and Lithuania. Particularly welcoming was the Polish king Casimir III, the Great, who had a long record of defending Jewish communities, and who now offered a refuge that was eagerly welcomed. It was especially from this period that we see the main concentration of Jews in what would in later times become the western lands of the Russian Empire, and then the states of Belarus and Ukraine. This was the classic geography of the small-town Jewish world of the shtetl, as it was known in the nineteenth and twentieth centuries.[38]

Christians Hunt Christians

Christians also inflicted persecution on fellow believers. Of course, intolerance was nothing new to Latin Europe. But violent heresy-hunting escalated in degree and character during the ugly years of the early fourteenth century, and especially in that post-1314 decade. Two factors were at work. In the desperation of the times, believers espoused more fervent and perfectionist views and practices as a means of placating God and escaping the sins of a failed and failing world. Often, such rigorous piety went awry of official church doctrine. On the other side, the authorities were ever more sensitive about suppressing heresies, which they believed aggravated the assaults of hunger and disease. As positions hardened, each side denounced the other in literally apocalyptic terms, and looked to the imminent end times. By 1320, the book of Revelation stood at the center of Latin Europe's religious and political struggles. The Latin church now suffered one of its worst political and spiritual crises before Luther's Reformation itself, two centuries afterward.[39]

At the heart of the controversy was a crisis of poverty, and the church's neglect of poverty. The key symbolic figure was St. Francis of Assisi, whom moderns commonly recall as a wonderful figure of holiness, fully in tune with the animal kingdom and the environment. It is curious, then, that for many faithful Europeans, he became an apocalyptic or messianic figure, devotion to whom led many to torture or the stake. After Francis's death in 1226, the order founded in his name became divided, as dissidents protested that both the order and the church had compromised far too much with worldliness and wealth. As controversies grew, the pro-poverty faction became increasingly disaffected from the wealth of the church itself. One brother named Peter John Olivi framed the conflict in cosmic terms in a commentary on the Book of Revelation that would provide a revolutionary manual for generations to come. Like many before and since, Olivi divided the ages of history into particular eras, with the lesson that we were now living in the last times, a sixth age, before the final Judgment of the seventh. He treated Francis himself as a heavenly figure, the new Elijah, "who is, after Christ and under Christ, the first and principal founder and initiator and exemplar of the sixth period and its evangelical [gospel] rule."[40]

From the end of the thirteenth century, the church increasingly condemned and stigmatized these hyper-pious Little Brothers (Fraticelli), who were driven underground. The movement found sympathy from devout lay believers variously known as Beguins/Beguines or Beghards, who followed lives of strict piety, of prayer, poverty, and good works, whether living as hermits or in small communities. They followed very much the same impulses as would a century or two earlier have led people into monastic orders or the new orders of friars. Many termed themselves "poor brothers of penitence of the third order of St. Francis." For Little Brothers and Beguins alike, the early fourteenth century was in every sense a much colder and harsher environment, as authorities became more punitive and intrusive. The unlicensed and unregulated nature of Beguin lives aroused deep suspicions about their orthodoxy. Ideas that in one setting might have led an individual to canonization as a holy mystic would in this context of spiritual free enterprise lead to charges of gross heresy, and to imprisonment or death.[41]

Although the Beguin tradition dated back to the early twelfth century, after 1310 it began to attract inquisitorial attention as a major religious peril. I have already mentioned the Council of Vienne in the context of the Knights Templar. The same council condemned "an abominable sect of wicked men, commonly called Beghards, and of faithless women, commonly called Beguines, [which] has sprung up in the realm of Germany." One key source for the religious currents of the age is the inquisitor Bernard Gui, who around 1323 compiled a sweeping manual, the *Practica inquisitionis heretice pravitatis* (Conduct of inquiry concerning heretical depravity). Of the Beguines, he wrote that

> their erroneous opinions began to be exposed around the year of our Lord 1315, more or less, although they were considered suspect by many even earlier. During the following years, in the provinces of Narbonne, Toulouse and Catalonia, many of them were seized, held in custody and, their errors having been detected, many of both sexes were judged heretical and burned.[42]

After 1317, Pope John XXII intervened decisively on the side of the Franciscan order against the Fraticelli. By 1318, recalcitrant brothers were being burned alive. But imposing order was no simple task at a time of very widespread popular discontent and disaffection. Franciscan dissidents gained wide public admiration and sympathy because of their obvious piety, which promised to please God and reduce his obvious fury against the human race. The Fraticelli became an underground messianic sect, with all the internal wrangling and fragmentation that implies. The Beguins regarded these suffering Little Brothers as God's holy martyrs, victims of an evil church order. In this view, the Fraticelli, not the church hierarchy, were the true Catholics. Beguins formed their own underground resistance, to help Fraticelli escape the Inquisition and flee to safer lands. The Fraticelli/Beguin networks constituted a clandestine church, with its own hierarchy.[43]

Although the Franciscan conflict might seem like an internal affair within the clergy—what moderns insultingly dismiss as "just theological"—it became a deeply divisive issue in international affairs, as Europe's rival powers became involved in the controversy, siding with one or another church faction. So did rival claimants to the Holy Roman Empire. Resulting controversies continued well into the fifteenth century, and there were mass burnings of Fraticelli as late as the 1420s.[44]

Facing torture and execution, Fraticelli leaders saw themselves as the persecuted true followers of Christ facing the fearsome powers of the Beast, in a terminal spasm of cosmic agony and violence. According to an orthodox investigation in 1319, Beguin commentaries on Revelation contained "many articles considered heretical, as well as many others containing falsity, intolerable error, temerity, or prediction of uncertain future events." The Beguins turned lovingly to Olivi and the traditions he supposedly passed on through his disciples. Like the Fraticelli, the Beguins held that "the carnal church (that is, the Roman Church) was Babylon the great whore which was to be destroyed and cast out just as the synagogue of the Jews was when the primitive church began." The movement dreamed of a glorious event to occur on the 1,300th anniversary of Christ's Resurrection, in 1333, when Muslims would be converted, the Antichrist (the Papacy) would fall, and Christ and Francis would reappear in glory to establish God's kingdom on earth.[45]

The Free Spirit

In these same years, church authorities targeted another supposedly widespread offshoot of orthodox faith, in the form of the so-called Free Spirit movement. In the crisis years following 1310, church authorities postulated the existence of yet another clandestine church hidden among the orthodox and pledged to the poisoning of Christian truth. If such a sect really did exist, then any failure to eliminate it would fully justify the divine anger that was so plainly manifest in the hunger and cold of the time.

The controversial ideas in question originated among Beghard and Beguine circles, which strove for perfection and mystical union with God. In 1311–1312, the Council of Vienne listed a roster of heretical beliefs about achieving perfection in this life that removed the need for true believers to follow the commandments of the church or to pursue most of the practices normally required of Christians. According to inquisitorial accounts, some believers taught an ultra-radical blend of pantheism and antinomianism. As pantheists, they held that God is Nature and Nature God. Once believers realized that God really was all things, and all things were God, then they too became God (autotheism). As God in human form, they were not subject to the Law or to mere human laws; at least in theory, they claimed the right to do anything they chose. This view was antinomian (literally, "against the Law"). Knowing that the present world was all that existed, they spurned fables of Judgment or an afterlife: Heaven and Hell were here and now, and, like God himself, those states existed only within us. Free Spirit adepts scorned the church and all its teachings and sacraments.[46]

Free Spirit ideas actually existed, to the extent that they can be identified in the recorded words of certain mystics and of some suspected individuals who were clearly expressing their opinions free of coercion or pressure. But we can certainly challenge the investigators' accounts that presented the Free Spirit as an organized movement, if not an alternative church, that operated across much of Europe. The church's war against the Free Spirit began at the end of the thirteenth century and became actively homicidal after 1310. In 1308, the Paris Inquisition began an investigation of Beguine mystic Marguerite Porete, who was burned in 1310, and the Council of Vienne condemned the group's key ideas. Over the next two decades, some powerful clergy led a near crusade against suspect mystics, notably the activist bishops of Strasbourg and Cologne. Thereafter, Free Spirit believers joined the fast-expanding catalogue of perceived foes, as the church pursued its ever-expanding quest for enemies and pseudo-Christians.[47]

Crisis in Islam

The experience of Christians under Islamic rule was a close facsimile of what Jews suffered in Europe at this time, and the chronological parallels are striking. The Islamic world, like its Christian counterpart, was entering a much harsher and more polarized era of inflexible intolerance. In both worlds, the number of real and imagined enemies was escalating—including many who saw themselves as devout members of the established faith.

As in Europe too, climate and environmental factors were decisive. The Middle East had suffered gradual depopulation and economic decline from the end of the thirteenth century, but the crisis became acute during the 1310s. Large parts of the region suffered a generalized environmental collapse as climate change combined with human action, to disastrous effect. Across the Middle East, societies had for centuries waged a constant battle between "the desert and the sown," with irrigation as the critical weapon. Incessant wars and massacres plus social and governmental breakdown all took their toll, making it difficult to maintain irrigation and thus to defend the arable lands won a thousand years earlier. Climate change now offered the coup de grâce. Nomads prospered, at the expense of settled farmers and city dwellers: Bedouin cultures spread over what had been fertile lowlands. When the legendary world traveler Ibn Battuta crossed the Middle East in the 1320s, he repeatedly listed all the once-great cities now characterized as only "a total ruin" or "totally uninhabited." Where cities survived, they covered only a paltry share of their historical area. Well before the full onslaught of the Black Death, societies were declining and populations were contracting.[48]

Military threats, above all from the Mongols, compounded climate-related disasters, with the result being the creation of harsh and intolerant new currents in Middle Eastern Islam. Those attitudes found an eloquent spokesman in the crucially important thinker Taqī ad-Dīn Ahmad ibn Taymiyyah (1263–1328), who even today remains a deeply polarizing influence in the Islamic world. Throughout the first quarter of the fourteenth century, Ibn Taymiyyah asserted many staunchly conservative or fundamentalist positions that sought to restore what he saw as the primitive glories of the faith in the decades following Muhammad. He insisted on rigidly literal readings of the Quran and condemned the customs and innovations that had grown up around the faith, such as visiting the tombs of prophets and saints. Based successively in Syria and Egypt, he condemned any and all Christian influences and contacts, and wrote stern anti-Christian polemics. His most daring innovation was in condemning the Islamic credentials of many self-described Muslims, including not just Shia believers but also recent converts to his own Sunni tradition. If these were not in fact the Muslims they claimed to be, then genuine Muslim believers could legitimately launch jihads against them. Ibn Taymiyyah was in effect reading large populations out of the faith and claiming the right to determine who was and was not an authentic believer. There are obvious analogies to trends in Catholic Europe, where orthodox and dissident believers were likewise stigmatizing each other as apostates and false Christians.[49]

In his turbulent lifetime, Ibn Taymiyyah was extremely controversial, and spent much time in prison. In later centuries, he won the fervent devotion of successive conservative and reactionary Islamic movements, including the Wahhabi sect that presently dominates Saudi Arabia, and the larger current of Salafism. Like Ibn Taymiyyah, Salafis venerate the stern and simple version of the faith practiced by its earliest adherents, the "pious predecessors," from whom they take their name. Particularly influential was the precedent he set in denouncing supposed Muslims as kaffirs, or unbelievers, an idea that today characterizes most radical Islamist sects. Osama bin Laden quoted Ibn Taymiyyah's opinions to justify the overthrow of conservative Islamic regimes, and the fourteenth-century sage was an equally powerful influence on the Islamic State and its modern-day caliphate. In their confrontational and intolerant quality, the ideas of Ibn Taymiyyah reflect the atmosphere of generalized crisis that so marked the years around 1320.

Christians and Muslims

That crisis, and the cultural atmosphere it produced, proved disastrous for the region's Christians. As far back as the seventh century, Muslim forces had conquered the then largely Christian Middle East, and conversions to Islam became commonplace. Even so, this was a slow process, and it is unlikely that Christians even became a minority in the region until the tenth or eleventh centuries. By 1300, they were definitively a minority, but the Christian presence was tolerated and acknowledged. As key administrators in the Muslim states, individual Christians enjoyed power and wealth.

Complaints about Christians grew from the start of the fourteenth century and reached a crescendo in 1320–1321, the exact time of the bizarre plots and seditions reportedly coming to light across western Europe. In Egypt, many Coptic churches and monasteries were sacked, never to be restored, with 1321 a notoriously violent year that lives in infamy in the memory of modern Coptic Christians. Several decades of further suffering followed, dramatically reducing Coptic Christian numbers. By the end of the century,

Copts made up a minority of perhaps 10 percent of the population, a level they would roughly maintain until modern times.[50]

The once-powerful Christians of Iraq/Mesopotamia were likewise subject to brutal pogroms, and forced conversions became commonplace. Churches suffered mass closure or leveling, even at such venerated Christian centers as Tabriz and Arbela, Mosul and Baghdad. Bishops and clergy were tortured and imprisoned. New laws demanded that Christians wear distinctive garb in public, very much like Jews in Christian Europe. The ancient Church of the East (the so-called Nestorian church) was headed by the Patriarch of Babylon, who since the ninth century had actually had his seat in Baghdad. During the fourteenth-century crisis, those Christians were forced out of the city, preferring to take up residence on the safer soil of northern Mesopotamia. In later centuries, the Patriarchs made their home at a remote and highly secure monastery in the mountains near Mosul.[51]

Throughout these conflicts, violence was repeatedly driven by paranoia, by suspicion of plots launched by minorities against the mainstream society. In the Middle East, that meant labeling and demonizing Christians. At one point in Egypt, Christians were blamed for setting fires across Cairo, allegedly aided by Byzantine monks armed with ingenious incendiary bombs. When some of the accused confessed under torture, the authorities were forced to support the popular movement. At one point, the sultan faced a mob some 20,000 strong, calling for the suppression of Christians and the destruction of churches.

Muslim writers now developed a whole catalog of anti-Christian charges that closely resemble contemporary European diatribes against lepers—indeed, they prefigure scabrous anti-Jewish tracts such as the later *Protocols of the Elders of Zion.* According to writers such as al-Asnawi, Christians were spies ever on the lookout for opportunities to betray the Muslim cause, and cases in both Egypt and Syria proved they were serial arsonists. Given modern-day stereotypes of Islam in the West, it is ironic that Christian minorities were so feared because they were allegedly plotting terror bombings against prestigious symbols of Muslim power.

Asian Crises

If the growing climatic difficulties of the fourteenth century were not absolutely global, they did find a surprising number of echoes far from Europe or the Mediterranean. East and Central Asian societies were very hard hit by the Black Death, which cost China alone between a third and a half of its population. But well before the 1340s, the agricultural systems of East and Southeast Asia were facing harder times, for reasons ultimately connected with the forces driving Europe's cooling. As in the Christian and Muslim worlds, the result was greatly intensified religious conflict, and the persecution and expulsion of faith minorities.[52]

Given the region's reliance on a narrow range of food products, above all rice, those circumstances were even harder to overcome than in Europe, with its versatile mixed agriculture. I have already pointed to the linkage between the El Niño system and the monsoons that do so much to determine the availability of water supplies. Monsoons vary in intensity, and they are affected by atmospheric conditions as well as by shifting geology; naturally, they are vulnerable to the sort of disruptions produced by major volcanic blasts. Societies depending on monsoons can find themselves facing either droughts or extremely heavy rainfall. Matters deteriorated from the mid-thirteenth century onward, reaching critical proportions in the fourteenth. These calamitous events assailed the societies of the region, ending some states and gravely weakening others.[53]

The effects of such changes, and their chronology, can be illustrated from the great Khmer Empire, in what is now Cambodia. At its height in 1150, the city of Angkor Wat had a population of some 750,000, making it larger than the ten largest European cities of the time combined. Yet by the fifteenth century, the empire's ruling elite had abandoned the decaying city. Water was central to that story. The city depended on elaborate building works to control floods and support irrigation. Reconstructing the region's climate history shows a series of critical monsoon events from the late thirteenth century onward, with the effects of the Samalas eruption as a notable turning point. There were some significant droughts, but most harmful were several ruinously wet monsoons throughout the fourteenth century. The resulting rainfall overwhelmed the city's carefully planned water infrastructure and made the city unable to retain its previous significance. Population halved in the century after the 1250s and fell steeply through the disastrous fourteenth century. As the number of people collapsed, so did the city's ability to mobilize forced labor to control its water defenses.[54]

The Khmer Empire had no religious minorities to trouble itself with, but China assuredly did. In terms of population, China was by far the world's most important center in this era, and from 1279 through 1368, it was ruled by the Mongol Yuan dynasty, founded by Kublai Khan. Kublai's reign dated to 1260, and he gradually expanded his power over the whole nation. In 1368, the Yuan was overthrown by the native Ming dynasty, which held power until 1644. That story of revolutions and transitions can be told in terms of ethnic conflict, or even nationalist resentment at foreign rule, but it is incomprehensible without its climate dimensions. In the century after 1260, China suffered repeated crises and disasters, which in both their nature and their chronology closely reproduce what we have already seen in Europe. The evidence here is actually more precise because the highly bureaucratic Chinese regime kept excellent records of weather and temperature. This shows, for instance, that "between 1260 and 1424, only one abnormally warm year is registered, 1312, as compared to sixty cold years." As in Europe, the years from 1311 to 1325 were unnaturally wet, but droughts also struck with agonizing frequency. As in Europe also, China recorded many episodes of dearth and famine in the Yuan years, reaching cataclysmic proportions after 1315. The 1320s were historically dreadful, with a "shocking nadir" in 1324. This decade was a time of political crisis, with several weak and short-lived emperors.[55]

Extreme cold, droughts, and famines repeatedly struck the empire in the following years, with deadly famines raging through the early 1330s. Millions perished. The resulting discontent and disaffection provoked mass insurrections through the 1350s and 1360s. Many of the rebels belonged to religious sects of messianic and apocalyptic cast, drawing on Buddhism as well as local Chinese traditions. In many ways, the revolutionary upsurge resembled the European insurrections we encountered earlier, such as France's *pastoureaux*. In the Chinese instance, the revolution succeeded, as the key peasant leader founded the new Ming dynasty in 1368.[56]

The Fate of Christianity

The fourteenth-century crisis was far more than a local European affair, and as in Europe, the religious consequences were clear. Through Chinese history, Christian missions had repeatedly enjoyed sporadic success in the country, before eventually being expelled or suppressed. In this sequence, the twelfth and thirteenth centuries were a time of notable success both by the Asian-based Church of the East and also by Latin Catholic missions. The Nestorians had by far the better-established Asian presence, and for several centuries they had evangelized among peoples of Central Asia. Those activities reaped a rich reward with the Mongol expansion from the end of the twelfth century, as many Mongol leaders were either influenced by Christianity or had Christian family members. When the Mongols expanded their power over the whole of China, Christians were widely tolerated. Those ventures find a powerful visual representation in a symbol commonly found in India and China that combined a cross with a lotus, integrating the sacred signs of Christianity and Buddhism.[57]

Meanwhile, the Catholic Church had high hopes of winning major conversions in the distant empire. The Popes sent envoys to the Mongol court, and some hundreds of Franciscans ventured to China as missionaries. In 1308, at the apogee of Christian optimism, John of Montecorvino was consecrated as archbishop of Peking, *summus archiepiscopus*, chief archbishop, of those parts. John was a very active and successful missionary who even raised hopes of winning the conversion of the imperial court. Catholics long dreamed of achieving in China the kind of court-down conversion that had been achieved under Constantine in the Roman world.[58]

If Christians were not a mass movement in Yuan China, they had achieved some real successes, and were a strong presence in some important cities and trading centers. That happy time ended suddenly with the Ming revolution of 1368, when the new government strictly forbade any manifestations it associated with the bad old times of foreign Mongol rule, with its cold and starvation. Presumably not all Christians ceased practicing overnight, and clandestine churches may have survived. But avid research by subsequent believers and mission historians has failed to produce any significant evidence of Chinese Christianity between 1370 and the new wave of Latin Catholic missions from the 1540s onward.

Other minority faiths fared better, but they too had to conform with a stringent and inward-looking regime. Although many court officials were Muslim, they were required to adopt strictly Chinese ways and to marry Han Chinese wives. The country became much less welcoming to Muslim migrants, who had been so numerous in earlier years. Another target of intolerance was the Manichean religion, which had once been a major transcontinental religion in its own right, wielding wide influence across Central Asia. The faith first established its foothold in China in the seventh century, not long after Christianity. Like the Christians, it was tolerated by the Mongols, and with the Christians, it was forbidden by the Ming. Although it persisted in severely reduced form for some decades, it was largely absorbed into other spiritual traditions. To date, it remains the only example of a world faith that has effectively vanished.[59]

Conclusion

The downturn of the early fourteenth century set many disturbing precedents for later centuries. In religious terms, that experience showed how readily minorities of any kind could lose whatever tolerance they presently enjoyed. In extreme circumstances, such as the singular horrors after 1315, it also showed how quickly lethal paranoia could emerge, and how widely it would flail in search of possible targets for popular wrath. Those lessons would often come into play during the long following centuries of cooling. What changed, dramatically, was society's capacity to respond to such crises.

5

After Darkness, Light

> The tempest comes out from its chamber,
> the cold from the driving winds.
> The breath of God produces ice,
> and the broad waters become frozen.
>
> —Job 37:9–10

The year 1540 marked a significant transition in the struggles of the Reformation, which had begun two decades before. On the Catholic side, the year exemplified a new determination in the reform movement aimed at reestablishing Papal control, and in effect the start of the Counter-Reformation. The Papacy now recognized the Jesuit order, a controversial process that had been in the works for some time. The order became the vanguard of the attempt to recapture Europe for the church, and by the 1620s, it had more than 15,000 members. The same year, 1540, was also when the Spanish Inquisition executed its first Protestant victim.[1] But the greatest landmark of that year occurred in the city of Geneva, where city authorities were seeking to attract John Calvin back to the city he had abandoned. He accepted, and in the following year established a draconian theocratic regime, a City of God that was at once an example and a terror to the Christian world. Until Calvin's death in 1564, radical Geneva served as a subversive symbol comparable to what Bolshevik Russia was for the world's leftists after 1917. Outside Geneva, the Reformation movement won great victories in the ongoing confessional struggle, including the recruitment of Sweden to the cause in 1544. Religious controversies now entered a new age of militant confrontation and sweeping radicalism.[2]

In understanding these trends, it surely helps to appreciate the climate context. In 1540, Europe experienced a drought and heatwave of terrifying proportions, which in fact are still hard to interpret by existing climate models, and which left their impact for several years. Summer weather was as hot as any recorded in modern times, while rain virtually ceased for much of that year. Rivers great and small dried up in this megadrought, and shortages of drinking water drove people to seek sources even less hygienic than usual, resulting in the spread of serious maladies. In the cultural context of the time, the disaster inevitably had religious consequences, aggravating already bitter religious tensions, stirring paranoid accusations, and galvanizing militancy. In the context of Geneva itself, what made Calvin's authoritarian powers possible was the desperate need to feed a city overcome by the effects of drought and the resulting famines and epidemics, which continued through the mid-1540s. Not until 1547 did grain prices return to anything like normal conditions, by which point Calvin's authority was absolute. It is difficult to imagine such a dictatorial revolution being accepted except in the context of the clear signs of divine wrath that had been made so evident during the great drying.[3]

In terms of Christian history, the early sixteenth century was a crucial time of transition in the form of the Reformation, and the scarcely less important Catholic counterblast to that movement. Unlike in other eras, we cannot find a precise context for the outbreak of the religious revolution in any particular climate episode. Although chronologically this era is generally included in the Little Ice Age, some eras were relatively warm, even alarmingly so, as in 1540. Martin Luther's revolution of 1517 does not fit the pattern of an immediate response to natural catastrophe. But climate factors did play a decisive role in ensuring the survival of emerging Protestantism, both in Luther's lifetime and later in the century. In particular, a climate crisis created the conditions for the success of a truly revolutionary form of the new Protestantism—namely, Calvinism. Repeatedly, struggles over reform and reaction were driven by social crises, which clearly had a climate context. From the 1560s, the pace of change accelerated swiftly, opening the way to one of the greatest religious and cultural transformations in Western history.[4]

Martin Luther's World

On an admittedly trivial note, Martin Luther's career owed much to weather. In 1505, he was trapped in a dreadful lightning storm that made him fear for his life. Terrified, he swore a vow that if he survived, he would enter a monastery, which he ultimately did, with potent consequences. Obviously, such an incident has nothing necessarily to do with the larger story of climate, but other climate factors did set the scene for the larger movement.

The origin of the Reformation is conventionally dated to 1517, with Luther's activism in Wittenberg, and the subsequent spread of his movement across much of western Europe over the following decade. In this instance, no single climate factor serves as a magic bullet, no overnight transformation of rainfall or temperature, and indeed the first half of the century was a time of volcanic tranquility. But throughout these years, climate conditions served as a backdrop to the story. Luther was writing during a relatively cold era, during the Spörer Minimum in sunspots, which certainly had its effects. Colder sea temperatures in the Baltic harmed the ecological systems on which herring depended, and the decline of herring fisheries in turn undermined the recently flourishing and powerful trading cities of the Hanseatic League. The beneficiaries of this change were territorial princes and kings, including the king of Sweden and the German princelings on whom Luther would depend for patronage and protection. If it did not spark a religious revolution, climate change created the political environment in which the early reformers operated.[5]

But if the immediate challenge to church authority did not have an obvious context in natural events, the growing conflicts and mass discontent of the following years offer a very different picture. In many parts of Europe, the years around 1520 marked a downturn in climate, which gave rise to severe and systematic famine conditions that later generations would recall in horrible terms. Worst hit in the early 1520s were the Low Countries, Scandinavia, and Ireland, with Italy soon following. A disastrous era of plague and epidemic diseases stirred agonized debate among both theologians and scientists: some interpreted the crises as signs of divine anger, while others explored "natural" factors, though they integrated a great deal of what we would think of as occult or pseudo-scientific speculation. The plague crisis in 1521 was so severe as to force the imperial Diet or parliament to relocate from its planned venue at Nürnberg to a new setting at Worms, where Luther had his epochal encounter with secular authorities. It was at Worms, not Nürnberg, that he declared that "here I stand." Meanwhile, the recently acknowledged menace of typhus swept large sections of Europe, spread efficiently by the movements of armies. Nor were these conditions confined to Europe. In the history of Morocco, the years after 1519 were marked by historically dreadful conditions of famine and epidemic.[6]

Natural and social disasters had dramatic political consequences, which among other things ensured that Catholic authorities were too distracted to concentrate their full attention on the rising Lutheran challenge. These were tumultuous years, marked, for example, by serious peasant risings in Hungary (1514) and, on an immense scale, in Germany (1525); the rise of truly extreme religious radicalism, in the form of the Anabaptist movement and the Radical Reformation; the Turkish advances that destroyed the kingdom of Hungary (1526); and the Italian struggles that culminated in the sack of Rome (1527). Europe was passing through a true decade of revolution, and those multiple other demands and commitments prevented any secular ruler, such as the emperor himself, from bringing his full power to bear to snuff out the religious dissidence flowering in Germany.[7]

Global Crisis

Beginning a religious reform movement was one thing; its later development was a much more difficult issue. Although the Reformation is often recounted as a series of seemingly inevitable steady advances and victories, it was nothing of the kind, but was rather marked by repeated successes and failures, a series of great leaps forward and comparable falls backward. The crisis of 1540 showed clearly how climate change could provoke religious change and drive conflict. That lesson became strongly apparent as the Little Ice Age entered one of its most severe eras. The beginning of those terribly hard years might be dated to Europe's dreadful harvests of 1556–1558, with the attendant famines and pestilence, but many parts of the world were suffering. In 1557, an influenza pandemic that began in Asia became truly global, afflicting the Americas as well as Europe. By 1560, signs of decline and crisis were unavoidable. The transition finds a striking visual symbol in the much-reproduced painting "The Triumph of Death," by Pieter Bruegel the Elder, which he created in Antwerp in 1562. Bruegel's panorama depicts a landscape terrorized by a merciless army of living skeletons, slaughtering all humans who come before them. Whatever its philosophical message—and yes, all will ultimately fall victim to death—the painting offered an apt augury of the wars and calamities then just beginning.[8]

In terms of climate, the post-1560 period is technically known as the Grindelwald Fluctuation, from the name of the Swiss town where glacial advances in this time were measured, and that era persisted from 1560 through about 1628. Those Alpine ice fields reached their farthest advance around 1600. By way of historical context, that age of intense climate stress roughly corresponds to the life and career of Shakespeare (1564–1616). The fluctuation—the very cold spell, or Hyper-LIA—was aggravated by the extreme volcanism that I have already described. Four eruptions in particular cast very wide shadows: Billy Mitchell in the southwest Pacific, in 1580; Kelut (1586) and Raung (1593), both in Indonesia; and Huaynaputina in Peru in 1600. The first and last eruptions of this series were extremely large, measuring 6 on the VEI. That Huaynaputina event remains the largest eruption ever recorded in the Western Hemisphere. Nor does that list include other level 4 blasts such as Nevado del Ruiz (1595), of a kind that became almost too commonplace to be worth noting. The relatively short interval between blasts gave the world little time for the effects to clear before the next assault. Volcanism contributed to creating the severe and protracted El Niño events of the mid-1590s, while the North Atlantic Oscillation entered a strongly negative phase. Extreme conditions were recorded in many parts of the globe. In the American Southwest, an agonizingly long megadrought persisted from 1570 through 1597.[9]

Human action played some part in creating this frozen depth. Scholars refer to the modern era in which human beings have so shaped the climate as the Anthropocene, the "human-recent" age, but perhaps that shaping began earlier than we usually suppose. The epidemic diseases that European conquerors and settlers introduced into the New World reduced native populations by the millions, obliterating the villages and the fires they would otherwise have produced. In Mexico alone, millions perished in epidemics in the 1540s, with a new wave of mass deaths in the 1570s. The consequent reductions in carbon emissions further contributed to cooling, although not sufficiently to explain the whole change. It should also be said that reconstructed numbers for pre-Columbian populations in the Americas are quite speculative, making any assessment of impact very debatable, but some impact certainly occurred.[10]

Frozen Europe

From 1560 onward, Europe endured some of the most brutal weather in its recorded history. The winter of 1564–1565 beggared belief. Contemporaries listed the great rivers that were now frozen hard enough to become highways: the Rhône and Seine, Thames and Scheldt. When the ice melted, heavy flooding added to the general misery. The year 1566 brought heavy rain in the spring and a drought in the summer, so famine naturally followed. The year 1569 was viciously cold across Europe, with the lagoon of Venice remaining frozen until March. The winter of 1572–1573 was atrocious: Lake Constance was under deep ice well into the spring. Such conditions were echoed in many other societies, including China and the Islamic Middle East. In 1621, the Bosporus at Istanbul froze over, making it possible to walk from Europe to Asia. In much of Europe, the cold reduced the growing season for crops by several weeks, with disastrous consequences for food supplies. Different regions suffered rain in quantities that were crushingly large or painfully insufficient. So savage were the climatic assaults and their consequences that they are difficult to enumerate in any kind of comprehensive way.[11]

Famines affected most or all of Europe in 1569–1574, and on a somewhat smaller scale in 1585–1587. Besides outright famine, we find all the customary indices of despair: surges in economic crime, hunger protests, peaks in judicial executions, and starving peasants flocking to neighboring towns in quest of food after their own crops failed. The numbers of beggars swelled to the point that virtual armies of the underclass wandered from town to town.[12]

As we have seen, significant climate changes rarely occur without biomedical consequences. Europe now suffered some of the worst outbreaks of epidemic disease since the near-terminal experience of the 1340s. Just to take the English experience, London suffered appallingly from plague in 1563–1564, 1578–1579, 1592–1593, 1603, 1625, and 1636. The 1603 outbreak killed perhaps 30,000 Londoners, with 35,000 in 1625, and comparable numbers in the kingdom as a whole. Three of those episodes—1563, 1603, and 1625—were roughly on the same scale as the better-known episode of 1665, which is remembered as the uniquely horrible Great Plague. However, that episode bears that title only because it attracted the literary skills of Daniel Defoe, while earlier events found less sparkling chroniclers.[13] Such conditions ravaged the continent. Military movements ensured that an epidemic of "Hungarian fever" raged across much of Europe. France suffered repeated waves of plague during the civil wars of the 1570s and 1580s. Italy was assailed in 1629–1631. That event in particular had far-reaching consequences for European history, as it ruined the fortunes of Venice, which up till then had been an economic powerhouse for much of the Western world. In Morocco, climate-related blows struck in the form of drought, which coincided closely with Europe's worst times. The year 1569 brought famine and epidemic to the Fez region, with further onslaughts from epidemics in 1581 and 1601–1602. Besides plague, other newer or more obscure diseases also had their effects. In 1580, a new influenza pandemic spread out of Asia.[14]

Triumphs of Death

Several periods in particular were especially agonizing. One of the worst lasted from the mid-1560s through the early 1570s, and I will return to this era shortly. Also dreadful were the 1590s and the 1620s, and I will discuss the first of these in greater detail to give a sense of how different kinds of pressure combined to ruin societies and states.

The decade of the 1590s was a truly dreadful time to be alive, as volcanic blasts darkened the skies in many parts of the globe. Europe suffered from heavy and seemingly incessant rain, and famine conditions afflicted much of Europe between 1590 and 1598. In *A Midsummer Night's Dream*, probably written in 1596, Shakespeare offered a catalogue of the contemporary nightmares:

> Therefore the winds, piping to us in vain,
> As in revenge, have sucked up from the sea
> Contagious fogs, which falling in the land
> Have every pelting river made so proud
> That they have overborne their continents.
> The ox hath therefore stretched his yoke in vain,
> The ploughman lost his sweat, and the green corn
> Hath rotted ere his youth attained a beard.
> The fold stands empty in the drownèd field,
> And crows are fatted with the murrain flock.

The "murrain" refers to the animal diseases that so often accompanied human diseases, and which contributed so much to hunger and misery. Quite apart from west European conditions, such a panzootic was raging throughout the Ottoman Empire through these very years.[15] In England, harvests failed in four successive years from 1594 through 1597, and these same years marked the highest inflation of prices in the sixteenth and seventeenth centuries. Italy in the 1590s suffered one of the worst famines in its history, and it was far from isolated. Similar nightmares visited northern Europe by mid-decade. El Niño conditions inflicted droughts and catastrophic famines in the mid-1590s in South and Southeast Asia. Geoffrey Parker writes aptly of the "Nasty Nineties."[16]

Those accumulating horrors placed enormous strains on states, stirring wars and rebellions and threatening the dissolution of the political order. In some cases, conditions became so extreme as to make modern observers apply the language of failed states. As we will see, the crisis that began in the late 1560s provoked turmoil and revolt across much of western Europe, and also brought Russia to the brink of collapse. Famines and epidemics so weakened the state that the Muslim Tatars were able to ravage much of the land and to burn down Moscow in 1571.[17]

In the popular history of several nations, the decade of the 1590s is recalled with shudders. In Russia, the years from 1598 through 1613 were the "Time of Troubles," an era of dynastic battles, foreign wars, and popular rebellions. Between 1601 and 1603, a famine likely provoked by the Huaynaputina eruption killed Russians on an enormous scale, probably 2 million people. The country was reduced to anarchy until the accession of the Romanov dynasty in 1613. Between 1590 and 1610, the Ottoman Empire suffered its Celali Rebellions, as warlords, provincial governors, and bandit chiefs made Anatolia ungovernable. From 1593 through 1603, Ireland was the scene of a revolt by Catholic aristocrats against English Protestant rule. In terms of casualties, this was one of the most ruinous conflicts of the whole era: war and famine claimed perhaps 150,000 lives, out of an Irish population that could not have much exceeded a million.[18]

The crisis of cold continued until 1628, another year without a summer, and that was followed by some years of very heavy rain, in a notably heavy El Niño period. Far-flung crises followed between 1628 and 1632, both in Europe and farther afield. India, for instance, had always been accustomed to sporadic famines, but little had prepared the country for the hammer blows that afflicted the Deccan and Gujarat between 1630 and 1632, and which killed between 3 and 7 million. In China, food crises spawned tax revolts, army mutinies, and local insurrections, which fatally weakened the regime. The Chinese Ming empire that came into existence among such bloodshed in one climate-driven cataclysm in 1368 was overthrown during another in 1644. This crisis in particular was a true slayer of empires.[19]

Although we can study such horrors in the context of certain notoriously severe years, such as the early 1570s, late 1590s, or late 1620s, we must also stress the unrelenting quality of these disasters, with few years of intervening relief. Across Europe, and indeed much further afield, catastrophe became normalized.

Plots and Paranoia

As in the 1320s, climate-driven disasters sparked conflicts and excited widespread popular terrors. Of course, not all conspiracy-mongering was the result of baseless paranoia. In an age of starkly divided political and religious factions, quite authentic plots and seditions were never too difficult to find. Plenty of people genuinely were plotting to kill kings and to massacre believers of different views. But paranoia on a massive scale became a mainstay of European culture and of its religious thought. When crops failed, when herds died, when plague ravished the land, when storms sank ships, the common and predictable human response was to find the malignant individuals or groups who were causing these phenomena and tormenting ordinary decent people.

In 1540, costly fires proliferated across Europe, as we might well expect in a year of extreme dryness. In the context of the time, however, human intervention seemed a more natural and acceptable interpretation. Organized bands of arsonists—in German, the *Mordbrenner,* or murder-burners—became a primary source of social and religious terror. When the Imperial Diet met that year in Regensburg, Protestants urged the emperor to act against the elaborate conspiracy to burn their cities, villages, and forests, part of a diabolical Catholic scheme masterminded by the Pope and leading aristocrats. Alternatively, perhaps Anabaptists were starting the fires. In 1540, magistrate Ambrosius Trota published an investigator's guide to the arsonist networks and their secret signs and codes. The book was likely printed in Wittenberg and would have had Luther's approval. Jews (or possibly Muslims) were suspected in other related plots to spread plague, and Geneva was one of many centers to prosecute deliberate "plague-spreaders."[20]

Jews featured in many other scares in these years. The problem in discussing such events is that anti-Semitic campaigns were such a standard feature of European life that it is difficult to find eras when they were lacking. Even so, the post-1560 years were richly productive of conspiracy charges, usually involving versions of the blood libel that had become so prominent in the fourteenth century. Especially from 1560 onward, many European Christian kings and states expelled or purged their Jewish populations, or confined reduced communities to tightly regulated ghettos.[21]

The Darkest Age of Witchcraft

By far the main culprit blamed for the ongoing crisis was the witch. I have already described the formation of the witchcraft mythology in response to the fourteenth-century crisis, and such ideas were revived in the later fifteenth century with the publication of the witch-hunter's manual, *Malleus maleficarum* (The hammer of witches; 1486). Usually we can identify periods when witchcraft was of particular concern because some enterprising publisher thought to reprint this ghastly tract. After enjoying initial success, the *Malleus* was not reprinted between 1520 and the early 1560s, when witchcraft prosecutions reached a curious low point. But the new wave of crises brought it back to the mainstream, with multiple new editions from 1574 onward.[22]

That midcentury hiatus in witch-hunts reminds us that witchcraft fears were not a constant of early modern life: fears could come and go, or they might be channeled to target some alternative enemy. But in the decades between the 1560s and the 1630s, the witch again occupied center stage. This is scarcely surprising given the particular evils for which such offenders were believed to be responsible, so many of which were linked to climate—droughts and floods, hailstorms and prolonged frosts. All those forms of suffering were abundantly in evidence in these baleful years. In fact, the upsurge of the new panic is generally dated to 1562, which we have already seen marked the most obvious escalation of the climate crisis of that era.[23]

The seven decades between 1562 and 1632 were the absolute height of the west European witch craze, with the most intense and wide-ranging investigations and persecutions and the best-remembered cases. (The movement would later spread to the north and east, to countries like Poland and Sweden.) As I remarked earlier, one key variable in determining the severity of such cases was the means by which investigators could seek information, and Roman-law countries such as Germany and France produced vastly more victims than England, where judicial torture was prohibited. That resulted in the rapid expansion of a network of alleged perpetrators, as suspects named multiple alleged associates and friends. Typical German panics in this era might execute alleged witches in the dozens, while England was killing offenders in the ones and twos.[24]

Eras of social crisis and near-collapse were uniquely fruitful in generating very large and bloody mass trials. From 1581, a new archbishop in the German city of Trier decided to eliminate the three great menaces of the era, Jews, Protestants, and witches, but the last of these became a primary obsession: several hundred people were burned. The 1590s brought notorious cases in Scotland, which was a Roman-law country and tortured suspects. In the new century, there were major witch-hunts in Fulda, Germany (from 1603), and the Basque witch trials made the town of Zugarramurdi as enduringly notorious in Spanish history as Salem would become in the United States. The German trials reached a crescendo with the sprawling investigations at Würzburg and Bamberg between 1626 and 1631, which we have already seen were uniquely horrible years for purely secular conditions, with famine and plague. At least a thousand perished in the Würzburg trials, a similar number in Bamberg.[25]

Persecutions varied in their nature and emphasis, but chiefly it was women rather than men who were targeted as malefactors, to the point that some modern writers use terms such as "femicide" or "gender terrorism." The reasons for that disparity are much debated, but a large part of the explanation is that women were directly in charge of the objects and places that most aroused suspicion in an age when sudden and inexplicable death had become so agonizingly commonplace. In all classes and settings, women's sphere of action focused on the oven, the cradle, and the herb garden, all potential settings for malevolence and criminality against family or neighbors. Women stood in the front lines of death. The more women were accused, the more the emerging stereotype concentrated on women as potential offenders, and the more attention theorists paid to witchcraft as a feature of unregulated femininity.[26]

Each of the set-piece show trials produced its share of writing and artwork, which have subsequently become the major sources shaping images of witchcraft in the Western mind. One key figure was Pierre de Lancre, who was a leading investigator in the Basque country and whose writings are a critical source (whether acknowledged directly or not) of virtually all later writing on the topic. That includes accounts of the Witches' Sabbat, which now became a central part of the mythology, and which, in these fevered years, was regularly depicted in engravings and paintings. In 1581, the otherwise intelligent and humane French jurist Jean Bodin published his *De la démonomanie des sorciers* (On the demon-mania of witches), which acquired a European influence comparable to the older *Malleus maleficarum*. The 1590s cases terrified the Scottish king James VI, later James I of England, who in the dreadful year of 1597 published his *Daemonologie*, a formative influence on Shakespeare's *Macbeth* (1606). In turn, writings about witch cases helped drive future incidents. Books exposing bogus acts of possession and bewitching served as practical how-to manuals for later fraudsters and deceivers seeking to prove the truth of the supernatural.[27]

Witchcraft panics had a significance far beyond the suffering they inflicted on particular families or communities. By reasserting the very widespread presence of supernatural evil, the reporting of such incidents reinforced fundamental ideas about the nature of faith and of its enemies. They taught the reality of the concept of the devil and his angels and, by extension, of the true church that those forces were seeking to subvert. The cases, endlessly retold, proved how natural conditions were affected by malicious individuals working in unholy alliance with evil forces: plagues and dearths did not just happen, they were related to supernatural attacks. The witch wars proved the necessity for specialized professionals to protect ordinary people from those lethal menaces, professionals whose work depended on a tight alliance between the forces of the state and the church.[28]

At a time of constant religious conflict, the cases demonstrated the unchallengeable realities of faith, and of providential interpretations of the world and its fate. Further, by proving the reality of diabolical attacks on the Christian order (however it was construed in any particular society), witchcraft cases offered a rhetorical foundation for attacks on rival churches that could likewise be portrayed as agents of the Devil. Witchcraft cases were in themselves profoundly theological statements, which exactly suited the mood of an era of violent religious polarization.

Wars of Faith

Such prolonged decades of crisis had predictable political consequences, which were largely defined in religious terms. In the context of Europe and the Mediterranean, several international confrontations stand out. One was the struggle between the Muslim Ottoman Empire and the great powers of Christian Europe, especially Spain and the Holy Roman Empire. But conflicts between rival Christian groups—Catholic, Calvinist, and Lutheran—were also deeply troubling. (We cannot use the word "denominations" here, as that suggests an amicable situation of coexistence: in this era, each grouping viewed itself as the true and only church.) Through the 1540s, Protestant and Catholic states had repeatedly fought wars. As the Reformation era progressed, several nations found themselves with substantial populations who dissented from the official faith of king and state. The most explosive situation was in France, where Calvinist Protestants (Huguenots) represented a powerful faction among the country's political and social elites, with special strength in certain regions. Meanwhile, the Low Countries—which we today call the Netherlands and Belgium—were ruled by the Catholic Spanish Habsburgs, but Protestant dissent was growing.[29]

From 1560, those internal tensions became sharply and suddenly more marked, with the outbreak of deadly violence, both local massacres and civil wars. In France, open warfare between Catholics and Calvinists dragged on through the 1590s, culminating in the notorious massacre of tens of thousands of Protestants on St. Bartholomew's Day in 1572. France's Wars of Religion claimed some 2 million lives in one of the bloodiest conflicts in European history before the twentieth century. Each side had its roster of crimes and massacres committed against their particular community, and those memories served to drive further hatred and retaliation. In the neighboring Low Countries, long-standing tensions escalated into full-scale revolution in 1566 and the creation of an independent Dutch polity in 1581. The resulting war between the new Netherlands and the Spanish Empire persisted, with only short breaks, into the 1640s. That confrontation was central to European politics over what we call the Eighty Years' War.[30]

The chronology of these events should be stressed. Religious tensions across Europe dated back to the beginning of the Reformation in 1517, but the full savagery of generalized European warfare arrived only after 1560. Some years in particular stand out as singularly disastrous, a point that emerges only when we overcome the familiar boundaries that separate social, political, and climate history. In France, the years of the bitterest warfare were 1562–1563 and 1567–1580, with new spasms through the 1590s. In each case, we recall how these eras of spectacular violence coincided with times of plague and severe climate stresses. I have already noted how atrocious the late 1560s were across Europe, and France was no exception: the country suffered extremely hard winters in 1565, 1568, 1570, and 1573. In the disastrous hunger year of 1565, religious divisions spilled over into the New World, as French Protestants sought to establish a New World colony in Florida, from which they were bloodily expelled by Catholic Spain.[31]

The popular quality of these violent outbreaks in France especially demands emphasis. Historically, many wars and conflicts remained largely matters of the elites, as ordinary people turned out faithfully to follow their feudal lords into battle. The wars of this era were very different in that so much of the endemic violence was the work of feral mobs, of those same ordinary dwellers in town and country, who felt the need to slaughter fellow subjects, with or without the approval of the lords and magnates. Just to take one example of many, in the spring of 1562, the French city of Toulouse suffered an egregious manifestation of this escalating insanity when several thousand perished in street fighting between Catholics and Protestants. It is one measure of the loathing that divided Europe's faith factions that by the mid-1560s, Protestants in the Netherlands were appealing to the (Islamic) Ottoman Turks for military help against Catholic Spanish Christians. Radicals used the slogan "Liever Turks dan Paaps" (rather Turkish than Papist).[32]

In such periods, we see not only the aggravation of hostilities in the well-known war zones but revolts, conspiracies, and massacres elsewhere, and they could easily have degenerated into open warfare that imperiled states and dynasties. In December 1568, southern Spain suffered a broad revolt from its Moriscos, those Muslims who had been forced to convert to Christianity. Over the next three years, that turned into a general war in the region, as thousands of foreign Muslim fighters joined the combat. In 1569, a large-scale revolt in northern England posed a potentially deadly danger to the Elizabethan regime, and other related plots and assassination schemes festered over the following three years. Such high-level conflicts coexisted with more obscure confrontations at the city or village level, which manifested in witchcraft panics.

The Calvinist Revolution

So many of these conflicts were carried out explicitly in the name of religion. In any or all of those cases, we are certainly free to doubt the religious content of the particular events, or the motivation of individuals. But the consequences for religious patterns and organizations were very marked, and the fate of Calvinism offers a clear example. Today, nonspecialists may know Calvinism as the basis of Puritan thought and as the theology underlying historical denominations such as the Presbyterians. In the context of European history, Calvinism matters enormously as a dynamic political and cultural force, which for a century represented the cutting edge of the Protestant movement. Later, moreover, the key Calvinist nations or regions—the Netherlands, Scotland, Switzerland, and New England—played a crucial role in the emergence of the Enlightenment. We can debate the exact linkage between the two phases—sixteenth-century Calvinism and the eighteenth-century Enlightenment—but the continuities are impressive. As we explore the history of Calvinism, its influence and survival, we see it is inseparable from larger social and economic trends, and especially from the influence of climate.[33]

The fact that social crisis generates religious responses is not surprising, but the form taken by that response is subject to the opportunities and constraints of the particular time and place. These factors involve the cultural traditions of the society in question and the strength or weakness of government, but also the state of the media through which information and ideas are circulated. Among other things, that determines how movements are formed and disseminated, and to what extent they can be kept within the control of any central structure. In the sixteenth-century case, we are dealing with a far more literate society than hitherto. Printing permitted the circulation of sophisticated theological debates and manifestos, and that literary culture enabled the growth and spread of very widespread religious movements, as activism and grievances in one nation readily found echoes in neighboring states.[34]

In the 1520s and 1530s, the Protestant explosion spawned multiple new currents, among which Calvinism was one of the most systematic and extreme. To understand just how radical the movement was, we must contrast it with what had been the Christian norm for a millennium. That old Catholic order was liturgical, with a critical role for ordained clergy, who represented a whole independent hierarchy. Christian life was rooted in ritual acts, in the veneration of the Virgin and saints, who were depicted in multiple media, and churches expressed their holiness through their images, whether in stone, plaster, gold, or glass. Pre-Reformation believers had ample access to the Christian tradition and its teachings, though usually it was mediated through nonliterate forms, such as drama and visual culture, rather than Scripture. The performance of faith was geared to the cycle of the church year, with a potent role for pilgrimage and the attendant shrines and holy places.[35]

When we tell the story of Protestantism, we often do so in terms of theology, through concepts such as justification by faith or works. But in terms of the movement's impact, the crucial question was how far different kinds of Protestantism accommodated those older ways, such as the liturgical year, the status of clergy, the adornment of churches, or the role of formal music. Lutherans were often quite accommodating in those ways, as were Anglicans, albeit selectively. Calvinists, however, absolutely rejected those older church institutions and hierarchies, even in modified and reformed models. They did not tolerate material vestiges of the old devotional life, which assumed the sanctification of times and places: ritual and liturgy were to be wholly replaced by the religion of the book. This was a media revolution par excellence. The Reformed (Calvinist) order represented a transformation of consciousness, perception, and behavior. It was a total break with history, a new order of worlds. In words adapted from the Vulgate Latin version of the book of Job, the Calvinist motto proclaimed, *Post tenebras lux*: after darkness, light. It was also the light by which one read.

A Calvinist upsurge in a particular country or region was usually accompanied by widespread iconoclasm, the smashing and burning of images of all sorts. Such assaults predated the mature Calvinist movement, and several spectacular outbreaks occurred in the late 1520s, but these increasingly represented a trademark of the Reformed, particularly after 1560. One explosive incident occurred in the French city of Lyon in 1562, when Calvinists sacked all the churches. This holy vandalism was commemorated in widely disseminated prints and cartoons that depicted the burning or spoiling of the old ritual world, all the statues, images, and stained glass; these images created expectations for future revolutionaries. In the rioting and mayhem, a millennium-old religious order was visibly, physically, and comprehensively smashed.[36]

Calvinism demanded a strict church-run order that governed every aspect of life, with moral laws enforced by draconian punishments. Calvinism was anything but democratic in its ideology, but in its emphasis on giving power to the godly and their congregations, it offered a thoroughly radical revision of social roles and power. Although in numerical terms they might be only a small minority, believers and their churches represented a disciplined and highly motivated force, which could achieve real successes when traditional authority stumbled. When the economic order was threatened, those churches offered an organized alternative in terms of distributing material aid. If we look for modern analogues, it is difficult to avoid drawing parallels with radical Islamism and its theocratic ideals. In every sense, Calvinism represented a cultural revolution, so much so that it could only have been instituted in conditions of revolutionary social change and political turmoil. It was a religion of crisis.[37]

Faith in Crisis

The crisis of the early 1540s allowed John Calvin to establish his regime in Geneva, and the wider movement spread rapidly from the late 1550s as the most militant and uncompromising form of the faith. But it was above all in the decade 1565–1575, during the various civil wars and revolutions, that it achieved its crucial political and cultural bases, most obviously in France and the Netherlands, but also in Scotland and Hungary. In Scotland, the Calvinist aristocracy secured their hold on the state following a messy domestic crisis in the country's royal family in 1566–1567. Also in 1567, Hungary's Calvinists acquired a new organizational sophistication with a famous synod at Debrecen. From 1563, the movement also developed a vital new political and cultural center in the German Rhineland state of the Palatinate.[38]

From the mid-1560s, England's Reformed mobilized into what their enemies termed the Puritan movement; the word "Puritan" first appears in 1564 or 1565. From 1570 onward, those Puritans became ever bolder and more inflammatory in their demands and their petitions to a hostile monarch. By the mid-1570s, the Puritans were spawning alternative religious and clerical structures that looked unnervingly like a seditious parallel to the state church. In the seventeenth century, the fiery Puritan movement that became a revolutionary force throughout the British Isles and New England was absolutely rooted in Calvinist ideas and practices. What divided the various groupings were questions of polity and organization, and that debate variously spawned Presbyterian, independent, and Baptist traditions. The Puritan movement achieved a political triumph during the next great General Crisis, that of the 1640s, which tumbled states and monarchies across Europe and farther afield. And again, more countries experienced their own new waves of sweeping iconoclasm.[39]

Just how radical the Calvinist movement became in these years is suggested by the burgeoning literature on political theory and on justifying political violence. Faithful Calvinists knew all the biblical texts justifying royal authority and requiring submission to properly constituted superiors. But what happened to such doctrines when the governments in place were so self-evidently targeting God's holy people (namely, themselves) and serving Satan and the Antichrist? Some influential thinkers now explored ideas of tyrannicide and the legitimacy of assassination. Scottish Calvinist leader John Knox exalted the biblical story of Phineas, who won God's favor by an act of righteous homicide against those who violated God's commands, and in so doing removed a plague from the land. In the context of the time, the obvious target for any such action was a Catholic monarch. Significantly, this example assumed the righteous decision of one faithful vigilante, who did not wait for the consent of a parliament or jury before striking. To that extent, the label of "tyrant" was a subjective designation.[40]

Around 1570, Scottish Calvinist George Buchanan wrote his explosive *De jure regni apud Scotos, or, A dialogue, concerning the due privilege of government in the kingdom of Scotland*, which circulated in manuscript for some years before eventually being published in 1579. This was a significant argument in favor of limited government, but critics condemned its message that "wicked kings and tyrants ought to be put to death." About 1572, a still anonymous French Calvinist extended the argument to justify acts of tyrannicide carried out by lone assassins where necessary. Such theories were all the more daring given the number of instances in these years when kings and prominent leaders on both sides of the religious divide actually were assassinated during political conflicts. In fairness, it should be said that in these very same years, Catholic thinkers evolved very similar ideas about the removal of unjust rulers.[41]

We think of the ideologies of this era in terms of the divine right of kings. But under the extreme strain of social crisis and confrontation, some thinkers came close to proclaiming the divine right of lone assassins.

Revolution in the Netherlands

The Dutch revolt indicates the relationship between climate-driven disaster and the growth of radical religious movements. In the mid-sixteenth century, the Low Countries were an extraordinarily valuable part of the Habsburg

Empire, but they were also the setting for rising tensions. Aristocrats resented imperial taxation, and the growing Protestant minority feared the growing intrusion of militant Catholic authorities, symbolized by the Inquisition. Even so, in no sense was a militant Calvinist party organizing revolution, and many of the key aristocratic leaders were Catholic, or else moderate Protestants. Activism grew rapidly in the 1560s, with popular pressure driving active insurgency. The key turning point was the disastrous winter of 1564–1565, followed by harsh frosts that ruined food production and drove food prices to impossible levels. Food riots followed. Mass popular misery created an audience sympathetic to hearing grievances, and as a government minister wisely warned, "If the people rise up, the religious issue will become involved." Making that scenario still more likely was the arrival of substantial numbers of French Calvinists fleeing massacres and persecutions in their own country. Open rebellion erupted in the Netherlands in 1566 when Calvinist militants launched comprehensive attacks on churches and their contents in what would be remembered as the *Beeldenstorm*, the evocatively named Storm of Images. The cities spiraled out of control.[42]

Spanish authorities responded ferociously with repression and mass executions, and for some years it seemed that the insurgency was under control. Calvinists occupied an ever-larger role in the continuing resistance, which gained strength in the terrible crisis years of the late 1560s. Calvinist lords mobilized as the Gueux (the beggars), and in 1572 those revolutionaries seized a port, which served as the nucleus of a steadily expanding core of liberated territory. At this stage, the resistance leadership was still religiously diverse, with Calvinists, Catholics, and moderates, but as so often happens in revolutionary crises, the most militant hard-liners came to dominate political life. In 1573, the revolutionary leader William of Orange, whose personal religious views were distinctly moderate, proclaimed himself a Calvinist. Even so, the revolutionaries were cautious about moving too fast in a way that alienated other factions. Not until 1581 did the rebellious regions proclaim their independence as the United Provinces, the nation that would later be known simply as the Netherlands.[43]

The United Provinces increasingly became a solidly Calvinist state, where Reformed clergy occupied an ever more visible role, with a shrinking and relatively powerless Catholic minority. Overt Catholic worship was prohibited. From the 1580s, the new nation became firmly established as a major military and commercial force, with incalculable consequences for every aspect of European life and thought—its economic and scientific development, its global and imperial role, and the origins of the Enlightenment. The Calvinist republic of the Netherlands has a solid claim to have invented modernity.[44]

At every stage of this story, climate-related factors were critical to the history, and that narrative has been expertly told by historian Dagomar Degroot. His book's title, *The Frigid Golden Age*, constantly reminds us of the extremely severe conditions in which the revolt occurred, and the new nation was born. The long decades of the Eighty Years' War coincided with some of the coldest and most damaging years in European history.[45] Degroot describes the climate's impact on multiple incidents in those struggles, but several key points stand out prominently. One is the general impact of food supply and prices, which so often sparked discontent and insurgency, most broadly in 1565–1566, and again with the horrendous winter of 1572–1573. Agricultural crises resonated through the whole social system, undermining finances and commerce. Those conditions continued long after the initial revolutionary upsurge, with lasting impact on the conduct of the war. Ultimately, all wars are about logistics, about keeping armed forces fed and supplied, but that was especially true of the long-drawn-out Dutch conflict. In order to feed soldiers in the Low Countries, the Habsburg empire had to maintain lengthy supply routes from northern Italy, which passed through the Rhineland. Such an enterprise would have been very difficult for any early modern state, but the climate crisis made it all but impossible. In 1576, ill-fed and unpaid Habsburg forces mutinied, sacking what had hitherto been one of Europe's wealthiest trading cities, Antwerp, where Bruegel had recently painted his prophetic vision "The Triumph of Death." The fall of Antwerp forced a fundamental realignment of European commerce and economic life and effectively made the fortunes of Amsterdam as the capital of the later Dutch golden age.[46]

But climate shaped the war in countless other ways. To oversimplify, the Spanish and Dutch fought in different ways, reflecting their historical traditions and geographical context. Both on land and at sea, the Dutch benefited militarily from conditions that were cold, wet, and stormy, which neatly characterized the Europe of the late sixteenth century. On occasion, the cold worked against them, as when Spanish forces were able to make dramatic advances across unexpectedly frozen waters. But normally it was the Dutch who profited. If the Spanish were the acknowledged experts at besieging fortified cities, little of that expertise mattered when torrential rains made digging trenches out of the question. Dutch cities succeeded in holding out as they would normally never have done. The Dutch survived the unequal struggle and built a nation.

Winners and Losers

In the same years that Calvinism was expanding and gaining its victories, the Catholic Church was at the height of its efforts to reform, restructure, and rearm. The reforming Council of Trent began its efforts in 1545, but it was in 1563, as the continent's social crisis was becoming acute, that the assembly concluded and its transforming edicts were promulgated. A new profession of faith, a new missal, and a new breviary all followed shortly, creating and consecrating what would be known as Tridentine Catholicism (from the Latin name for Trent, Tridentum). In 1564, the bull *Benedictus Deus* demanded strict obedience from all the faithful, condemning unauthorized interpretations on pain of excommunication. In the same year, the church began listing censored writings in its notorious Index of Prohibited Books.[47]

Between 1563 and 1575, the Catholicism asserted by Rome became significantly more militant, more demanding in its requirements, and more expansive in the doctrines to which it demanded unquestioning assent and obedience. Catholicism and Calvinism looked like mirror images of each other. While Calvinists were pressing for social and theological revolution, Catholics were envisaging a spiritual and military reconquest of Europe. That new militancy found aggressive expression through Catholic sovereigns and secular leaders, as demonstrated, for instance, in the savage response to the Dutch unrest in the mid-1560s. In 1570, the Pope formally excommunicated Elizabeth of England, challenging the legitimacy of her whole regime and encouraging Catholic dissent to the point of revolt or assassination.

Across Europe, insurrections and warfare acutely intensified religious hostilities and benefited the strictest and most uncompromising factions, the movements least open to toleration. A vicious circle soon became apparent. As intolerant regimes of whatever persuasion strove to eliminate dissent, repression drove the rival groups to rebellion, which in turn confirmed impressions of them as seditious and dangerous. That in turn provoked further violence. In some cases losing movements were expelled from their older footholds, and in other cases they were altogether eliminated from the map.

The religious wars of the era were rarely a zero-sum game, in the sense that losers would be completely destroyed. As the Dutch story illustrates, minorities did persist, even if they lost their power and privileges. But in some cases, the losers suffered appallingly. In hindsight, we think of Protestantism as distinctive to northern and western Europe, while being at best a tenuous presence in "obviously Catholic" lands like Italy or Austria. Such an outcome was anything but predetermined in the sixteenth century, when Protestant dissent manifested in many surprising corners of the Christian world. That dissent did not die naturally of its own accord but rather was eliminated by conscious and ruthless action from above, through campaigns that coincided with economic and social strains. In just the years that regions were seeking witches for execution, many were also targeting faith minorities as obvious causes of God's wrath on the land. In the Austrian Habsburg lands, attempts at coexistence and mutual tolerance came under heavy strain from the mid-1570s, with growing restrictions on Protestant preachers and publications. From the 1580s, Austria's Protestant populations faced local acts of mass expulsion and religious cleansing. England's Catholic populations never recovered in prestige or security after the crises of 1569–1572.[48]

Ireland offers a clear example of the religious consequences of these struggles. I have already described the brutal wars of the 1590s, those years of systematic crisis and hunger. The defeat of Catholic rebels led to the flight of their aristocratic leaders into exile and the English seizure of their lands. That offered the opportunity for a new Anglo-Scottish settlement or "plantation" in the province of Ulster, and in effect the creation of a new Calvinist enclave. Catholics were systematically displaced and expelled. Across the island, Catholics who remained loyal to their faith were subject to harsh and steadily increasing disabilities and discrimination. The "Irish problem" that so often resurfaced over the following four centuries has its origins precisely in these years.[49]

By the end of the sixteenth century, decades of strife had created certain fundamental assumptions in the European Christian world. Beyond particular conflicts, such as the forever war between Spain and the Netherlands, all right-thinking people understood the utter polarization between Protestant and Catholic causes, each of which found its harshest expression in its most militant and effective believers. Each side saw the ideological destruction of its rival as a realistic goal, if not through conversion then through ruinous violence. Where accommodations were reached—as in France from the late 1590s—there was always the realization that a delicate balance could be overthrown by changing circumstances beyond the frontiers. The scene was perfectly set for the appalling Thirty Years' War, which killed still more millions.

Counterfactuals are always perilous. Any attempt to reconstruct how European history might have developed without the ferociously cold weather of the late sixteenth century involves juggling an impossible number of variables. But what we can legitimately say is that at many critical points, climate factors decisively shaped political events, with the dramatic results that we know.

6
A Faded Sun and a Wider World

> Then he gave him a parchment roll, and there was written within, "Flee from the wrath to come."
>
> —John Bunyan, 1678

Between 1678 and 1682, Great Britain and Ireland experienced a national political and religious trauma known as the Popish Plot, an upsurge of anti-Catholic fury, violence, and vigilantism. Reputedly, Catholic clergy (led by Jesuit priests) were plotting to kidnap or assassinate the king, Charles II, as part of a coup d'état that would place his Catholic brother on the throne. The resulting panic led to the deaths of some dozens of Catholic clergy, through either execution or systematic maltreatment. Political conflicts arising from the crisis came close to igniting a civil war.[1]

Historians tell the story of these years in many different ways. They might discuss the long background of anti-Catholic sentiment in Protestant England, or the rivalry between court factions in the late 1670s, or conflicts within particular families that were deeply divided between Protestant and Catholic wings. Each of these is a legitimate approach. But this affair was also part of a larger international context. Between 1677 and 1682, French elites were no less bitterly divided over the sensational Affair of the Poisons. The case focused on a group of what were loosely called witches but which we might term a mixture of fortune-tellers and poisoners-for-hire. The case revealed a court culture in which powerful individuals targeted rivals for murder while using love potions to secure the affections of the king. Following an investigation by royal officials, dozens of participants were killed and others exiled. The carnage would have been worse if the king had not feared the scandalous effects of any resulting publicity, which might have threatened the stability of the monarchy itself.[2]

At first sight, these cases seem to be wholly independent. The French cases never involved Protestant-Catholic tensions, and the English Popish Plot never delved into witchcraft. But beyond the general chronology the two affairs had much in common: an atmosphere of raging paranoia, and a furious quest for scapegoats. Both hinted at the fear of sudden murder by sinister cabals, who operated within a recognizably religious framework. If you traveled between London and Paris in those years, you would have had a powerful sense of déjà vu.

Very similar events occurred in such different societies, and with a quite different cast of villains, while many other countries in these same years experienced rumored conspiracies and seditions. But as we have seen from earlier periods, the parallels make sense when set against the background of agricultural crisis and economic catastrophe resulting from climate pressures. The accumulation of nightmares that developed in the late 1670s echoed through the social and political system not just in Europe but on the other side of the Atlantic as well. The years between 1675 and 1710 were marked by repeated disasters driven by climate change, including wars and revolts, dearths and plagues, and unprecedented weather conditions. Many believers imagined the fast-approaching end of the existing world and avidly sought out evildoers and demons, literal and figurative.[3]

Once again, the resulting conflicts and persecutions had the effect of relocating religious centers of gravity, with the most acute effects reshaping the Islamic presence in Europe. The same years resulted in the redistribution of Protestant Christians across both Europe and the New World. Much of the later religious history of North America has its roots in these dreadful years.

The General Crisis, Continued

I have already cited Geoffrey Parker's 2013 book *Global Crisis* as a brilliant and pathbreaking contribution to integrating the history of the environment with the conventional story of human societies and their political and social developments. Parker demonstrates incontestably that climate change supplies the essential context for the wave of revolutions, wars, and disasters that overcame many societies at midcentury, in Europe but also as far afield as the Ottoman Empire, India, and China. For Parker, this crisis was at its most acute between roughly 1635 and 1665. Much of modern European political theory grew out of the midcentury turmoil that collapsed multiple states, as thinkers demanded a radical new approach to such basic questions as the legitimate foundations of authority and the balance of rights and duties between sovereign and subject. Arguably, European modernity is a direct product of this General Crisis of the mid-seventeenth century.[4]

But dating that phenomenon presents challenges. Like most scholars, Parker focuses intensely on the early and mid-seventeenth century, saying little about conditions from the 1670s onward. Yet in fact, most of the climate-related horrors that caused ruin in 1650, say, were still very much in evidence later in the century—arguably, still more so in these latter decades.[5] The years after 1675 proved extremely difficult, with all the social consequences we might expect. The year 1675 itself was a catastrophically cold "year without a summer." In a Parisian July, French author Madame de Sévigné complained, "We suffer horribly from the cold and have the fires lit," and she speculated sagely that "the behavior of the sun and of the seasons has completely changed." So bad were the 1670s in Egypt that Cairo's elites took to wearing furs. Record-breaking cold returned in 1684, in the mid-1690s, and again in 1709—in each instance, reaching levels that were actually worse than anything seen in the 1640s. The winter of 1695 was the worst in centuries, and 1709 was little better. Yet most accounts of the seventeenth-century crisis, including Parker's, do not address the far-reaching political and social effects of these later disasters. Many ignore such catastrophic near-meltdowns as Britain's Popish Plot, or the near-constant great-power wars that raged between the 1670s and 1710s.[6]

In fact, events very much like the midcentury crisis were reproduced with high fidelity in those later years, which makes the years around 1650 less singular than might otherwise be the case. To take an example from the realm of health, not until 1720–1721 did western Europe have its last encounter to date with a major outbreak of bubonic plague. The parallels between eras were very strong in matters of religious change and innovation. What changed between the 1640s and 1680s was not that climatic conditions eased—quite the contrary. Rather, states became better able to ride out these storms, both literal and metaphorical.[7]

A Cold Sun

A climatic context for these crises is not difficult to find: indeed, the main problem is a surfeit of possible suspects. The years from 1645 through 1715 were the time of the Maunder Minimum, when sunspots were few or entirely lacking, and that situation reached an extreme stage precisely in the mid-1670s. Coincidentally or not, volcanic activity reached strikingly high levels during those decades of the quiet Sun. Long Island in New Guinea produced a shattering level 6 eruption in 1660, and four more level 5 events occurred between 1663 and 1680, all in Japan or Indonesia. One in particular—Gamkonora, in 1673—was probably a sizable Plinian eruption, characterized by gigantic amounts of pumice and other volcanic debris, with gases ejected high into the stratosphere. That is a strong suspect for the miseries that Europe suffered over the following years. A duet of very large explosions followed in the early 1690s, inflicting a historically cold epoch on many parts of Europe. One extreme El Niño event occurred in 1660–1661, and a mega–El Niño struck in 1686–1688, with ruinous effects in South Asia and historic famines.[8]

Whatever the precise causes, the consequences were dreadful. Sea ice menaced the North Sea, ruining trade and fishing. And the cold was no localized phenomenon: glaciers advanced around the world, affecting both hemispheres. In Europe, glaciers made historic advances in the eastern Alps, and populations fell in areas imperiled by glaciers. But similar expansions occurred also in both North and South America, in China, and even in New Zealand.[9]

Freeze Again to Death

It is small consolation to note that the dreadful cold offered a theme for some of the great artists and musicians of the era. In 1677 the French court watched Jean-Baptiste Lully's opera *Isis*, with its timely references to the appalling winter and its chills, its *mortels frissons*. In England in 1691, Henry Purcell's semi-opera *King Arthur* featured an appearance by the Cold Genius (the Spirit of Winter), who sang:

> See'st thou not how stiff
> And wondrous old
> Far unfit to bear the bitter cold
> I can scarcely move
> Or draw my breath . . .
> Let me, let me, let me
> Freeze again to death.[10]

Perhaps humor was the only way to cope with such horrors. But in these same years, people genuinely were pleading for relief from freezing conditions that made breathing miserably difficult.

I have already described the wrenching winter that England suffered in 1683–1684, the time of the great Frost Fairs on the Thames. Diarist John Evelyn recorded that England that December experienced "one of the severest frosts that has happened of many years." Smaller towns held fairs on their own frozen rivers. Yet if the London fair, "Great Britain's wonder," was a potent tourist attraction, other effects were much grimmer. Evelyn was troubled at what seemed to be

> a bacchanalian triumph, or carnival on the water, while it was a severe judgment on the land, the trees not only splitting as if the lightning struck, but men and cattle perishing in divers places, and the very seas so locked up with ice, that no vessels could stir out or come in. The fowls, fish, and birds, and all our exotic plants and greens, universally perishing. Many parks of deer were destroyed, and all sorts of fuel so dear, that there were great contributions to preserve the poor alive. Nor was this severe weather much less intense in most parts of Europe, even as far as Spain and the most southern tracts. London, by reason of the excessive coldness of the air hindering the ascent of the smoke, was so filled with the fuliginous steam of the sea-coal, that hardly could one see across the street, and this filling the lungs with its gross particles, exceedingly obstructed the breast, so as one could scarcely breathe. Here was no water to be had from the pipes and engines, nor could the brewers and divers other tradesmen work, and every moment was full of disastrous accidents.[11]

Across the country and in much of Europe, planting and plowing became all but impossible. The early 1680s also saw memorably frigid winters in North America, the coldest in more than forty years.

Every Moment Was Full of Disastrous Accidents

For many historical periods, our ability to measure the impact of social crises is quite limited, and we have to depend on impressionistic accounts or anecdotes. That problem is far less pronounced in Europe's seventeenth century, a time of state churches and compulsory church membership. Parish records were very good at collecting evidence of key life transitions: births, marriages, and deaths. Using such documents, modern scholars can identify times of feast and famine, the singularly good or bad periods in the long span of history. At their worst, some years stand out for the sizable surfeit of deaths over births, the times of high mortality or, most tellingly, of crisis mortality, defined as years in which mortality rates ran 40 percent or more above the normal trend. At such times, famine and epidemic struck together to produce an ugly surplus of deaths over births.[12]

The years after 1675 were alarmingly productive of such extreme crises. France suffered one such period of very high mortality in 1676, and parlous conditions afflicted France, Italy, Spain, and the Low Countries between 1678 and 1680. Based on a sample of five hundred parishes in southeastern England, historian Mary Dobson found that just three years in the seventeenth century reached this stage of extreme crisis: 1625, 1638, and 1679. Combined horrors reached a nightmarish crescendo between 1678 and 1682, with crisis mortality in 1679. If we look at the whole period from 1601 to 1710, then four of the worst mortality years fell between 1678 and 1681, the most sustained period of very high death rates for the whole century. Even the 1640s offered nothing comparable. In England at least, the crisis year 1679 was the last of its kind measured by Dobson for the whole period up to 1800. (Scotland and Ireland followed different trajectories.)[13]

It is all but impossible to disentangle the effects of diseases and plagues from those of hunger. The year 1679 featured "the most widespread epidemic or group of fever epidemics in seventeenth and eighteenth century England . . . August to December 1679 was the period of severest local mortality crises on the national series." At various times between 1678 and 1681, England suffered outbreaks of enteric fever (possibly typhoid), smallpox, epidemic ague, and influenza, while 1679 saw "the most widespread epidemic of fever epidemics in 17th and 18th century England." That was followed by deficient harvests. Conditions improved marginally in 1680 and 1681, when deaths were at high rather than crisis levels, but "average" conditions did not return until 1682—and then the great cold took hold. But much of Europe suffered terribly. An influenza pandemic struck in 1675, the same year that central and eastern Europe suffered a new outbreak of bubonic plague. That gradually spread over much of the continent over the next decade, and 1680 was a notorious plague year, recalled among other things for the Great Plague of Vienna. During the European winter of 1683, many countries suffered from so-called hungry fever, which particularly struck Germany. In frigid

1684, John Evelyn noted that "the smallpox was very mortal." Elsewhere, Persia suffered terribly: "The 1670s witnessed drought, harsh winters, locust swarms, famine, and earthquakes." Plagues and famines continued to strike the country through the mid-1680s. Meanwhile, the vast area of the African Sahel suffered prolonged drought and famine.[14]

Across Europe, the mid-1690s were horrific. In 1693–1694, more than 1.3 million died in France's *grande famine*, some 6 percent of the population. Between 1695 and 1697, 300,000 perished in Sweden and the Baltic lands, and Finland lost a third of its people. Scotland lost 15 percent of its population in its "seven ill years," and particular regions suffered a fatality rate of 25 percent. Many thousands of others—perhaps 15 percent of the population—abandoned their homes to wander the roads in search of food. The years 1698–1699 saw severe volcanic-related cold spells. Observers varied as to which particular horror year in this series proved the worst. In New England, at least, the years 1696–1698 were the coldest of the century. Diarist Samuel Sewall recorded that "to Horses, Swine, Net-Cattell, Sheep and Deer / Ninety and Seven prov'd a Mortal yeer." Droughts afflicted western North America.

A new series of cataclysms struck around the Euro-American world in 1709–1710. Famine in East Prussia cost 250,000 lives, and a new *grande famine* in France killed 600,000. Influenza raged. The same year marked the start of a dreadful panzootic, which killed millions of Europe's cattle over the following years.[15]

Such accounts offer obvious parallels to the notorious General Crisis. That event, which supposedly hinged on the 1640s, was marked by wars, revolutions, and the collapse of regimes, together with mass starvation and epidemics. As I noted, famines continued to rage well into the 1710s, and Europe was scarcely more peaceful in this period. Just to take the greatest European power of the time, France was only rarely at peace internationally between the 1660s and 1713. In the opening years of the new century, the country faced a bloody and widespread Protestant revolt. Most European nations were drawn into at least one of the engulfing general struggles of the era: the Dutch Wars (1672–1678), the Great Turkish War (1683–1699), the War of the Grand Alliance (1688–1697), the Great Northern War (1700–1721), and the War of the Spanish Succession (1701–1714). The mighty Swedish conqueror Charles XII had the misfortune to fight the Russians at the epochal Battle of Poltava in 1709, after losing much of his army to the cold and starvation of that horrific year. His defeat, which in its European impact is often compared to Waterloo a century later, marked the end of the Swedish Empire and the ascent of Russian power. Reflecting the colonial endeavors of the time, some of these struggles reverberated around the globe, making Europe's struggles transcontinental, if not yet fully global. Dreadful winters such as that of 1709–1710 also left a legacy of profound discontent and popular fury, which commonly found its way into political and religious struggles. Even in prosperous England, a political crisis in 1710 sparked extensive interreligious rioting, with numerous attacks on the places of worship of Presbyterians, Baptists, and other dissenting Protestants. Political chaos loomed, and many feared a return to the civil wars of the 1640s.[16]

Reports that the seventeenth-century General Crisis ended around the 1670s were very premature—or should we in fact count this as a whole separate crisis?

Signs in the Sky

However we define our historical periods, the post-1675 crisis swiftly acquired spiritual and intellectual dimensions. Drawing readily on the circumstances they witnessed around them, major scholars and theologians produced highly influential works on apocalyptic. Who could deny the stark evidence of God's wrath in these years of agony? It was in 1678 that the first part of John Bunyan's *Pilgrim's Progress* described the humble Christian beginning his quest after discovering the powerful text "Flee from the wrath to come!" Throughout the politics of these years, we often see echoes of apocalyptic doctrines, especially as persecuted groups turned to Revelation to comprehend their sufferings and defeats.[17]

If all the other disasters were not proof enough of the Last Times, 1680 actually brought a shattering heavenly sign in the form of the Great Comet, one of the brightest of the century. The word "disaster" itself derives from "bad star." If its appearance at the time of such climate upheavals was purely coincidental, that lack of connection was not obvious at the time: disasters were mounting daily.[18]

That comet in itself became a potent cultural phenomenon, which contemporaries contextualized together with the assaults from the climate. If not actually a sign of the imminent end, the comet was a direct warning from God that humanity should mend its ways. In the fifteenth century, the Pope had urged Christians to pray for protection against "the Devil, the Turk, and the Comet." Such fears remained very much alive in 1680. As Scots minister Robert Law remarked,

> No history ever made mention of the like comet, and it is doubted if ever the like was seen since the Creation, and is certainly prodigious of great alterations and of great judgments on these lands and nations for our sins; for never was the Lord more provoked by a people than by us in these lands, and that by persons of all ranks.[19]

When French thinker Pierre Bayle asked his mentors what the meaning of the sign was, he heard that "God shows forth these great phenomena in order to give sinners time to ward off by their penitence the evils that hang over their heads." Hundreds of pamphlets presented a similar message. In London, John Evelyn was deeply engaged in the violent controversies of the time, including the unjust executions arising from the Popish Plot. Right in the middle of those events, he observed the comet, and recalled that the last time he had witnessed anything like that was in 1641, in the lead-up to the great Civil War. "I pray God avert his judgments!" he added. The government responded to accumulating crises by proclaiming solemn public fasts, to demonstrate national penitence.[20]

The World's End and the New Birth

Turmoil and violence begot apocalyptic views, but by no means among the usual suspects in the radical Puritan sects. We might expect a devout Baptist such as Bunyan to imagine the end times, but more educated and rational believers surely would be more skeptical. After all, the later seventeenth century saw the origins of the Enlightenment. In England, this was the heroic age of London's Royal Society and the towering intellects of the Cambridge Platonists. But apocalyptic ideas survived strongly among the mainstream and orthodox in 1680, and they enjoyed a particular boom among such otherwise respectable Puritan clerics as Richard Baxter, who was assiduously studying prophetic works including the books of Daniel and Revelation. Another of the great minds of the age was Henry More, the Platonist and fellow of the Royal Society. Yet his publications at this time included his detailed study of Revelation, *Apocalypsis Apocalypseos* (1680), and his 1681 exposition of the prophecies in the book of Daniel. One of More's enthusiastic readers was Isaac Newton, who had a lifelong interest in apocalyptic and millenarian themes. In the early 1680s, just as he was working on his epochal *Principia*, he was also painstakingly annotating More's thoughts on Daniel and the end times. Apocalyptic thought coexisted easily with modernity and even Enlightenment.[21]

If such elite and academic figures were convinced of the world's imminent end, it is not surprising that such doctrines appealed to a mass audience who knew only their Bibles. In the Germanic world, debates over the end times sharply divided the mainstream churches. One celebrated prophet in Germany in the early 1680s was the brilliant theologian and astronomer Johann Jacob Zimmerman, who predicted the imminent end of the world, occurring no later than 1693. He was ejected from his post as a Lutheran minister in 1685, and he urged faithful Christians to separate from a dying society. His views were widely influential, especially among radical Lutherans and Pietists (whom I will discuss shortly). Zimmerman's most famous disciple was Johannes Kelpius, whose observations of the Great Comet were respectfully cited by Newton himself. Like other German mystics of the era, he combined apocalyptic thought with highly developed astronomy and mathematics while delving deeply into astrology, alchemy, the occult, and the magical properties of plants and stones. As we will see, Kelpius and his followers brought these apocalyptic and mystical doctrines to North America.[22]

Figures such as Kelpius might be well known only to fellow scholars, but other figures from this age enjoyed a wide popular influence, to the point of reshaping mainstream Christian faith. The year 1675, with its savage cold and growing apocalyptic concern, was marked by the publication of the *Pia desideria* (Heartfelt desire for God-pleasing reform) by Frankfurt-based Lutheran pastor Philipp Spener (his other major works appeared shortly afterward, his *General Theology* in 1680). The title of *Pia desideria* gave its name to the massively influential Pietist movement, which burgeoned between the 1670s and 1690s; Kelpius was an early recruit. Describing Spener's ideas today makes them sound almost too commonplace to be worth noting. He was deeply uncomfortable with the very formal and hierarchical nature of Protestant churches, which gave so little scope to the laity or to any kind of spontaneity. Spener favored replacing the intellectual and theological approach of mainstream sermons with appeals to the heart and emotions. Going beyond the shared worship of congregations, Spener wanted to bring devout laypeople and clergy together in small groups where they could share intense prayer and Bible-reading, with a view to promoting individual holiness and a religion of the heart as well as the mind. Ideally, believers would achieve an inner conversion, a new spiritual birth—in short, they would be born again.[23]

Emotional sermons, heart conversion, small-group piety—little here sounds controversial. But at the time, such a vision was radical to the point of being attacked as heretical. If the language of "born again" is in the New Testament, the specific program presented by Spener and his disciples in the 1670s and 1680s was wildly innovative, especially when it was accompanied by so much transgressive spiritual excitement, in which women played a key role. Through these years, we find the first of what would become such a common genre: believers describing those critical moments when they felt that God had transformed them to new life, to new birth. In its origins, Pietism, which ultimately became the foundation of evangelical thought in North America, is incomprehensible except in the context of the apocalyptic crisis of these decades. (I will return to this American dimension.) It was not just that a single religious thinker presented such an idea, but that it was so avidly received by so many ordinary believers desperate to hear the conversionist message, to be born again. With the world so evidently entering its end times, the approaching Spirit could no longer be contained within formal institutions. Inner fire was essential to rescuing a spiritually frozen world.[24]

Fear and Blame

Conceivably, a society of impassive saints might humbly accept such nightmarish conditions, might learn to live with constant hunger, deprivation, and the ever-present reality of death, especially among the weakest. In reality, most human beings are neither saints nor stoics, and they seek explanations for what they see around them. Their desire for solutions becomes ever more desperate as a crisis drags on into a fourth or fifth year with no obvious hope of an end or any glimpse of cosmic mercy. It would have been astounding if there had not been persecutions and panics of some kind beginning in the mid-1670s and enduring through the next decade. Of course, there was tension, desperation, paranoia, and fear, and the only question was just how these appalling forces were going to be directed. Predictably and inevitably, there was going to be a religious and cultural explosion around 1680.

Popular fears often found expression in witchcraft panics. After all, witches were blamed for visiting evils upon their neighbors, and mass deaths and sickness naturally spawned a quest for culprits. Americans naturally think of the traumatic Salem upheaval of 1692, by far the worst outbreak of its kind in their colonial history, with nineteen executed. In England, the year 1682 brought a sensational case in Bideford, which produced some of the last judicial executions of witches in that country. Even so, this was quite limited in its effects when compared with matters in Continental Europe, where the conspiracy charges that first emerged around 1320 had subsequently become ever more ornate.[25]

European witchcraft inquiries of these years offered a stunning repertoire of charges and nightmares—secret murder and poisoning, heretical and anti-Christian practices, labyrinthine conspiracies. Sweden suffered several sensational cases from the late 1660s, with allegations of great Sabbats at which Satan held his earthly court. This began an era of panic remembered as Stora Oväsendet (the Great Noise), which culminated with the Torsåker affair of 1675. Seventy-one suspects were executed in a single day, June 1, beheaded and then burned. That massacre claimed the lives of a fifth of the women in the three parishes affected. Other executions followed over the next year. In 1678–1679, cases were afflicting Moravia, Scotland, and Iceland. A hundred perished in Liechtenstein. A series of witch-hunts that began in Salzburg, Austria, around this time claimed perhaps 140 lives.[26] This list does not include minor instances of individuals being prosecuted for nonorganized witchcraft, cases that proliferated in these years on both sides of the Atlantic. Nor does it include the French Affair of the Poisons, the themes of which overlapped at so many points with the classic language and imagery of witchcraft and witch-hunting. Allegedly, some of the main perpetrators actually used black masses and human sacrifices to advance their causes at the royal court, making it a defining moment in the invention of the mythical religion of Satanism.

One common theme in these many cases is the use of witnesses who likely would have been ignored in more placid eras. The Torsåker proceedings in Sweden were notorious in this regard, as fanatical clergy mobilized bands of children as trained witnesses against random suspects. In the Salem cases a few years later, courts admitted so-called spectral evidence, events that were glimpsed in dreams or visions but which were nevertheless cited as eyewitness testimony. At the time, raising objections to such atrocities was a profoundly dangerous enterprise, as it invited charges of being allied to the Devil.

The spike in cases that were reported and prosecuted arose not from any particular change in the behavior of ordinary people but rather the acutely heightened sensitivity to social dangers by elites and investigators. The same impression emerges from explicitly political cases such as England's Popish Plot, which was revealed by a number of informers and supposed defectors, most notorious of whom was the loathsome manipulator Titus Oates. Informers of that kind are a perennial feature of any society, but only at times of real crisis and alarm are desperate elites likely to take them seriously, however ridiculous their assertions. Together, the various investigations demonstrate a real sense of existential panic.[27]

Not only did those who believed in the booming allegations of witchcraft maintain their views, but they doubled down on defending the whole intellectual system that implied. That defense was explicitly linked to contemporary end times fears. In western Europe, educated opinion had since the 1660s become more skeptical about witchcraft charges and accounts of ghosts and apparitions, but the new atmosphere demanded a rethinking. In 1681, the sophisticated intellectual Henry More was instrumental in the publication of *Saducismus triumphatus*, one of the most significant works ever written in English on the subject of witches and the occult. Although published posthumously under the name of the original compiler, Joseph Glanvill (who had died in 1680), it was extensively edited by More. The book takes its title from the ancient Jewish sect of the Sadducees, who held "that there is no Resurrection, and that there are neither angels nor spirits," and the suggestion was that such hyperskeptical beliefs had gained power in contemporary Europe. In order to challenge prevailing skepticism and to assert the imminence of apocalypse, *Saducismus triumphatus* offered a stunning (and thoroughly credulous) array of case studies of witches, ghosts, apparitions, and poltergeists. Among other lasting impacts, the book exercised a potent influence on Cotton Mather, who some years afterward had to interpret the events at Salem. The book is still a critical resource for anyone trying to reconstruct the occult beliefs of preindustrial England.[28]

God's Enemies

Across Europe, despairing people targeted unpopular groups and individuals, and religious minorities were a natural choice. By deviating from the national religious consensus, such stubborn deviants showed clearly their resistance to divine will. Mainstream religious believers from majority communities become very open to conspiratorial theories that demonized outgroups and rivals. In some cases Jews suffered acts of violence and massacres, but at least in western Europe this occurred at a level no greater than had been customary over the previous century. In the new environment, most of the most grievous violence was directed by Christians against other Christians.

These conflicts and resentments had deep historical roots. As we have seen, the era had left most countries divided between those who accepted the new religious order and others who opposed it. In theory, states followed one approved religion, but most contained minorities who followed the rival faith. Those minorities could be substantial: although France would ultimately become overwhelmingly Catholic, its Protestant (Huguenot) minority amounted to perhaps 10 percent of the population in 1580, falling to 4 percent a century later. By the 1670s, Catholics were a tiny minority in Protestant England, and a sizable majority in British-ruled Ireland. In most cases too, minorities were visible in the sense of being publicly identified, and usually worshipping at well-known public or semipublic facilities. The degree of official toleration varied over time, but a time of surging fear and resentment created plenty of targets for persecution. In several key realms, the crisis of the 1680s was so severe that it all but eliminated minorities, marking a decisive end to Reformation conflicts. Although Protestant-Catholic conflicts are best known, intolerance was a multifaceted affair, and Protestants and Catholics alike struck at troublesome sects, such as the Anabaptists.[29]

Protestants and Catholics

Just as France was recovering from the Poisons crisis, its government turned its attention to the Protestant minority, the Huguenots, who still amounted to some 800,000 people. Their religious practice was officially tolerated under the royal Edict of Nantes (1598), which had ended the horrendous Wars of Religion. From the late 1670s, the ambitious King Louis XIV (1643–1715) became ever more determined to remove those dissidents who thwarted his efforts to make France the unified flagship of Catholic Christianity.[30]

In 1681, the Most Christian King Louis began a heavy-handed policy of quartering soldiers in Protestant households, with the expectation that these "missionary dragoons" would force Protestants either to convert or to flee the country altogether. Instances of violence, plunder, and sexual assault were commonplace. Memories of these *dragonnades* remained bitter for later Protestants, which incidentally explains why the little-known Third Amendment to the US Constitution prohibits quartering soldiers in civilian households in peacetime. Sporadic religious persecution continued until 1685, when Louis formally revoked the Edict of Nantes and ended even the shadow of toleration. Most Huguenots fled the country, including Pierre Bayle, who took refuge in the Netherlands; his brother, who stayed behind, died in a French prison. But others who remained waged a stubborn rural guerrilla war that persisted until the 1710s, under the leadership of "prophets." Those hard-line resisters—the Camisards—spawned a vigorous tradition of militant faith, rooted in apocalyptic doctrines and Bible texts.[31]

In France, Catholics persecuted and murdered Protestants, but in other nations, the sides were reversed. In England, simmering anti-Catholicism became ferocious from the mid-1670s onward and was expressed in mass popular celebrations. In 1677, London mobs denounced the Pope by burning great effigies of the pontiff himself, accompanied by devils, or of the apocalyptic figure of the Whore of Babylon. Such demonstrations acquired sound effects in the form of live cats burned within the effigies, and the poor creatures "squalled most hideously as soon as they felt the fire." In 1678, informers exposed what they claimed were extensive plots for a Catholic putsch, and the suspicious death of one of the lead investigators appeared to show the truth of even the most outrageous accusations. The following year, priests started going to the gallows. In 1681, the purge acquired its most visible victim in Oliver Plunkett, the Catholic primate of Ireland.[32]

As smoldering resentments and tensions burst into new life, they were reflected in the popular culture of the time: poems and ballads, incendiary pamphlets and handbills, posters and cartoons. For several taut years the British political world remained on a knife edge, as any new accusation might further destabilize the court or government. Through a mixture of wise policy and good fortune, the Crown avoided such a catastrophe, and even won a political comeback. The persecution of Catholics in the Popish Plot was followed by a pro-Stuart and monarchist revival in the mid-1680s, what we today call a right-wing reaction. That in turn led to the persecution of Protestant dissenters, especially the most radical groups, the Quakers and Baptists.[33]

Different religious conflicts prevailed in one portion of the British Isles, namely Scotland, where both sides were Protestant. But an Anglican establishment dominated a more militant and Calvinist Presbyterian population, which became ever more militant in the face of economic crisis and social desperation. Presbyterians condemned their Anglican rulers as crypto-Catholics, symbols of the evils delineated in Revolution. Drawing on Old Testament precedent, they pledged to a covenant that would keep the nation true to God's law. Such militancy conjured terrifying memories of the 1630s, when an earlier generation of Covenanters defeated the army of King Charles I. In his attempt to reconquer Scotland, Charles provoked a civil war with his English subjects, which killed hundreds of thousands and ultimately cost that king his life.[34]

In the 1670s, Covenanters and radical resisters developed a powerful alternative culture of prayer and devotion outside the churches and royal centers that they regarded as tainted, as preachers addressed mass meetings in fields and the countryside. Their ideology developed a fiercely apocalyptic tone, with themselves as the righteous remnant resisting the Beast. As elsewhere, matters came to a head in the hunger year of 1679, when Covenanters launched a national revolt against the regime of Charles II, son and namesake of the earlier royal martyr. Among other actions, they assassinated the leader of the established church, the archbishop of St. Andrews. On this occasion, though, the script played out quite differently. Royal forces bloodily suppressed the revolution, defeating the rebels in the pivotal Battle of Bothwell Brig, and violence continued through the savage repression and executions of the next decade. Particularly targeted were the revolutionary hardliners, the Cameronians, dozens of whom were executed in a purge in 1685. In Scotland, the 1680s were notorious as the "killing time," an era of persecution that shaped Presbyterian thought and attitudes for two centuries afterward. As for other religious minorities, this was a time of martyrs, and of painstakingly collected martyrologies.[35]

The New States

The analogies between these events and those of the 1640s, the time of the so-called General Crisis, are very strong, but the differences from midcentury are no less striking than the parallels. If the degree of popular unrest remained, the state mechanisms that confronted it had changed. Partly this was a simple matter of learning from bitter experience. If Charles II had acted less judiciously than he did and followed the advice of his senior ministers in 1678–1679, then he would inevitably have faced a civil war like the one that had flared in his father's time and cost his father his head. Charles had learned what not to do.

Crucially, most countries had responded to those earlier crises by developing much stronger state mechanisms, in the form of expanded bureaucratic government, reliable financing and taxation, economic regulation, and (in some cases) the abolition of representative assemblies and the rise of absolutist monarchy. If England was not an absolutist state, it deployed far more resources than it had in midcentury. The British monarchy acquired permanent armed forces, ensuring that government would never again be as vulnerable as it had been in 1640. The military response that faced the Scottish rebels meant that the political script would develop on utterly different lines. Each of these developments was in its way a response to the lessons learned in the midcentury crisis, and a way of ensuring that such disasters could never recur. In consequence, fewer regimes actually collapsed in the 1680s or 1690s than in midcentury, and fewer kings lost their thrones. If the French suppression of the Huguenots met violent resistance, the opposition never came close to challenging the state, as might have occurred fifty or a hundred years previously. The frequent international wars from the 1680s onward further strengthened states and their military resources.[36]

The character of persecution and violence had also changed substantially from earlier eras, in that it was now more commonly undertaken by states rather than mobs. France offers an ideal example. Looking back at earlier eras, we see the mass popular movement of the shepherds, the *pastoureaux*, in the fourteenth century, or the unchecked mob violence directed against Protestants during the St. Bartholomew's Day slaughter of 1572. In such episodes, states and public authorities were close to invisible, except where they had been appropriated by local factions. In the 1680s, it was emphatically the royal government that sought to eliminate Protestants, using a sizable standing army and an extensive police apparatus. Anything like the earlier mob violence would have been regarded as an intolerable threat to public order and been snuffed out quickly and ruthlessly. West Europeans could still express their fears and miseries in religious form, but the options available to them had changed quite dramatically since earlier times.

That growth of states explains other long-term European trends, such as the sharp decline in anti-Jewish pogroms in much of Europe after the mid-seventeenth century. The great exceptions to this statement chiefly occurred in eastern regions. In the 1650s, tens of thousands of Jews were murdered during the Khmelnytsky uprising in Ukraine, on the borders of Poland-Lithuania. Politically as much as geographically, that was far removed from the increasingly well-organized states of the rest of Europe. At the bitter end of the century too, the worst anti-Jewish atrocities again took place in the east and particularly during times of warfare, when civilized restraints collapsed. Beyond Europe, it was Islamic states that followed the once-familiar European pattern of blaming Jews for plagues and natural catastrophes and penalizing them accordingly: Yemen brutally expelled its Jews in 1679, and Algeria did so in 1706.[37]

But that relative stability in Europe did not mean that the later decades faced easier situations or fewer challenges. Rather, states had better means with which to cope. In the newer world, rebellions and popular outbreaks were more likely to lead to the defeat and repression or exile of the protesters. That was a historic change, and one with enduring consequences for the development of European states through modern times.

The Road to Vienna

France's religious persecutions found a close analogy further east in the lands of the Holy Roman Empire, the other great European power of the era, which was ruled by the ardently Catholic Habsburg dynasty. This situation would be so significant because persecution and insurrection attracted armed foreign intervention, and that in turn detonated large-scale wars. The religious consequences were far-reaching.

As in France, Protestant (and mainly Calvinist) doctrines had made extensive advances in the empire despite the rule of a solidly Catholic monarchy, most convincingly in Hungary. During the seventeenth century, Catholic emperors made systematic efforts to re-Catholicize their territories, a process represented by the spectacular Baroque churches that now appeared so widely. Although we may think of them today as symbols of unquestioning Catholic orthodoxy, at the time their main purpose was to impress, attract, and reclaim a population fallen deep into Protestant error. But if religious tensions were endemic, hunger and social desperation threatened to turn those strains into armed revolution and open warfare.[38]

Efforts at militant Catholic evangelism were reasserted under the zealous Emperor Leopold I (1658–1705), who was thoroughly convinced that economic disasters and plagues reflected God's displeasure. He loathed Jews, expelling them from Vienna. As the economic situation deteriorated in the 1670s, Leopold violently persecuted Protestants, to the point of sending Calvinist pastors into galley slavery. (As in France, the persecution came from the throne, not from mobs or the streets.) The emperor faced major religious and national resistance in his Hungarian lands, which revolted repeatedly, while peasant revolts erupted in Bohemia and elsewhere. In 1678, the Transylvanian Protestant noble Imre Thököly took command of the Hungarian revolt. Insurrection spread over the following years as crops failed and people starved, and protests metastasized into a full-scale national revolution. At its height, Thököly commanded some 30,000 rebels, who took the name of *kuruc*, Crusaders, as he sought outside allies who could provide a counterweight to the awe-inspiring military strength of the Habsburg state. The result was an alliance between these mainly Protestant Crusaders and the (Islamic) Ottoman Empire against the Catholic Habsburgs. The sultan recognized him as king of Upper Hungary, tributary to the Ottoman state.[39]

Further complicating the matter was the devious role of the French Catholic king Louis, who was currently persecuting his own Protestant subjects. But Europe's power politics revolved around the clash between the French monarchy and the Habsburgs, and Louis saw huge benefit in an alliance with anyone of any faith who would weaken the power of that hated dynasty. At this very time, Louis was fighting to extend the French frontier to the Rhine, which meant pressing on the empire's far western possessions. His agents supported the (Protestant) Hungarian/Magyar revolt, and in 1679 and 1680 his envoy was pleading with the Ottoman grand vizier Kara Mustafa to intervene against the Habsburgs. Louis then let the Turks know that he would never fight on the Habsburg side, and he massed troops at the eastern frontier of France. That is what gave the Ottomans the confidence to launch the assault on Vienna, although at the last minute in this campaign Louis shifted his support to the Habsburgs.[40]

Such an account may make it seem that religion was a marginal force in the larger world of realpolitik and dynastic struggles, but the resulting wars transformed Europe's religious realities. The various plots and schemes culminated in 1683, one of the legendary years of European (and world) history and a decisive turning point in the relationship between Christianity and Islam. Leopold's internal struggles persuaded the Ottomans to launch a massive invasion of the empire, with some 150,000 troops, and to besiege Vienna. For some months, Vienna really was at the pivot of global history.

This remains one of the enduring might-have-been moments in history. If Vienna had fallen, then Islamic power would have penetrated into what we today think of as Germany, and perhaps beyond. Hungary, meanwhile, would have emerged as a Protestant-dominated statelet, under Islamic sovereignty. In reality, the Habsburgs were saved by the intervention of the heroic Polish king John Sobieski, who that September won a victory that effectively broke Muslim power in central Europe. (Less sensationally for European history, it also marked a disastrous moment in the history of Hungarian Protestantism.)[41]

The consequences were far-reaching and, for Christians, intoxicating. The ensuing Great Turkish War (1683–1699) pushed Christian military strength deep into the Balkans. One key victory was the 1686 recapture of Buda, the core of later Budapest, and the whole territory of modern Hungary soon followed. In Buda as elsewhere, the Christian reconquerors launched brutal massacres of infidels, killing thousands of Jews as well as Muslims. In 1686, the Russian Empire joined the Christian coalition. This was the first occasion on which Russia had participated in a western European alliance, and it conveniently marks the entry of Russia into European politics. The following year, a new Christian victory briefly raised the prospect of a total reconquest of Islamic lands in Europe. That vision soon faded, but the Ottomans never regained the threatening position they had held for the previous 250 years. Again, it is difficult to tell this story except in the context of climate factors, and particularly that great El Niño. It was precisely in 1686–1687 that the Ottoman Empire was suffering from ruinously cold conditions, and this marked the second time in the century that the Golden Horn froze over. Dry winters and soaking summers left an impoverished state unable to pay its army, which mutinied and forced the sultan, Mehmed IV, to abdicate. The Horn again froze in 1699, the year that brought the whole titanic struggle to its conclusion. If the Christian powers fought courageously, they had potent allies in the skies and the seas.[42]

The 1683 battle at Vienna is famous enough, both as reality and symbol. Even today, far rightists in Germany and Austria scrawl "1683" as a threatening graffito, intended to intimidate Muslim populations by reminding them of that epoch-making victory. But however we commemorate that year, whether as liberation or as catastrophe, the battle and the surrounding events cannot be understood except in the broader atmosphere of discontent, revolt, and inter-Christian religious persecution. We can never know exactly how the political situation might have developed if the weather had remained friendly or if temperatures had stayed broadly stable. But the climate crisis incited tensions and grievances that destabilized half a continent and rewrote the history of faiths.

American Crises

From a European perspective, the years around 1680 clearly fit the familiar pattern of a time of troubles, closely parallel to other epochs when climate changes destabilized the social order. But the same was true much farther afield, not least in North America. People really did share a common planet and a single global climate.

Apart from the commonplace symptoms of cold and crisis, parts of the Americas also suffered extraordinary storms and weather events that directed people's minds to prospects of apocalypse. The much-read New England leader Increase Mather gave a detailed account of a terrifying and baffling event that occurred in Cambridge, Massachusetts, in July 1680, which modern readers immediately identify as a tornado—in fact, the first tornado recorded in what would become the United States. Storms of astonishing ferocity proliferated around this time, and the summer of 1682 brought unforgettable hail and "the most amazing lightnings that have been known in New-England." Another tempest that same June—another tornado?—tore down "many thousands of trees" in Connecticut. Puritans struggled to understand such signs, especially when the lands affected were inhabited by pious Christians. Cotton Mather preached on *Brontologia sacra*, literally the sacred interpretation of the study of thunder and storms, or "the voice of the glorious God in the thunder."[43]

As elsewhere, climate-driven crises produced political upheavals and popular revolts, and in the Americas as in Europe, the mid-1670s produced the worst nightmares. As crop yields plunged in the English colonies, settlers pushed harder to claim fresh Indian land. In New England, tensions became explosive with the 1675 outbreak of war with the Native leader Metacomet, or King Philip, a savage conflict that was perhaps the greatest single trauma in the whole history of colonial New England. The war's conduct was largely conditioned by the extreme climatic conditions of the following year, when Indians starved en masse. As in the Dutch revolt a century before, frozen swamps and streams allowed colonists to make startling advances across solid ice and seize fortified positions that previously would have been impregnable. The English victory reshaped the self-perception of the English, strongly encouraging ideologies of biblical chosenness and giving a warrant to expel or remove heathen Natives. In 1676, Nathaniel Bacon led his famous revolt in Virginia, which later historians often characterize as the forerunner of later anti-colonial and anti-royal sentiment in the English possessions. Causes were complex, but as in New England, weather issues were crucial. In a single year, the colony suffered from "hailstorms, floods, dry spells, and hurricanes." That in turn drove colonists to seek scapegoats, which inflamed tensions against Indians. When the English governor tried to soothe tensions, furious colonists were driven to revolt.[44]

The other great revolt in this era was in the Spanish dominion of New Mexico, where the native Pueblo people mounted a stunningly successful rising in 1680, one that took explicitly religious forms. Climate-related changes precipitated the revolt, notably the long drought of the 1670s. Famine forced the abandonment of pueblos, some permanently. Grim conditions drove some Native communities to wander over great distances and to engage in raiding, aggravating famine and discontent. In desperation, many Natives returned to the traditional faiths and practices that they had notionally abandoned as part of Christian conversion. From 1675, colonial authorities were engaged in mass prosecutions for witchcraft and pagan revivals among the Pueblo, in a striking parallel to the witch trials that had become so commonplace in contemporary Christian Europe. When it became so very difficult to grow or find food, people had little alternative but to turn to any religious or ritual systems that might offer the hope of greater success, even if such practices invited savage official reprisals.[45]

By 1680, the long-simmering situation broke into open revolution, which culminated with the rebel capture of the colonial capital of Santa Fe. Hundreds of Spaniards were killed, and most of the European population was expelled. The anti-colonial triumph had a powerful religious and spiritual component. During those years of independence, the Pueblos removed all vestiges of Christian worship and wholeheartedly restored their own indigenous traditions and rituals. This was one of the rare instances in the period where a Native rising actually did eliminate colonial rule and church power, if only for a short period, and restored native religion. In 1681, a Spanish attempt to reclaim the territory was thwarted by dreadful weather, in what we have already seen to be one of the epically cold years of the era. Not until 1692 could the Spanish regain their power.[46]

Fight or Flight

But the climate crisis had a still more extensive impact on North America in the form of the mass migrations that now resulted from the persecutions and repressions in Europe. Of course, there is a powerful irony here, in that so many people fleeing a stressed Europe chose to escape to a region so afflicted by its own climate shocks. But they did, and in large numbers.

In earlier centuries, persecuted dissidents and heretics might have taken refuge in border territories of their own kingdoms, or perhaps in remote regions blessedly separated from the evils of civilized government. Such short-distance migrations certainly did take place in Europe at this time, as Muslims fled from advancing Christian armies, while Christian populations fled from Ottoman vengeance. In the Balkans, the 1680s mark the beginning of the so-called Great Migration of the Serbs, northward into lands firmly held by the Christian Habsburg forces. But by the seventeenth century, new maritime technologies and well-established colonial trade patterns allowed travel over much greater distances, even on an intercontinental scale, and the persecuted took full advantage of these imperial opportunities. Driven from their homelands, those migrants not only founded or strengthened overseas colonies but also imprinted them with their own distinctive religious ways, which in many cases were the very practices and beliefs that had originally set their governments against them. The experience of persecution and exile ensured that colonial territories would be founded on ideologies deeply hostile to state religion or imperial power. That antipathy would have its greatest impact in later decades and later revolutions.[47]

France's Huguenots demonstrate the wide scope of the new diasporas. Those exiles spread their Calvinist-derived religious traditions into many corners of the world, including Britain, the Netherlands, and Scandinavia, and farther afield to North America and South Africa. The Huguenots who went to Africa became crucial to the development of the Afrikaaner/Boer tradition, with its strongly Old Testament idea of true believers as God's holy people, pledged in a divine covenant. Huguenots brought with them a sense of martyrology, persecution, and the need for communal self-defense. That tradition shaped the politics of white South Africa right up to the 1990s and beyond. Although the Afrikaans language is basically Dutch in origin, most Afrikaaners have some Huguenot blood. Many of the families who dominated Afrikaaner society until recent times bear French names.[48]

Huguenots settled widely in the American colonies, where they integrated so rapidly into the larger Protestant population that their distinctive origins were often forgotten. Many early names were anglicized, so (to take one example of many) a Rivoire became the father of Paul Revere. One tiny settlement in particular epitomizes the larger story. New Paltz, New York, was an early Huguenot settlement in the Americas, and it dates exactly from the bitter year of 1678. Although the settlement was small, it contains an evocative history. So much of the religious tension and anti-Protestant persecution took place along the Rhine, in what we would call western Germany and Switzerland. A major center of violence and intolerance was Pfaltz, the Palatinate (modern-day Rheinland-Pfalz). Hence, New Paltz was to be the New Palatinate, much as New England was to England.[49]

America and the Sects

The growth of the British Atlantic empires offered many new opportunities to relocate dissidents, willingly or otherwise. After a failed rising by radical Protestants in southwest England in 1685, many were hanged, but the great majority were dispersed as indentured labor, either to the American colonies or to the Caribbean. It now made excellent financial sense to preserve the lives of religious resisters, with the added advantage of building up emerging colonies.[50]

The creation of the Pennsylvania colony in 1682 is often cited as a pivotal moment in the growth of England's overseas empire, as well as a landmark in the history of religious toleration. Often forgotten is how precisely that event fitted in the crisis that Europe was then suffering, and which was driving religious minorities to seek safe haven. In a highly localized society based on agriculture, it takes real incentive to induce ordinary people to uproot themselves and relocate thousands of miles away by means of a hazardous sea crossing. The political and climatic conditions prevailing at this time made such a movement thinkable and necessary. Adding enormously to the appeal of the new land was its strong and explicit assertion of religious liberty, welcoming all who believed in God and granting full political rights to believers in Christ. Such proclamations can only be appreciated in the context of the persecutions in progress in these very years in much of Europe. Much of that colony's success resulted from that principle, which would in turn strongly influence the later United States.[51]

Quakers, of course, were central to establishing the new colony, in the very years that the British government was turning its hostile attention to radical Protestant Dissenters and sectaries. The resulting migration relocated the centers of radical religion across the Atlantic. To take one example, this movement largely uprooted the old centers in Wales, as local Quakers migrated en masse to Pennsylvania, to the Welsh Tract (1684). Some of the Welsh-sounding place-names found along the Philadelphia Main Line are in fact of nineteenth-century origin, but plenty of authentically older names survive to commemorate a lost radical heartland in Wales itself. By 1700, the Welsh made up a third of Pennsylvania's population, as against one-third English and one-third German. If the early numbers were still small—perhaps 20,000 European settlers in the colony in 1700—Pennsylvania's population was growing fast, more rapidly than in any other free New World colony. By the 1770s, Pennsylvania had 430,000 people, making it second only to Virginia in British America.[52]

Beyond just Quakers and Pietists, much of America's later religious history traces its roots to congregations founded in and around Philadelphia. Baptists from all parts of the British Isles likewise sought new homes in Pennsylvania. In the 1680s, Pennsylvania's Baptists formed the pioneering churches that would be significant in shaping the later history of that tradition in many more distant regions, including the South. If they never supplanted the traditions already well established in New England, the Pennsylvania churches contributed powerfully to America's Baptist heritage, and especially its Particular Baptist strand.[53]

One exile group in particular left a long tradition. The 1680s were a dreadful time for the Covenanter Presbyterians in Scotland and for their allies in Northern Ireland, the Scots-Irish. This began a migration to North America, which continued after the Covenanters triumphed in Scotland itself. They brought with them the custom of mass field-preaching meetings that they had developed during the years of persecution. In the American context, there is a direct line of continuity from those field-preaching meetings to later revivals and camp meetings, to the Great Awakening of the 1740s, and even more starkly to the Second Awakening in the 1790s. Those camp meetings were especially common across western Pennsylvania and throughout Kentucky and Tennessee, regions heavily populated by Scots and Scots-Irish migrants. Those same Presbyterians bore with them the martyrologies they had acquired in the 1680s, together with a strong sense that such official repression should never again be tolerated. Some observers at the time of the American Revolution referred to that event as the Presbyterian Rebellion or the Presbyterian War. Much like the Afrikaaners, Calvinist Scots and Ulstermen have long historical memories.[54]

German America

The German-speaking lands likewise had their Protestant sects, which faced intolerable pressure in the persecutions of the post-1675 decade. William Penn lived in Germany in the mid-1670s, where he encountered the Pietists as well as other devout Protestants. When his new colony of Pennsylvania was established, its authorities avidly tried to recruit German believers, who were drawn both from mainstream churches, the Lutheran and the Reformed, and also from the sects, such as the Mennonites and Anabaptists. The key settlement of Germantown (north of Philadelphia) was founded in 1683 as a magnet for German believers of all shades and denominations. The region's various German churches became seedbeds for national denominations that in later years would claim many millions of members. These early migrants included strong representation from the recently emerged Pietist movement, and that element grew enormously with later Lutheran immigration. The venerated founder of Germantown, Francis David Pastorius, was a close friend of Spener: he joined the Pietist movement in 1679 after fleeing a revolutionary upsurge in his home city, and then moved to America. Born-again Christian faith flourished in the new province.[55]

The emerging German world became a haven for beliefs that simply could not survive in Europe's repressive atmosphere. We have already encountered the apocalyptic mystic Johannes Kelpius, who in 1694 led the sect's emigration to the Philadelphia area. Following a cryptic passage in Revelation, they founded what they called the Society of the Woman in the Wilderness. Those "mystics of the Wissahickon" made southeastern Pennsylvania a center for religious experimentation through the following century.[56]

One famous surviving sect from this era must be understood in the context of the persecutions of the crisis years. Through the seventeenth century, Mennonites had often been harshly persecuted, but matters now became much more acute. Some resisted government pressure to the point of martyrdom. Others, meanwhile, sympathized with the sect and offered material assistance but would not take the final step of a public declaration of faith, with the lethal consequences that entailed. Churches disagreed on the proper response to these "good-hearted" believers and on how strictly to discipline weaker members and fellow travelers. The most intransigent demanded they be shunned and avoided. In 1693, this issue caused outright schism, as the hard-liners followed Jakob Ammann; from his name, they became known as the Amish. The Amish still flourish across North America, although they are extinct in their European homeland.[57]

The United States is legendary for its seemingly limitless religious diversity, for all its faiths, sects and churches. Within the Christian traditions that still remain numerically dominant, that religious story cannot be told except in the context of those late seventeenth-century crises and conflicts, which drove exiles beyond the seas.

Conclusion

Historians naturally write about events that happened far more than they address themselves to considering why other seemingly probable things did not occur, why alternative paths were not taken. As I have remarked, counterfactual history is a perilous endeavor. Yet in the context of the seventeenth century, some of those non-events do merit consideration. The crisis of the 1640s is one of the best-known facts in early modern history, and it unquestionably had its origins in climate factors. But climate conditions that were actually worse than those of the hungry forties failed to generate anything comparable later in the century. If crises, plots, and insurrections proliferated, most were contained or defeated, or at least failed to overthrow states as they would assuredly have done some decades earlier. This resilience showed just how much elites had learned from their earlier experiences, and the scale of that forced education was deeply impressive. Forged in that crucible of suffering, Western states became much better able to withstand catastrophe, even on the horrendous scale of the late seventeenth century. That set a powerful precedent for later generations, who would have to deal with further disasters, but with much greater confidence than hitherto in states and civil authorities.

What had not changed was the predictable range of religious and supernatural responses to future crises. Henceforward, though, governments were anxious to prevent the rise of violent or confrontational forms, anything resembling mob upsurges that might challenge state power. Religious responses became less overtly political. Meanwhile, new forms of media and technology allowed the rise of innovative religious structures, some of which would become very influential.

7

Who Can Stand Before His Cold?

> He giveth snow like wool: he scattereth the hoarfrost like ashes.
> He casteth forth his ice like morsels: who can stand before his cold?
> —Psalm 147:16–17 (KJV)

The years between 1739 and 1742 constituted a critical era in American religious history. Besides Jonathan Edwards's *Sinners in the Hands of an Angry God* (preached in July 1741), this was also the time of George Whitefield's immensely popular preaching tours in British America. So extreme was the perceived spiritual emergency that preachers proclaimed that it had to take priority over any worldly institutions or hierarchies. The revival issue starkly divided denominations. It was in March 1740 that Gilbert Tennent preached the sermon later published as *The Danger of an Unconverted Ministry*, which denounced those clergy who resisted revival and inner spiritual conversion. Tennent saw those more conservative clergy as "the great crowds of these orthodox, letter-learned, and regular Pharisees." They were "false apostles, and deceitful workers" who did no more than imitate the apostles of Christ. His words provoked open schism among Presbyterians the following year. Such episodes demonstrate the attitudes of the revival preachers, and their sense of spiritual crisis—a word that in its origins means simply "judgment." The Awakening spread widely through the British colonies over the following decade, and Europe recorded many similar events.[1]

We do not have to look too far to find other kinds of crisis shaping attitudes in these years and focusing people's minds very sharply on issues of survival. Even by the standards of the Little Ice Age, this was a period of climate catastrophe, one that broke centuries-old records across Europe and the Atlantic world. Millions of survivors were reduced to terrified despair as they desperately sought to comprehend the tribulation. In secular terms, no less than religious, talk of the end of the world did not seem hyperbolic. Of course, such events in the material world drove concern about spiritual well-being and the right road to take for the afterlife. No less natural was the need to pursue solutions at the expense of social assumptions and clerical privileges, even if that implied a cultural revolution. Ordinary believers avidly welcomed spiritual leaders who preached a message of the world's Judgment and condemnation, while offering believers hope and comfort in the supernatural realm. Established institutions were quite inadequate to cope with the passionate enthusiasm that resulted, which inevitably found expression in new sects and structures. These were life-and-death decisions.[2]

The Worst Years

In Europe, the time from December 1739 through September 1741 was marked by awful harvests, freezing winter weather, and prolonged spring and summer droughts. The winter of 1739–1740 left evil memories for decades to come: social historian W. G. Hoskins called it "the most hellish in the memory of man." The cause of the catastrophe remains uncertain, but such a sudden, nearly overnight change did not result from any kind of long-term trend within the larger "ice age." Other precedents persuade us to look to a volcanic eruption, particularly given the sudden onset of the crisis and its impact over three years or so. Yet no single culprit leaps out, no gargantuan parallel to Samalas or Tambora. Japan's Mount Tarumae did erupt in August 1739, scoring a 5 on the VEI scale, but something on that scale should not have caused such global havoc: other comparable eruptions certainly have not. Perhaps other, less noticed eruptions might have occurred around the same time as Tarumae, combining their effects, and an El Niño role is also likely.[3] Whatever the cause, the effects in Europe and North America were cataclysmic. In climate history, the winter of 1709 is usually singled out as among the very worst and coldest in generations, but in many regions, the 1740 low temperatures were actually below those of that earlier year of ill omen.

Some of the consequences could be remembered romantically enough. Of course, Londoners again held a fair on the frozen Thames, as part of another "Great Frost." But for most people, these years were a nightmare beyond imagination. In Finland—in climatic terms, one of the best-studied nations—scholar Timo Myllyntaus remarks, "The Finnish winter of 1740 was cold, and it was followed by the coldest spring and summer of the eighteenth century; in fact, the spring of that year was the coldest of the past five hundred years in all of Europe." Across Europe, rainfall was far below normal in the spring and summer of 1741, creating an epic drought and ruining farmers' hopes of recovery. Glaciers advanced in western and northern Europe. Weather observers—and by this stage there were many, both amateur and professional—watched with astonishment as outdoor temperatures fell below zero degrees Fahrenheit. When that scale had been perfected, in Amsterdam in 1714 (by Daniel Gabriel Fahrenheit), that zero point was assumed to be the lowest level that temperatures could reach in nature. People had a lot to learn. On the last day of 1740, an observer in Plymouth, England, recorded succinctly, "Coldest day in the memory of man."[4]

Although the climate horrors were most evident in Europe and North America, there were echoes farther afield. If the North Atlantic world froze hard, extreme drought afflicted other regions. The 1740s marked an epochal drought across the Sahel. Hundreds of thousands died, and the vital trans-Saharan trade routes were badly disrupted. Extraordinary drought conditions also affected the American Southwest and the Mexican borderlands (the ecologically sensitive region scholars today call Aridoamerica), generating a crisis in food supplies. That in turn contributed to political unrest, and a widespread Indian revolt in northern Mexico between 1740 and 1742 resulted in grave setbacks for the colonists. Several thousand perished on both sides in the most successful indigenous rising since the earlier Pueblo revolt in 1680, during the preceding climate onslaught.[5]

Contagion, Famine, Death, and Deadly Shocks

Many regions of Europe experienced a mortality peak—in other words, mass starvation, aggravated by epidemics—and food riots were widespread. In 1741, the British government took the crisis measure of embargoing exports of grain, a desperate step they had not taken since the horror year of 1709. In his classic scholarly analysis of this era, John D. Post observed that "a shortage of food and high cereal prices constituted the proximate problem. . . . The combined consequences of climate shock, social disarray, prolonged undernutrition, and military operations brought about the crisis mortality." Although the military angle had no direct connection to the climate crisis,

Europe from 1740 onward was involved in the bloody War of the Austrian Succession, which drew in most of the great powers and further disrupted a society already under severe stress. That in turn came to absorb ongoing peripheral struggles, such as the simmering conflict between England and Spain, as well as their respective American colonies.[6]

I have already mentioned Mary Dobson's analysis of death rates in a large sample of English parishes. She notes an upsurge of disease in Britain in 1741, mainly typhus and dysentery, "the classic famine fevers." Together with typhoid, smallpox, and influenza, those diseases wrought havoc between 1740 and 1742. Dobson continues, "The mortality peak of 1740–42 made an outstanding impact on European demographic history. In many European countries, 1741 marks the last major demographic crisis of the early modern period." It is often difficult to distinguish deaths that arose directly from hunger and those from hunger-related conditions, while cold and hypothermia claimed their victims.[7]

In Ireland in 1740 and 1741, outright famine raged: "Multitudes have perished and are daily perishing under hedges and ditches, some of fluxes and some through downright cruel want." At least 400,000 died from famine-related causes, one-sixth of the population, and some estimates of the death toll run higher. As a proportion of the population, the situation was actually worse than the notorious potato famine of the 1840s. One modern book on this event is aptly entitled *Arctic Ireland*. In the words of contemporary Anglo-Irish poet Laurence Whyte in his "Famine,"

> The Earth lock'd up her Treasures under Ground,
> And Dearth began to spread itself around:
> The Horn of Plenty flew up from the Earth,
> And left behind it Poverty and Dearth,
> With Evils equal to Pandora's Box,
> Contagion, Famine, Death, and deadly Shocks.

Even the soundscape changed, as the mass death of Ireland's birds left an uncanny silence: "No lark is left to wake the morn, / Or rouse the youth with early horn; / The blackbird's melody is o'er." Although the effects there were less dire, Scotland too suffered atrociously from cold and hunger, with a full-scale harvest crisis and mortality peak. This was also a disastrous time for livestock, with the failure of fodder crops. The year 1740 marked a strong new upsurge in the panzootic that would wipe out so many of Europe's cattle, in a bovine equivalent of the human Black Death. Between 1709 and the 1780s, the continent lost perhaps 200,000,000 cattle.[8]

Frozen America

North America was hard hit. After the long winter of 1739–1740 came one of the coldest summers of this century. The following winter, of 1740–1741, broke most records for cold. New England and the middle colonies froze, and an abundance of written records and diaries demonstrate the full impact in what would become the epicenters of religious revivalism. From late 1739, New England was hit by a series of catastrophic snowstorms, followed by major flooding. As floods refroze, the ice fields spread, and people resorted to their sleighs to travel once unthinkable distances. Long Island Sound became passable over the ice. Francis Lewis (later a signer of the Declaration of Independence) drove his sleigh along the shore ice from Barnstable, on Cape Cod, to New York City, some 200 miles. Frigid conditions affected areas little accustomed to snow and ice: the York River froze near Williamsburg, Virginia.[9]

In Rhode Island, Governor William Greene reported that Narragansett Bay was frozen over, and people could easily cross the ice from Providence to Newport. In early 1741, "it was frozen from the main to Rhode Island and from thence southward out to sea. It was reported by the inhabitants that they could see nothing but ice." A decade later, Rhode Island minister James MacSparran recalled how at this time "I have seen [the ocean] froze as far as the human eye could reach." Ice still covered rivers and bays until well into April 1741. Livestock perished in huge numbers, and the shipping business became impossible.[10]

One valuable source for New England history is the *History of Newbury, Newburyport, and West Newbury*, by Joshua Coffin, who drew on extensive contemporary records. Throughout his account of 1740 and 1741, Coffin was reaching far back in history to find some kind of precedent for the conditions he witnessed around him. In 1740, he noted, "the summer and fall of this year, were as remarkable for the rain, which fell and flooded the country, as the subsequent winter was, for the severity of the cold. It was probably the most severe winter ever known, since the settlement of the country." In November, a freshet (flood) struck the Merrimack River; "the like was not known by no man for seventy years." Foot-deep snowfalls became a regular occurrence. In

December, "shipping was all froze in and this severity extended to New York government." In 1740–1741, he noted,

> there were twenty-seven snows this winter, the hardest winter that ever was known. . . . In February the streets were full of snow to the top of the fences and in some places eight or ten feet deep. . . . February twenty-eighth, the ice at Deer island the strongest place of the tide was thirty inches thick.[11]

In Bolton, Connecticut, by the start of 1741, "traveling was almost wholly suspended by reason of the extreme cold and deep snow, and God had sealed up the hand of every man." The results were predictable:

> A great number of cattle and horses died, and near half the sheep, and about two thirds of the goats. . . . Exceeding scarcity followed, partly by reason of abundance of Indian corn being ruined by the long rains in December, and partly by people giving their corn to their creatures to save their lives. We suppose the ensuing summer was the greatest scarcity as ever the English felt since the first settlement of this government. Indian corn rose in the price from ten to twenty shillings, and what was commonly sold for twenty shillings, till at last all buying and selling utterly ceased.[12]

Even respectable families turned to begging.

In March 1741, Pennsylvania observers recited their litany of disasters:

> March 5, very cold; sleighs crossing the Delaware; severe winter throughout the country; cattle dying for want of fodder; many deer found dead in the woods and some came tamely to the plantations and fed on hay with the domestic animals; March 13, river navigable; winter had been very long and severe; snow in Lancaster County more than three feet deep; back settlers suffered for want of bread; many families had little else to subsist on than the carcasses of deer found dead; very deep snow until the 19th of April.[13]

Sermons of Catastrophe

Contemporaries inevitably turned to religious faith to understand what they saw around them. Although they found few specific biblical texts referring to extreme cold, they regularly turned to one refrain that they found in Psalm 147, quoted at the start of this chapter. As a Bolton writer reported a sermon in 1741, "We had a very sensible consideration of... Who can stand before His cold!!!"[14]

In March 1741, Anglican clergyman James MacSparran preached in Narragansett, Rhode Island. He had ample grim matter on which to discourse, including the effects of the ongoing British war with Spain (of which more shortly) and also a series of epidemics, including smallpox. But it was above all the cold that drew his alarmed attention, as he framed the ongoing climatic assaults in supernatural terms and in the context of divine Providence. As MacSparran declared, "The elements have been armed with such piercing cold and suffocating snows as if God intended the air he gave us to live and breathe in should become the instrument to execute his vengeance on us for our ingratitude to his goodness and our transgression of his law." The world was under siege by the forces of cold. Even the Sun, "the great luminary that rules the day," could make no headway against these oppressive forces: "So faint are his armies, tho' innumerable and each atom harnessed in fire, that they cannot force the frost to give ground nor dissolve the intrenchment of snow." "Intrenchment" is one of many military siege metaphors that contemporaries deployed to portray their conditions.[15]

Normally, said MacSparran, it was a pleasure to witness the animals and plants flourishing with the springtime blessings God provided. In contrast, people now saw those herds and flocks starving dismally, until they dropped and died. Even if some melting was now visible, "are not the cattle now corrupting in the fields, and that after they have consumed most of the corn that might have maintained us to that time?" As yet there were no signs of outright famine, but that must be a concern. It would be a dreadful vision, "a sad spectacle to behold numbers of faint and famished creatures like walking ghosts and inhabitants of the grave with nothing to allay their hunger." He hinted at cannibalism when he warned that "hunger will drive men to the most desperate designs." As an immigrant from Ulster, MacSparran would have been aware of conditions in his Irish homeland, especially as he lived in a colony so closely attuned to the transatlantic trade.[16]

MacSparran later earned notoriety for a tract he published in 1753, *America Dissected*, in which he warned British and Irish people to think very carefully indeed before migrating to the colonies, because of the many dangers and disadvantages they might face. First among his reasons was "the Intemperance of the Climates; Excessive Heat and Cold, and Sudden Changes of Weather":

> In New England, the Transitions from Heat to Cold are short and sudden, and the extremes of both very sensible. We are sometimes frying and others freezing; and as men often die at their Labor in the Field by *Heat*, so some in Winter are froze to Death with the *Cold*.

Painful memories of 1740–1741 lingered.[17]

Resistance and Paranoia

Such extreme conditions made people tense and fearful, as well as hungry and sick, with obvious nutritional deficiencies. This was an age of conspiracy nightmares, and of plots and sedition, both real and imagined. In the American setting, the British imperial conflict with Spain provided a disturbing context. The two countries were at open war from 1739 through 1742, with raids and invasions between the rival colonies of Florida and Georgia. Those did much to define the shape that tensions would take. Spain was a Catholic power, raising fears of Catholic plotting within the Protestant British possessions. Also, the struggle between colonies stirred fears that slaves would take advantage of the crisis to escape or to organize insurrections.

In 1739, South Carolina was the setting for the Stono Rebellion, as slaves hoped to escape to Spanish lands. The resulting outbreak was the largest and bloodiest single slave revolt in Britain's North American colonies. South Carolinians blamed George Whitefield and the revivalists, among other scapegoats, for unsettling the colony and causing the insurrection. Not only was that charge of religious manipulation inaccurate, but it actually gave far too much credit to the preacher, who was alarmingly sympathetic to slavery in practice. Whatever the causes of the outbreak, in the following year the colony passed its infamous Negro Act, placing draconian and unprecedented restraints on the behavior of slaves, who were forbidden to learn to write. Rebellious slaves could be killed outright if their owners thought it necessary. In varying degrees of severity, that act was widely imitated in the fast-expanding slave territories of the southern colonies. In South Carolina itself, it remained in force until 1865.[18]

But if real threats did exist, they were dwarfed by the nightmares that now besieged the minds of a population exhausted after months of privation, hunger, cold, and economic chaos. Matters came to a head in New York City, which through the spring of 1741 suffered a series of mysterious fires. In normal times, there would have been no reason to inquire too deeply into such accidents, which were a common feature of a largely wood-built community. The more people were confined to those houses by the extreme cold, the more likely were accidents involving fires and stoves. But now paranoia was rampant. Investigators of the fires thought that they were dealing with the early stages of a slave insurrection, and as in South Carolina, that also implied activity by subversive religious forces. In New York, suspicion turned to Catholic priests, and this led to savage reprisals against white Catholics and alleged Spanish agents, as well as against slaves themselves. Although whites would be suspected as accomplices in later insurrections, this affair was unique in American racial history in the execution of white co-conspirators.[19]

Just how seriously New York authorities took matters is suggested by a judge's questions to Black prisoners before sentencing: "What then could prompt you to undertake so vile, so wicked, so monstrous, so execrable and hellish a scheme, as to murder and destroy your own masters and benefactors? nay, to destroy root and branch, all the white people of this place, and to lay the whole town in ashes?" The city at the time had a population of 12,000 whites and 2,000 Blacks, numbers that put the resulting penalties into horrifying perspective. Some 200 were arrested in all. Between May and August 1741, seventeen Blacks were hanged, and thirteen Blacks were burned at the stake. Such burning alive was a very uncommon atrocity in English law, but New York looked to the Roman/Dutch tradition. Four whites were also hanged. Seventy Blacks and seven whites were deported.[20]

New States and New Worlds

Cold, starvation, despair, paranoia . . . the sequence is familiar enough, but the exact consequences differed from earlier years in crucial ways. Intergroup rivalries and hatred were as much in evidence as in any crisis period, and food shortages provoked violence and grain riots in Britain, France, the Low Countries, and elsewhere. But the contrasts with earlier eras are also marked. I have already noted how nation-states in this era were far stronger than in earlier centuries, and those states had a powerful vested interest in snuffing out any possible manifestations of public unrest or disorder. Those states grew significantly stronger as the century progressed, in large part due to the incessant wars that increasingly developed a transcontinental aspect. States organized to manufacture the artillery and ships they needed to fight enemies, and—even more crucial—to build the financial resources and structures to pay for them. That meant a giant leap toward political modernity.[21]

Europe's powers had far better means than hitherto to respond to crises, and greater incentives to avoid chaos or disorder. However inadequate they might appear today, systems of poor relief were far better established, and governments were better able to direct food supplies to the worst-hit areas. As the most advanced of the powers, England by the later eighteenth century was conspicuously a welfare/warfare state, anticipating the familiar twentieth-century model. Internal security was also much stronger. Though common people might fervently wish to attack their differently believing neighbors, armies and even police forces were available to suppress potential mass pogroms and riots, or (as we will see) witch-hunts.[22]

The issue of government control and police power does much to explain the religious manifestations of this particular crisis, and its geography. By far the best-known spiritual explosion of these years occurred in the English-speaking world, where internal controls were weak by European standards and a high degree of religious freedom and self-expression was accepted, at least de facto. That was assuredly not the case in European states such as France or Prussia, where states not only distrusted and feared religious excesses but had elaborate mechanisms for enforcing internal security. Through the early eighteenth century, French authorities had waged an internal war against religious dissidents, some of whom engaged in wildly extravagant behaviors that we might term cult-like, including the ecstatic sect of the *convulsionnaires*, with their healing miracles. Unlike in the British world, those French believers who might have wished to pursue a spiritual revival or new Awakening around 1740 would very rapidly have fallen afoul of a tough-minded police force, complete with informers, secret agents, and draconian powers of imprisonment. And although Pietists originated in the German-speaking lands, they enjoyed some of their greatest successes in the religiously tolerant British-ruled world. Revivals could and would occur only where opportunity permitted.[23]

Toward Enlightenment

The decline of supernatural and religious themes in scapegoating and internal conflict was striking, and in fact it points to an apparent paradox. Explicitly religious politics were declining, while authorities were striving to regulate or suppress outbreaks of what they saw as spiritual fanaticism. Yet in at least some nations and some regions, the acute crisis resulted in a religious upsurge, with enduring consequences. Was that great revival actually an outright rejection or flouting of those larger cultural trends? In fact, the story is more complex, and must be placed in the context of fundamental changes in intellectual and cultural life across much of the Western world, including the emergence of what we can call Enlightenment beliefs and assumptions. Those changes did not hamper the revivalist phenomenon but rather shaped the particular forms that religious revivalism would take. If the new political order constrained the kinds of behavior that would once have been tolerated, other opportunities arose to present and promote new ideas and movements.[24]

These cultural changes were grounded in growing wealth and economic sophistication across Europe and North America, with the marked expansion of cities and the trade on which they depended. Societies became more complex and diversified, with an expansion of urban elites, crafts and trades, and middling classes. Although mass industrialization would not develop until the 1760s, scientific and technological growth were already making great strides from the start of the eighteenth century, and there was a ferocious popular hunger to know and understand the latest discoveries and insights. A great many ordinary, non-elite people were engaged in the skilled and careful observation of the natural world, including weather-related changes, indicating how such phenomena were incorporated into a scientific worldview. The barometer was invented in 1643, followed by mercury-based thermometers in 1714, and these tools came into very wide use. Meanwhile, education became more readily available and sought after, literacy rates rose, and aspiring classes were served by a boom in media and publishing, with floods of books, pamphlets, and popular reading material of all kinds. These changes coincided with the intellectual and cultural developments that we associate with the Enlightenment, although that term is often used chiefly in the context of elite thinkers. Scarcely less important than the creation of radical and secular ideas was their acceptance by large and influential sections of society.[25]

Early Enlightenment thought grew out of a reaction against the extremism of the crisis that occurred during the bitterly cold years of the later seventeenth century. That is evident in the political thought of the time, where philosophers such as John Locke reacted so vigorously against the political and religious repression of the time, and advocated principles of toleration and individual freedom. More broadly, thinkers attacked the kind of providentialism that so directly associated worldly catastrophes with divine displeasure at human sins. Huguenot refugee Pierre Bayle used the panic over the Great Comet of 1680 as a reason to publish his *Pensées diverses* (Various thoughts) in 1682, a sweeping diatribe against superstition and, indeed, against a good deal of Catholic orthodoxy. He placed the comet firmly in the realm of natural science, and showed why God would never use such a thing as a cosmic sign to instruct his earthly subjects. The *Pensées* became a potent influence on Enlightenment thought and religious skepticism. Bayle also published his *Dictionnaire historique et critique* (Historical and critical dictionary), a vital source for all later Enlightenment philosophy and religious thought.[26]

Through the early eighteenth century, we see a general challenge to religious extremism of the kind that had stirred such tumult and injustice in early years. That involved, for instance, an attack on extravagant religious manifestations by people claiming to be prophets or even messiahs, who were now dismissed as fanatics or enthusiasts (literally, people claiming to be possessed by God, *en-thous*). In England, the rejection of enthusiasm focused on the case of the French Prophets of 1706–1707, a group of radical French Protestants derived from the Huguenot communities expelled during the 1680s. Words and actions that might once have inspired mass support were now received as likely indicating mental illness. Of course, such new attitudes were most marked among educated metropolitan elites, but they were also reflected in the rapidly growing world of mass media, with its newspapers and prints that told lower but aspiring classes what they should think.[27]

Governments, and mass publics, learned to be more critical of extravagant supernatural claims and charges. Significantly, the crisis around 1740 resulted in very little by way of the trial or execution of alleged witches, actions that in earlier times assuredly would have been a natural consequence. France generated a panic in the familiar mode precisely during the crisis of 1742–1743, when twenty-seven people (including three priests) were implicated in a large case involving Black Masses. But this affair was very isolated, and most European countries produced nothing comparable. The decline of witchcraft beliefs illustrates a general transformation of social attitudes, especially among elites. Since the 1690s, critics of witchcraft beliefs became ever more public and overt, and their views achieved a wide hearing. Retrospective analyses of the Salem cases or their Swedish counterparts were very damaging and made it all but impossible for such cases to recur on anything like that scale. Active at the start of the century, German philosopher and legal scholar Christian Thomasius undertook an incisive demolition of witchcraft prosecutions, and of the use of torture that made possible the customary range of ludicrous charges. Thereafter, most European countries limited or ended the witch persecutions. Thomasius in fact deserves to be far better known as an authentic hero of cultural progress. The last witch to be executed in Sweden perished in 1704; in England, in 1716; and in Scotland, in 1727. The French cases of 1742–1743 were an isolated outbreak, and one of the executed priests became the last person to be legally killed for the offense in that country.[28]

That emphasis on "legally" executed is significant. Popular belief in witchcraft remained strong, particularly in the countryside and small towns, justifying mob actions and lynchings that faded very slowly. Even some educated thinkers held on to reactionary positions: John Wesley himself was appalled by enlightened approaches in such matters, and held that "the giving up of witchcraft is in effect giving up the Bible." What had changed was that states and ruling elites were now determined to suppress witch-hunting, seeing it as a form of criminal malfeasance far worse than anything that could be wrought by supposed witches themselves. Hatred and scapegoating could exist, but those passions were channeled very differently than how they had been in the past.[29]

The Rise of Enthusiasm

Elite skepticism was by no means uniform, and it did not necessarily reflect the sentiments of common people. That was particularly true in matters of religion: new religious movements emerged on the basis of immense popular appeal, and they spread widely, despite often meeting the disapproval of established religious authorities. Had elite society not expressed its scorn of enthusiastic faith?

But many aspects that made the new society so open to progress also helped the growth of new religious forms. The same social and technological changes that spread rational and scientific ideas also reduced centralized official control over the expression of popular beliefs. The media revolution laid the foundation for the phenomenon of mass religious revivalism beyond the control of state churches. In turn, a revived and energized populace provided an ever-growing market for published materials, both religious and secular. This unprecedented development opened whole new channels for religious excitement and desires. People could hear stars such as George Whitefield speak, but they could also read him and read about him, or venerate him through mass-produced prints or porcelain figures. As much as book printing, religious consumerism assisted the popular spread of revival.

Also, the growth of international travel and trade made it possible for people around the Atlantic world to hear the great preachers and revivalists firsthand. Whitefield, John Wesley, and others made regular preaching tours across that British Atlantic world. Such globalization had other effects as well. Even more than in 1680, it made it easy for troubled or persecuted groups to absent themselves from the worst areas of potential crisis. That mobility ensured that any religious movements that grew out of the crisis could quite rapidly achieve international scale—or at least within countries that did not immediately repress any non-approved manifestations.[30]

The Climate of Revival

The religious revival—the Awakening—did not begin during the climate crisis, but it received a massive boost from those conditions. As we have seen before, the pace of evolution accelerated greatly under the stress of climate shock. The movement had been germinating for some decades, in fact, ever since the previous crisis years around 1680. As we have seen, that era produced the reform movement of Pietism, which emphasized small-group devotion, individual conversion, and above all the born-again experience. That movement had an enormous impact on the Wesley brothers, who encountered Moravian Pietists while on a storm-racked transatlantic crossing in 1736 and who subsequently visited their German headquarters. John Wesley experienced his famous heart conversion in 1738 and began his sensational career of open-air preaching the following year. This laid the foundation for what would become the Methodist movement, and ultimately the very large churches founded in that tradition.[31]

Quite independently of that English trajectory, a movement was stirring in the American colonies. From the mid-1730s, preachers such as Jonathan Edwards and Theodorus Frelinghuysen (another Pietist) launched revivals in their churches, which had a critical regional impact, in turn inspiring other preachers. In 1737, Edwards published *A Faithful Narrative of the Surprising Work of God in the Conversion of Many Hundred Souls in Northampton*, which stirred interest on both sides of the Atlantic. Among other things, it influenced the direction of Whitefield's own revivalistic endeavors. A whole new cultural and spiritual environment was coming into existence, which would evolve into what we know as evangelical Christianity.[32]

At least in rudimentary form, an evangelical revival was already in progress by mid-1739, shortly before the climate declared war. That was the point at which the hunger for revival became evident, and when audiences of all kinds showed such fervor for words of inspiration and comfort. Inevitably, the question soon arose how far this could be reconciled with the structures of an official institutional church under royal or state control. The first great beneficiary of the new mood was George Whitefield, who in 1739 had won fame for his open-air preaching in the British Isles. (He in fact inspired John Wesley to adopt similar tactics.) Whitefield was a legendary orator, but whatever his personal skills, it was immensely beneficial to have an audience that so urgently wanted to hear words of promise and warmth at a time of cold and hunger.[33]

Whitefield's preaching tour in North America was an astounding phenomenon. He landed in Providence, Rhode Island, in September 1740, and over the following months preached widely in New England. Many accounts testify to the extraordinary excitement generated by his appearance. One observer of the meeting in Middletown, Connecticut, reported, "We went down in the Stream; I heard no man speak a word all the way three miles but every one pressing forward in great haste and when we got to the old meeting house there was a great multitude; it was said to be 3 or 4000 of people assembled together." A sensational gathering in Boston that October claimed an audience of 35,000, at a time when all the British American colonies combined could muster a population of only some 900,000, including both free and slave. From December, Gilbert Tennent joined what was emerging as a systematic revival campaign. From 1740 through 1743, "a great and general awakening" was much discussed in New England. Whitefield himself extended the movement through the colonies, riding horseback as far as Charleston, South Carolina. Despite some pockets of resistance, he won general praise and admiration, and his ideas were welcomed.[34]

We should never forget the landscape in which this Great Revival occurred, the physical landscape no less than the political and cultural. Only by combining these different elements can we understand the acute pressures under which people functioned, and the ill-focused terrors that resulted. Reading Joshua Coffin's unrelievedly bleak account of the incredible weather conditions of the time, we have a new appreciation of the comments that Coffin uses to frame his retelling. The summer of 1740 produced the incredible rains that threatened the crops; then in September he notes, "The reverend George Whitefield preached on this day, for the first time in Newbury." After describing the situation in March 1741, he continues, "Some time this year, commenced in this county and town, the remarkable revival of religion, which, commenced under the preaching of the reverend Jonathan Edwards, in 1735, and continued by Whitefield, Tennent, and many others, agitated not only New England, but the whole country." Revival occurred at a time when many had quite genuine fears about their mere survival. In mid-1741, Connecticut teenager Isaac Backus noted that "God by his Spirit was pleased in his infinite mercy to bring eternal things near to my soul and to show me the dreadful danger of delays." (Backus went on to be one of the most celebrated Baptist preachers of eighteenth-century America, and is often credited as sparking a new Awakening in the 1790s.) To quote Edwards, preaching about the "angry God" in July 1741: "In short, they have no refuge, nothing to take hold of; all that preserves them every moment is the mere arbitrary will, and uncovenanted, unobliged forbearance of an incensed God." The crisis created a perfect mass audience for the new Awakening.[35]

The Surprising Work of God

Edwards's own words illustrate the growing concern about Judgment and salvation. He traced the revival movement to the mid-1730s, which left a real legacy of spiritual concern in and around Northampton, Massachusetts, but he stressed that there had subsequently been "a very lamentable decay of religious affections, and the engagedness of people's spirit in religion." The real revival, the very large-scale social movement, could be precisely dated to

1740, as the region experienced repeated climatic onslaughts: "In the spring before Mr. Whitefield came to this town, there was a visible alteration: there was more seriousness and religious conversation, especially among young people." Whitefield preached several times that October, with sensational results: "The congregation was extraordinarily melted by every sermon; almost the whole assembly being in tears for a great part of sermon time." Through that winter, febrile concern with spiritual matters spread far beyond the town's usual suspects among the faithful, and reached many young people hitherto uninterested in religion.[36]

In May 1741, a sermon provoked something like a spiritual explosion, with wild expressions of emotion and enthusiasm.

> Many others at the same time were overcome with distress, about their sinful and miserable estate and condition; so that the whole room was full of nothing but outcries, faintings, and the like. Others soon heard of it in several parts of the town, and came to them; and what they saw and heard there, was greatly affecting to them, so that many of them were overpowered in like manner, and it continued thus for some hours; the time being spent in prayer, singing, counselling, and conferring.

Throughout his account of the following months, Edwards writes repeatedly of the physical manifestations of enthusiasm, all the "extraordinary appearances," especially among the young. He tells of "cryings out in the meeting-house," noting that "it was a very frequent thing, to see a house full of outcries, faintings, convulsions, and such like, both with distress, and also with admiration and joy." Those outbreaks, and many others, continued unchecked through 1742.[37]

Edwards's account is a classic revival narrative, which has influenced so many similar narratives through later American history. As later readers and sermon-hearers absorbed the details of his account, so they formed their impressions of exactly how they were expected to behave if and when revival struck their particular churches and communities, as they have continued to right up to the present day. This is where they learned the vocabulary of revival. What such readers did not necessarily appreciate was the worldly circumstances through which those "hearers" and "professors" were living at the time—the apocalyptic weather from which they were seeking some relief and comfort, and which brought them together with like-minded souls in hours of ecstatic release and communion.

Such extravagances became widespread. In Philadelphia in 1740, a typical anti-revivalist critic mocked new converts,

> filled brim full of enthusiastical raptures and ecstasies, pretending to have large communications from God; to have seen ravishing visions; to have been encompassed, as it were, with flames of lightning, and there to have beheld our blessed Savior nailed to the cross, and bleeding before their eyes in particular for them! These and such like enthusiastical extravagances some of our bigoted young zealots (who are not as yet distracted) have run into.

Conservative critic Charles Chauncy described the spiritual manifestations he witnessed. As he observed, those who heard the revivalist preachers responded with

> strange effects upon the body, such as swooning away and falling to the ground where persons have lain, for a time, speechless and motionless; bitter shriekings and screamings; convulsion-like tremblings and agitations, strugglings and tumblings, which, in some instances, have been attended with indecencies I shan't mention.

Dozens or even hundreds would be affected at a single time. When asked why they behaved thus,

> some say, they were surprised and astonished, and insensibly wrought upon, they can't tell how: others, that they had presented to their view, at the time, a sight of their sins, in all their number and desert: others, that they saw Hell, as it were, naked before them, and destruction without a covering; and that it seemed to them as though they were just falling into it: others, that they imagined the devils were about them, and ready to lay hold on them, and draw them away to Hell. The more general account is, that they were fill'd with great anxiety and distress, having upon their minds an over-powering sense of sin, and fear of divine wrath.

The converts were overcome by a despairing sense of their weakness and vulnerability in face of the absolute power of the divine, and the fearsome attacks of demonic forces of this world. In a different political setting, how easy it would be to imagine these passions manifesting themselves in attacks on scapegoated minorities, in something like the earlier Flagellant movement.

As it was, they merely became the controversial far fringes of a movement that later generations would laud and imitate.[38]

Throughout contemporary discussions of revival, we repeatedly encounter the metaphorical language of heat and cold, of fire and freezing. Conversion meant experiencing fire, and during his momentous conversion experience in London in 1738, John Wesley famously reported that he felt his heart "strangely warmed." A congregation was "extraordinarily melted" by a sermon. The unconverted individual, in contrast, was cold of heart, cold to the gospel. In the dark winter depths of January 1741, Yale student David Brainerd recorded that he "grew more cold and dull in religion," although he soon succumbed to the wider revival. In 1771, Edwards's grandson Timothy Dwight imagined zealous American faith spiritually reviving the world: "Hence o'er all lands shall sacred influency spread, / Warm frozen climes, and cheer the death-like shade." Such imagery had deep roots in the Bible, where analogies between fire and zeal are so frequent, and these figures of speech became familiar through successive movements of Puritanism, Pietism, and evangelicalism. One recent survey of Puritanism in England and America is aptly entitled *Hot Protestants*.[39] To the best of my knowledge, no contemporary observer of the revival drew an explicit analogy between the extreme cold of the natural world and the frigidity of the unconverted people. But for the traumatized audiences of 1740 and 1741, such parallels would have been difficult to avoid.

Enthusiasm Unchecked

For the religious-minded of the day, enthusiasm—hot faith—was a mixed blessing. At its best, and suitably disciplined, it offered the hope of pious fervor. But it could also manifest in paranoia or even challenge the sanity of inexperienced believers. The fraught mood of the time is exemplified by the sensational career of James Davenport, who briefly enjoyed superstar status as a preacher and revival leader. From 1739, he preached increasingly wild revivalistic sermons to his congregation at Southold, Long Island; one of those productions lasted twenty-four hours. In 1741, his career took a dramatic new turn as he became an itinerant preacher, traversing communities in New England. However familiar it would become in later history, that notion of itinerancy was radically new at the time, and represented a massive departure from older assumptions of learned clerics addressing settled congregations.[40]

Originally inspired by Whitefield and Tennent, Davenport violated many known rules of clerical behavior at the time. He denounced settled clergy and engaged in mass burnings of immoral books, objects, and clothing—his bonfires of the vanities. In Boston in 1742, a hostile (Anglican) minister complained that

> it is impossible to relate the convulsions into which the whole country is thrown by a set of enthusiasts that stroll about haranguing the admiring vulgar in extempore nonsense, nor is it confined to these only, for men, women, children, servants, and Negroes are now become (as they phrase it) exhorters.[41]

In an age when debates raged over an individual's predestination to salvation or damnation, Davenport offered brutally simple solutions: he could tell someone's eternal spiritual state just by looking at them. Contemporary observers worried that he was severely lacking in "the rational faculties of his mind," yet not until 1743 was he stopped. In retrospect, Davenport himself later admitted that something had been dreadfully wrong; what moderns regard as severe mental disturbance, he attributed to demonic possession. He issued a general retraction of his actions and behavior.[42]

For later observers, the question is not so much why a disturbed person engaged in weird and embarrassing behavior but rather why he was so long tolerated and even praised as an emissary of divine truth. He would almost certainly not have been so viewed ten years earlier, nor ten years later. Why did his career last four years, rather than four weeks? Something like Davenport's career could only occur when multiple audiences were prepared to abandon traditions and restraints and accept teachings suitable for desperate times, for what obviously seemed to be an era of terminal crisis. As economic normalcy returned after 1742, so the public mood became less willing to tolerate excess and extremism—or "enthusiasm."

Living with Revival

Although the New England experience is celebrated, there were many other local manifestations, and some had equally lasting effects. In Scotland, the town of Cambuslang (now a Glasgow suburb) became the epicenter for a famous revival. At its height in 1742, this movement, the Cambuslang Work, reputedly drew some 30,000 hearers, at a time when Scotland's population was around 1.2 million. The ministers who launched the movement were in close touch with American conditions, and Whitefield himself had recently visited the area. Together with other revivals in these same years, Cambuslang began a general evangelical wave that lasted through the century, and which had a special impact through the expanding British possessions overseas.[43]

Meanwhile, the social crisis gave a major boost to transatlantic migration, and particularly brought to America migrants whose distinctive religious traditions predisposed them to revivalist faith. This especially meant the mainly Presbyterian Scots and Ulster people who had long familiarity with field preaching and open-air meetings, dating back to the previous crisis around 1680. Their homelands were hard hit by the food shortages around 1740, which drove new waves of exodus. By the 1770s, the Scots-Irish made up perhaps a third of the population of Pennsylvania, and they were beginning to move into regions such as Ohio, Tennessee, and Kentucky. Here they offered a substantial audience for successive new waves of fiery revivalism, which explicitly drew on the foundations laid by Whitefield, Edwards, and the rest.[44]

An explosion of revivalist enthusiasm fueled the famous Great Awakening, with tens of thousands of new members added to Congregational churches. When fervor faded in New England, the movement spread south and west. This in turn laid the foundation for the Baptist and Methodist expansion that so dominated the nation's religious history for the next 150 years. Narrow issues of theology merged into larger questions of the role of institutions and of authority, and even of the rights of individuals. The sense of an outpouring of Spirit drew many lay and unlearned people to preach and speak publicly, including teenagers and even women, all to the horror of established leaders.

Meanwhile, the spiritual upsurge divided many churches and denominations between pro- and anti-revival factions, between New and Old Lights (or New and Old Sides). New Light and New Side ministers and itinerant preachers invaded the territories of their conservative counterparts, who persuaded secular justices of the peace to enforce order by arrest where necessary. From the early 1740s, Virginia especially experienced a slow-burning religious civil war, the alignments in which profoundly influenced later political struggles. The struggle against the Anglican Church set the pattern for the later revolt against the British Empire. In religious terms, this is when the American colonies came of age. Many historians trace a direct line from that spiritual upsurge to the popular political enthusiasm that ultimately led to the American Revolution. Some have described Whitefield as America's spiritual founding father.[45]

Between 1739 and 1742, Europe and North America experienced a period of climate crisis, which coincided very closely with a revolutionary spiritual upsurge. In the cultural context of the time, such a linkage was natural and indeed predictable. Of course, early modern people assailed by horrendous weather, with its attendant evils of starvation and epidemic, would place those horrors in a spiritual context. The two climates—natural and spiritual—must be understood in a common context.

8

Darkening Heavens and a New World

Nature is often hidden, sometimes overcome, seldom extinguished.
—Francis Bacon

In 1820, the fourteen-year-old Joseph Smith experienced what has become known as his First Vision, which he portrayed as a transformative encounter with divine realities that laid the foundation for the Church of Jesus Christ of Latter-day Saints, and the Mormon tradition. But if Smith was distinctive in his enduring influence, he was anything but unusual in terms of his deep interest in visions, angels, and the end times. Such concepts were integral to the religious thought of the time. The roots of this obsession can be traced to a specific era of climate-based catastrophe in the years immediately following 1815 and the eruption of the Indonesian volcano of Tambora. The disaster caused sudden and brutal global cooling and seemingly endless rainfall, making 1816 "the year without a summer" or "Eighteen Hundred and Froze to Death." As we would expect, those conditions inspired the growth and mainstreaming of apocalyptic ideas, along with the rise of potent denominations and churches.[1]

Although Tambora was exceptional in its violence, other climate episodes around this time had far-reaching effects, and those in turn drove religious and cultural change. To that extent, this is a pattern we have seen before in earlier centuries, notably in the years around 1740. But the nineteenth century also marked a transition to a new and enduring climatic environment, which went far beyond the immediate response to a single brief crisis. For one thing, the climate itself changed decisively, with the end of the Little Ice Age—however we interpret that concept—and the beginning of a long-term warming phase, in which we live today. But the human activity that contributed to warming also changed the responses to climate, and to climate change. In 1320 or 1680, societies throughout the world were still predominantly agrarian, and hence utterly vulnerable to natural events. In Europe and North America, the century following the 1780s marked a revolutionary shift toward industrialization, modernization, and urbanization, as societies diversified their food resources. Over time, the direct and immediate consequences of short-term climate episodes became less obvious, allowing the industrializing world to develop a sense of security about such matters. At least in the West, well-informed people came to believe that climate and weather were concerns for bygone societies, as advanced nations could no longer find themselves "in the hands of an angry God." In retrospect, that sense of invulnerability, that supposed escape from the bondage of climate, looks like a dangerous illusion.[2]

Three Crises

To appreciate the scale of that change, we can compare the relative impact of three of the climate shocks that occurred between the 1780s and the 1880s, which are respectively associated with the eruptions of Laki in 1783–1784, Tambora in 1815, and Krakatoa in 1883. As I have said, volcanoes in themselves are in no sense the sole drivers of global change, but they are significant, and they are intimately linked to other phenomena. Each in its way resonated across the world, creating some kind of climate crisis, with strong cultural and religious consequences. But as time went on, those consequences diminished, as did the ways in which people understood their planet and its activities.

1783: Laki Haze

At the end of the eighteenth century, volcanic eruptions once again combined with other climatic upheavals to inflict widespread chaos and suffering around the globe. What had changed from earlier events of this kind was that the impact was sometimes expressed through secular movements that explicitly rejected the language of religion and faith.

In 1783–1784, the Northern Hemisphere suffered a cataclysmic downturn in its weather, traceable to an obvious culprit in the form of the Icelandic volcano Laki. The actual eruption was quite small by the scale of some recent competitors—a mere 4 on the VEI—but several months of sulfur dioxide and hydrogen fluoride emissions enhanced its damage to economies around the world. Those emissions were comparable to the industrial output of modern Europe, and matters were aggravated by at least one other Icelandic eruption in the following few years. The main immediate result was a "Laki haze," which soon became visible as far afield as China. In England, the learned naturalist Gilbert White described how

> the sun, at noon, looked as blank as a clouded moon, and shed a rust-coloured ferruginous light on the ground, and floors of rooms; but was particularly lurid and blood-coloured at rising and setting. At the same time the heat was so intense that butchers' meat could hardly be eaten on the day after it was killed; and the flies swarmed so in the lanes and hedges that they rendered the horses half frantic . . . the country people began to look with a superstitious awe, at the red, louring aspect of the sun.

Benjamin Franklin wrote of "a constant fog over all Europe, and a great part of North America." North American winter conditions resembled those of 1740. In New England, Noah Webster reported the winter of 1783–1784 as "the most extraordinary instance of extreme cold that I have ever known." In Europe, extremely hot summers preceded bitter winters and deadly flooding. European temperatures fell an alarming two degrees Celsius below normal. Tiny Iceland itself suffered the harshest direct impact, losing a fifth of its population.[3]

But the volcano was part of a much larger story, in which other forcing factors were at work over a period of three decades or more. Quite apart from Laki, we can also point to the interaction of the different oceanic phenomena—the North Atlantic Oscillation and El Niño—together with low solar activity. We are at the start of the so-called Dalton Minimum in sunspot activity, which lasted until 1820, and we have already noted the possible connections between such a phenomenon and El Niño cycles, and also volcanism. Meanwhile, the NAO was at an extremely negative point, which is associated with cold European conditions.[4]

That El Niño component accounts for the weakening monsoons that inflicted famine in widely separated regions. The Chalisa Famine in India killed several million people in 1783–1784, and that was just the impact in one region. Egypt lost a sixth of its people. New factors entered the equation over the following decade. Between 1789 and 1793, a historically strong El Niño had its global impact. (Some scholars extend the limits of this Great El Niño to 1788–1796.) Droughts as bad as any in living memory occurred as far afield as Africa, Australia, Mexico, and the Caribbean. In India, the monsoon failed and droughts reached levels not seen since the earlier depths of the mid-1680s; famine ensued. In 1791–1792, India lost millions through the chillingly named Skull Famine. In 1794, extensive famines in China precipitated the destructive White Lotus Rebellion, as radical sects promised the messianic coming of a new Buddha. A hundred thousand perished in the ensuing warfare. Europe too suffered famines in the early 1790s, although it is difficult to disentangle natural from political causes at a time of wars foreign and domestic. Observers in the newly independent United States recorded several years of disastrous cold and freezing conditions—the winters of 1784, 1788, 1792, and 1796–1797 were all parlous. In 1800, several southern states, including Florida and Louisiana, were astonished to report deep snow.[5]

Revolutions

From the mid-1780s, Europe suffered severe years of crop failure and hunger, which contributed powerfully to political conflict in several European nations. Without the global turmoil, France would not have experienced the agricultural disasters that drove the country into economic crisis and led to famine, food riots, and rural insurrection in the winter of 1788. General social panic manifested in the notorious Great Fear, when protesters attacked aristocrats and anyone else who could plausibly be blamed for the ongoing horrors. The French Revolution began the following year. But even before the tumultuous year of 1789, political disaffection and outright revolts were developing in several nations, as part of what has been called a larger wave of Atlantic revolutions. Although each local conflict had its own particular context and rivalries, the general climate crisis contributed powerfully to inspiring political dissent and undermining established orders—to subverting what would soon be known as the ancien regime, the old order.[6]

Religious effects of the catastrophe, and the "superstitious awe" it awakened, can easily be traced. As in earlier years, everything depended on the legal and political opportunities available to particular groups, and these were so much greater in the English-speaking world than in Continental Europe. Unlike in previous years, the beneficiaries of the crisis were not so much whole new sects or movements as existing groups who were already making progress, but that was now accelerated. In both Britain and the United States, the 1780s were a spectacularly successful time for revival, largely within the general framework of existing Methodist and Baptist denominations. Particularly given the revolutionary political atmosphere of the era and the American victory in the country's war of independence, millenarian and apocalyptic ideas were strongly evident. Although small in number, sects such as the Shakers enjoyed a boom and a surprising cultural impact. Very difficult climate conditions provide a context for the new wave of revivals that began in 1798, although the linkage is less clear and direct than with the predecessor movement in 1741. This movement—sometimes termed a Second Great Awakening—was again marked by enthusiastic outbursts of extreme physical behavior, including screaming and convulsions.[7]

Religious alignments were of course utterly different in most Continental European states, whether Catholic or Protestant, where religious dissent was usually strictly limited. Matters changed fundamentally with the French Revolution, with its ferociously anti-clerical and anti-religious tone. However much ordinary people may have felt that the crises of the time manifested God's anger with the world, this was no time for any kind of new religious movement. But if the chaos in the natural order did not provoke explicitly apocalyptic responses, with all the religious consequences we would expect, the secular outcomes actually looked remarkably similar. Again, to take the example of France, as violently anti-religious revolutionaries confronted the starvation and disasters of the early 1790s, they drew heavily on ideas that in a religious context we would immediately describe as apocalyptic or millenarian. As in earlier and more pious ages, they drew on such ideas to target and annihilate enemies who stood in the way of the creation of a perfect order. Commonly, these were religious believers, especially faithful Catholics. In the most notorious instance, in the Vendée in the catastrophic year of 1793, revolutionaries slaughtered perhaps 200,000 Catholic rebels and their supporters, in what some historians have called the first genocide in the modern West. Rival apocalyptic visions, Christian and militantly secular, clashed lethally.[8]

1816: The Year Without a Summer

Again, in the years around 1815, sudden climate change caused disruption around the globe, and had its impact on religious thought and belief. In particular, the evangelical tradition, which was forged in the crisis of the early 1740s, now achieved unprecedented influence.

In recent years, the crisis following the Tambora eruption has become familiar, with several book-length studies on the event. But that event was part of a larger and quite complex global phenomenon that preceded it by several years and which was only partly related to volcanism. Another still unlocated eruption occurred, presumably in the Pacific, in 1808–1809, which was at least in the 6 range of explosivity, and several lesser blasts followed over the next few years. Together, that contributed to some years of cooling. The United States recorded several bizarre happenings, such as New England's incredible Cold Friday in 1810, when temperatures dropped by sixty or more degrees Fahrenheit within a single day. The American winter of 1812 was appallingly cold, and as Napoleon discovered in his expedition to Moscow, Russian conditions were at least as bad. As I have remarked, the relationship between climate factors and earthquakes is controversial, but over a period of months in 1811–1812, New Madrid, Missouri, was the epicenter of a series of historically large tremors, the most intense of which was an 8 on the Richter scale. It is scarcely surprising that the tremors inspired a wave of apocalyptic concern and religious revivalism through the Ohio and Tennessee Valleys, the "Earthquake Revivals." However stupendous in its own right, Tambora should properly be seen as one event in a longer cycle of crises that spanned the years from 1808 through 1820.[9]

Tambora's emissions of sulfur dioxide were enormous, leaving Greenland's ice cores with the highest sulfate concentrations seen for millennia. In Britain, low temperature records were repeatedly broken. In the United States, heavy snow and freezing conditions persisted through June, as Thomas Jefferson reported "the most extraordinary year of drought and cold ever known in the history of America." Many countries recorded terrifying new temperature lows. Floods were followed by droughts that ruined farmers; a terrifying subsistence crisis ensued across the West, with the worst famine in nineteenth-century Europe. In Europe at least, this was the last continent-wide outbreak to date of premodern starvation conditions not directly caused by warfare. Food prices soared: wheat and rye prices doubled between 1815 and 1817, even rising fourfold in some regions. Desperate people made bread from sawdust and straw, and slaughtered horses and dogs for food. Starvation and undernourishment caused at least hundreds of thousands of deaths, and probably far more. Legions of beggars roamed the towns and villages, and Germans called 1817 "the Year of the Beggar." In 1819, the United States suffered a ruinous financial panic and an ensuing depression.[10]

The effects of systematic deprivation lingered through 1819, driving numerous protest movements and revolutionary upsurges, including many conspiracies and plots for coups and assassinations, often directed by clandestine secret societies. So multifaceted and so threatening were such threats in Britain that the country feared an imminent outbreak of armed revolution. The fact that those upsurges followed so directly from the tumult of the Revolutionary and Napoleonic Wars (1793–1815) means that they are usually seen as symptoms of postwar readjustment, demobilization, and economic restructuring. Until recently, rarely did historians see the turmoil for what it was—namely, the direct consequence of a climate-driven catastrophe.[11]

As so often before, pandemic followed famine, and in this case, the culprit was the new global menace of cholera. The bacterium itself occurs widely around the world, and usually harmlessly, but a lethal new strain evolved in South Asia around 1815, in the rapidly changing environmental conditions following Tambora and the disrupted monsoons. Over the next decade, the world suffered its first cholera pandemic, an insidious pestilence that first struck in India. This Asiatic cholera was then transmitted rapidly across Eurasia by a combination of imperial British and Dutch military forces, and by both Muslim and Hindu pilgrims traveling to their respective sacred sites. By the 1830s, the disease was taking a ghastly toll across Europe. Apart from cholera, other pestilences also had their impact in particular regions. In Ireland, perhaps 100,000 perished from typhus, and this "Irish fever" then struck Britain.[12]

Tambora's effects have now become part of standard cultural history. Readers with no great interest in climate issues have become familiar with the idea that appalling weather forced a group of British literati to take refuge in their Swiss villa, and their enforced leisure produced several literary achievements, including Mary Shelley's *Frankenstein*. Also in the party was Lord Byron, who echoed contemporary prophecies of the imminent end times in his poem "Darkness." Visualizing the last man on a frozen earth, he imagined all-encompassing despair and destruction amidst ruined and depopulated cities:

> All earth was but one thought—and that was death
> Immediate and inglorious: and the pang
> Of famine fed upon all entrails—men
> Died, and their bones were tombless as their flesh;
> The meagre by the meagre were devour'd.[13]

Besides *Frankenstein*, Mary Shelley left another monument to the dark years in her 1826 novel *The Last Man*, which likewise portrays the last representative of the human race, in this instance in a world ravaged by a plague.

Revivals

For religious and secular thinkers alike, the prospect of the end times—the "latter days"—became fashionable, indeed pressing. Skies darkened, astonishing clouds filled the heavens, crops failed, people starved, unrest flared: how could anyone not read these as apocalyptic signs? The crisis caused immediate religious upsurges, and revivals flared in 1816–1817, especially in the United States, but also in European countries where Protestantism had been in retreat. When Scottish theologian Robert Haldane visited Swiss seminaries in the dark summer of 1816, he launched a revival movement that spread widely across France, Germany, and the Netherlands, and then throughout much of Europe. Known under different names, this Réveil (Awakening) spread a close facsimile of Anglo-American evangelical thought and practice across the Continent. In Germany, Pietist influence reached new heights, and especially the movement's emphasis on holy living rather than confessional theology. That approach won a historic victory in the emergency situation of 1817, when the Prussian king was persuaded to merge the Lutheran and Reformed/Calvinist churches in his realm into a new united Evangelical church.[14]

In the United States, the years from 1816 through 1821 saw multiple outbreaks of evangelistic enthusiasm, most memorably in the lands of western New York State that were so often smitten with the fires of revival that they became known as the "Burnt-Over District." Thousands attended camp meetings, often held by Methodists, but also by several other sects and independent preachers. In 1819, the region experienced a "flaming spiritual advance," a "religious cyclone which swept over the whole region round about and the kingdom of darkness was terribly shaken." One influential alumnus of these movements was Charles Grandison Finney, who was converted to a radical new commitment in 1821 and became the leading exponent of enthusiastic revivalism. Quite apart from the sensational revivals, the era witnessed some key developments in existing churches, as social strains demanded innovative responses and a new activism. It was in 1816 that a number of disaffected Methodist believers formed the African Methodist

Episcopal (AME) Church, which would have an enormous impact on later US history. The country's first abolitionist newspaper dates from 1819.[15]

The long-term religious impact was still more critical. Through the 1830s and 1840s, the United States had a mighty efflorescence of sects with a strongly apocalyptic cast, and in most cases the leaders and primary members of those movements grew up during the post-Tambora horrors. They were commonly alumni of those 1816–1817 revivals. Joseph Smith was at an impressionable age when the heavens darkened, and it was the crop failures of those years that forced his family to move from Vermont to western New York. Critics who challenge the Book of Mormon's credentials as an authentic ancient text commonly cite the many examples that seem to reflect the world that Joseph Smith knew in the 1820s or remembered from the recent past. Memories of extreme climate events surface in some of the Book of Mormon's terrifying prophecies. In 3 Nephi, we read of the "tempests, earthquakes, fires, whirlwinds, and physical upheavals" that reputedly occurred at the time of Christ's crucifixion. The "vapor of darkness" that falls over the land suggests memories of 1816:

> And there could be no light, because of the darkness, neither candles, neither torches; neither could there be fire kindled with their fine and exceedingly dry wood, so that there could not be any light at all; and there was not any light seen, neither fire, nor glimmer, neither the sun, nor the moon, nor the stars, for so great were the mists of darkness which were upon the face of the land.

These prophetic accounts commonly include references to the shaking of the earth, which may recall overheard tales of the earthquakes of 1811–1812, distant echoes of which were felt as far afield as Boston.[16]

William Miller, founder of Adventism, was much older than Smith, but this was exactly the time when his thoughts were decisively shifting to religious concerns. After his discharge from military service in 1815, he settled in upstate New York and suffered a religious crisis that lasted some three years. After struggling to regain his earlier Baptist views, he immersed himself in biblical prophecies of the end times. By 1818, he was thoroughly convinced of his new chronological understanding, which unerringly predicted the world's end for 1843. The movement he founded faithfully preached that date, and their advocacy powerfully drove the nation's apocalyptic mood. Specifically, they opened the way to the very influential doctrine of premillennialism, the idea that Christ would return in a time of worldly crisis and catastrophe as the essential precursor to his millennial rule of peace and justice. When doomsday failed to materialize in 1843, the Adventists turned their attention to 1844. But the movement survived even that double disappointment and long remained a potent influence on American religious life.[17]

Apart from such key individuals, the disasters proved a major incentive to westward expansion in the United States. As conditions deteriorated in New England, settlers moved west en masse, into the Ohio country and beyond. The newcomers spread evangelical born-again religion with an apocalyptic flavor, and favored innovative practices such as the camp meeting. If such expansion was inevitable in the long term, the crisis greatly accelerated it, in the process giving rise to the nation's frontier faith.

1883: Krakatoa and Beyond

Still, in the early years of the nineteenth century, we find the familiar linkage between extreme climate conditions and religious upsurges or revivals. As other climate crises followed over the coming decades, what is most striking is how much less impact they produced. That lack of impact—that non-story—in fact reflects the fundamental shift in social and economic affairs.[18]

Through the twentieth century, the name of Krakatoa became part of popular culture across the West, as the legendary manifestation of the planet's uncontrollable wrath. The eruption occurred in 1883, killing tens of thousands in the East Indies and causing tsunamis, and it registered around much of the world. A 6 on the VEI, it clouded the skies and dropped global temperatures by a degree Celsius. Its exact impact is open to some debate. Global temperatures dropped for several years after 1883, in some cases causing blizzards and frozen seas in what looks like a classic volcanic-winter scenario. Still, that was apparently part of a pattern that had already begun in 1882, before the actual eruption, so Krakatoa was reinforcing and aggravating existing trends.[19]

Despite those caveats, Krakatoa had a potent contemporary impact. The alarming changes in the colors of the skies were depicted in Edvard Munch's iconic painting "The Scream." Alfred Lord Tennyson used the episode in his historical poem "St. Telemachus," which is set around 400 CE. After "the fierce ashes of some fiery peak [had] been hurl'd so high they ranged about the globe," as "the wrathful sunset glared," a Christian hermit "bathed in lurid crimson" is inspired to sacrifice his life in a confrontation with Roman imperial power. This is a pioneering and rather convincing account of how a natural catastrophe might inspire religious zeal and apocalyptic sentiment.[20]

But despite its fearsome reputation, Krakatoa produced nothing like the global chaos of Tambora, and we do not find the systematic crises of earlier centuries, none of the mass starvation or pandemics. Nor did the disaster have anything like the social or political effects that such a change would have had in earlier eras. Economies did not stumble or collapse (or if they did, it was due to factors unrelated to that eruption). We do not find mobs so alarmed by changing colors in the sky that they attacked social or religious minorities; there was no upsurge of apocalyptic sects or Flagellants, no wave of revivals or miracle crusades, no mass appearance of millenarian prophets. Or at least no such phenomena manifested in the increasingly hegemonic Western world, a distinction to which I will return shortly. Tennyson explicitly set his poem in an archaic context, when people might be expected to interpret cosmic signs in supernatural terms. That was what they did back then, and evidently the modern world viewed things very differently. Both author and reader knew very well that the colored skies are produced by a volcanic eruption rather than by divine fury.[21]

Similar observations about lack of impact can be made about two other volcanic events of very comparable size that occurred shortly after Krakatoa, yet which achieved nothing like the same central place in popular memory. Two other grade 6 eruptions occurred in 1902 (Guatemala) and 1912 (Alaska), and both affected climate in some measure. Yet neither created any kind of social crisis. Just how thoroughly volcanoes have dropped from our modern-day list of fears is suggested by the 1991 eruption of Mount Pinatubo in the Philippines, a grade 6 comparable to Krakatoa and an event that claimed perhaps a thousand lives in nearby areas. Over the next two years, it dropped worldwide temperatures by about half a degree Celsius. The eruption garnered some media attention, but its direct effects on everyday lives in other continents were close to nonexistent. If a European or American chose not to follow mass media, there was no reason to notice Pinatubo, and still less to be concerned. In 2010, the legendarily unpronounceable Icelandic volcano Eyjafjallajökull did indeed cause global disruption, but that was entirely because of its effects on transatlantic air routes.[22]

Other once-overwhelming climate factors lost their urgency. In modern times, El Niño events have occurred on a sizable scale, and with far-reaching effects. One major El Niño in 1982 inspired an upsurge in scientific research on the phenomenon, encouraging scholars to comprehend the scale of its consequences. That impulse was strengthened when a historically strong event occurred in 1997–1998. Producing violent storms on the US West Coast, the phenomenon brought the whole concept of El Niño into popular culture, and it was widely reported in the media. But for the great majority of North Americans and Europeans living at the time, El Niño had little direct impact in terms of threatening livelihoods or raising concerns about food supplies. The same was true of the very strong El Niño of 2014–2016, even though this was—together with 1982–1983 and 1997–1998—among the strongest and most consequential ever recorded. Anyone interested in the topic could follow these visitations as closely as they wished, but they did not impinge on how most ordinary people viewed their everyday lives.[23]

The Escape from Climate?

What had changed? Why did such later events have nothing like the cataclysmic quality of earlier eras? Partly it was that the climate itself was in the process of change, and in a direction that limited or counteracted those potential trends. From the mid-nineteenth century, steadily growing industry produced ever more greenhouse gas emissions, which began a warming process that decisively ended the Little Ice Age. The exact date of such an ending is much debated (as is so often the case), and experts have offered various dates between 1850 and the start of the twentieth century. A fair consensus would place it a little before the time of Krakatoa. No more were there long-term cooling trends that massive eruptions could aggravate to inflict global harm.[24]

But also society itself had changed, moving away from the total and direct reliance on agriculture of earlier eras. The proportion of people living in cities and industrial communities grew during the nineteenth century, a phenomenon seen first in Europe and then in the United States—although not until 1920 did American city dwellers outnumber rural people. Today, only some 11 percent of Americans work in agriculture and related industries, and the actual number working on farms or ranches constitutes just 1.3 percent of the population.[25]

Feeding those urban populations demanded a total restructuring of food supplies. Among other things, that meant new forms of industrialized agriculture, food storage on a previously unthinkable scale, a revolution in food retailing, and the globalization of food exports and imports. Canning and refrigeration technologies were just two of the obvious manifestations of this new era. Further new developments continued into the twentieth century. In 1913, the coming of the Haber-Bosch process allowed the large-scale chemical production of ammonia, and with it the fertilizers required to feed a fast-growing world population. In the short time since 1900, global population has grown from 1.6 billion to almost 8 billion. That population has also become far more urbanized, with the fastest rates of urbanization occurring in the global South. Around the year 2007, for the first time, a majority of the human population lived in cities, and that proportion will grow steadily in coming decades.[26]

In such an environment, most urban dwellers in the developed nations had no inkling of whether the previous year's harvests in their own countries had been spectacularly good or atrociously bad, beyond uttering complaints at the prices of particular seasonal fruits or vegetables. Even less were they concerned about harvests in the distant lands from which other parts of their diet derived. Vulnerability to famine and its attendant catastrophes had become a critical marker separating the advanced and developed world from its less developed and less prosperous counterpart. Growing food security combined with improvements in medicine and public health to ensure a sharp decline in infectious diseases and a general increase in life span. The impact of this process, the so-called epidemiological transition, has been so comprehensive, so transformative, that people in advanced nations assume it is an obvious and natural part of life.[27]

Of course, modern societies have known hunger and outright famine, in which millions perished, but that usually occurred as a result of warfare and occupation, or through sieges and other deployments of the food weapon. When starvation and epidemics did occur—when European nations suffered mortality crises on the once-familiar model, as they did between 1918 and 1921, or in Ukraine in the 1930s—those generally happened not because of changes in the oceans or the skies but as a direct effect of human action, because of wars or official savagery. Even so, I stress "generally," as climate still contributed to calamities in ways we are only beginning to grasp. We cannot find a simple or straightforward climate-based explanation for the Spanish Influenza epidemic of 1918, which caused so many millions of deaths around the world. However, recent research indicates that the effects of the disease were vastly aggravated by extreme climate conditions that had prevailed since 1914, marked by severe cold and torrential rain. (We recall the often-repeated images of the oceans of mud on the Western Front of the First World War.) That made for "a once-in-a-century climate anomaly." That linkage was not apparent at the time, and would not be so for a full century after the event.[28]

During the twentieth century, large sections of the world became immunized from the effects of short-term climate shocks, or at least came to believe that they had. Even when natural hazards continued to afflict humanity, their cultural meaning had changed fundamentally. Americans, for instance, suffered such natural calamities as the Galveston floods of 1900 or the San Francisco earthquake of 1906, which together killed some 10,000. Each incident attracted its share of spiritual excitement. Popular reactions to the San Francisco event contributed to the ecstatic passion driving the Azusa Street revival that was occurring in Los Angeles in these same months, out of which emerged the Pentecostal movement. Other terrifying events, including floods and epidemics, likewise had their religious resonances. But such responses were absolutely alien to the dominant scientific approach, which had no sympathy whatever for providential interpretations of natural events. By the mid-nineteenth century, any educated figure who proposed such a supernatural view of natural disasters—who laid the blame on the wrath of God or the Devil—was decisively exiling himself from the scientific community. Meanwhile, the scientific study of climate and climate history grew apace, drawing heavily on all those observations collected since the crises of the seventeenth century.[29]

Conversely, when religious upsurges did occur, climate factors became ever less salient or relevant. In the United States, for instance, we can trace religious declines in some eras and booms in others, and we can plausibly argue for some material context in terms of economic change or shifts in prosperity. But climate no longer played anything like the role it had in earlier centuries.

Earth Abides

This is not to say that climatic events ceased to afflict human populations after the mid-nineteenth century. They certainly did, in many places outside the Western and industrialized world. Other regions, especially in Asia, suffered repeated catastrophes through famine and pandemic, and in some cases the climatic role is clear. One appalling example followed the powerful El Niño of 1876–1878, one of the most severe episodes of its kind on record. The resulting drought combined with multiple other factors to create ruinous famines across China, India, northern Africa, and Brazil. By some measures, Asia suffered its worst drought in eight centuries. Responding to the conditions in India alone, Florence Nightingale described "a hideous record of human suffering and destruction the world has never seen before." The death toll is controversial, with estimates ranging from 15 million up to as high as 50 million, and if that latter figure is correct, that would constitute 3 percent of the human population at that time. Other climatic assaults in the 1890s covered equally broad swaths of the globe and killed tens of millions. Human intervention, social policies, and imperial arrogance undoubtedly aggravated these famines, which have even been termed "late Victorian holocausts," but their immediate causation lay in climate-related factors.[30] Over and above those episodes, China continued to suffer famines on a gargantuan scale, usually as a consequence of drought. Acute episodes occurred in 1907, 1911, 1928–1930, and 1936, and each of those cycles claimed several million lives. By some estimates, the 1907 event was among the worst famines in all recorded history.[31]

Since the Second World War, famine has been stereotypically a problem of the global South, and even then, the culprits were more commonly found in malevolent political regimes than in purely natural or climatic conditions. This was true of the extraordinary famine that swept China in the late 1950s, killing tens of millions, and atrocious examples occurred in Cambodia in the 1970s and Ethiopia in the 1980s. These were manifestations of mass murder or outright genocide rather than a mere inability to respond to shifting conditions. If not willfully intentional, other catastrophes could be directly blamed on wars or state failure, as in the Democratic Republic of Congo in the opening years of the present century.[32]

For the economically advanced nations, the constant litany of such horrors sent a potent (and pernicious) message about the racial geography of natural disasters and their causation. According to this view, these were associated with the weakness of states and social systems in the less-developed world, whether that was labeled the "Third World" or the "global South." The underlying assumption, rarely spoken, was that white people did not starve, because they had become independent of nature. Nor, of course, did they suffer from epidemics. Those advanced and prosperous societies utterly dominated both scientific research and global mass media. If those nations saw no cause for concern about larger climatic influences on human misfortunes, they were not likely to encounter dissenting voices from elsewhere in the world.

9
A Warming World

> The best way to suppose what may come is to remember what is past. The best qualification of a prophet is to have a good memory. Experience maketh more prophets than revelation.
>
> —George Savile, Marquess of Halifax

In 1988, climate scientist James E. Hansen, of the National Aeronautics and Space Administration, made a historic presentation to a committee of the US Senate. He warned that global warming was already occurring, and that the trend would continue unless remedial action was taken. Hansen claimed a 99 percent certainty that the trend "was not a natural variation but was caused by a buildup of carbon dioxide and other artificial gases in the atmosphere." That represented a broad scientific consensus. Further, he said, "it is time to stop waffling so much and say that the evidence is pretty strong that the greenhouse effect is here." His remarks had a special impact at the time, as the years 1988–1989 marked one of the worst droughts in US history, with accompanying heatwaves and damaging wildfires. If that was in fact a portent of the future, then a response was needed urgently. Other possible consequences, such as melting icecaps and rising sea levels, were no less threatening.[1]

Hansen was only one of many scientists making such arguments at the time, but the venue gave his words unique visibility and a special impact. Although detailed aspects of such projections have been attacked, the general model presented in these years is now widely accepted, and so are the dire consequences. In many nations, climate change has become a central issue in political life. But beyond general prognostications of disaster, we can legitimately ask about the cultural implications, and specifically the religious aspects. As we know from abundant historical experience, apocalyptic changes in climate frequently have reshaped religious thought and life—through mass migrations of particular faiths and sects, by stimulating millenarian and prophetic movements, by stirring revivals and awakenings, and also by inciting groups to demonize and attack perceived enemies. Extreme times bring extreme religion. And if Western nations have, at least in theory, moved far beyond providential interpretations of natural disasters, other societies around the world have not. Whatever other transformations climate change may wreak in coming decades, the world's spiritual landscape will also take on new forms. A knowledge of history can help us understand what these outcomes might be.[2]

Discovering Warming

Nineteenth-century scholars theorized about the human impact on climate, and especially the role of emissions. Debate focused on gases such as carbon dioxide, nitrous oxide, and methane, which together warm the planet's surface through the so-called greenhouse effect. In appropriate quantities they are essential to survival. In 1859, Irish scientist John Tyndall remarked that without the greenhouse effect "the warmth of our fields and gardens would pour itself unrequited into space, and the sun would rise upon an island held fast in the iron grip of frost." Mass industrialization rapidly increased levels of these greenhouse gases, and in the 1890s, Svante Arrhenius calculated just how much increases in atmospheric carbon dioxide would drive global warming. Apart from factory smokestacks, the main culprits are carbon-based methods of producing energy through fossil fuels, especially petroleum and coal. As recently as the 1950s, the world produced 5 billion metric tons of carbon dioxide each year (not counting other greenhouse gases), but that figure today exceeds 35 billion tons. The swift rise of human populations accounts for much of that growth, as has the emergence of wealthier societies in vast nations such as China and India. Between 1990 and 2017, China alone increased its emissions of carbon dioxide by over 350 percent. Presently, China accounts for over a quarter of the world's annual CO_2 emissions, the United States and the European Union combined make up another quarter, with India's contribution at 7 percent.[3]

Scientists have long warned that a greenhouse effect would cause warming levels that were harmful, indeed disastrous. That message was originally a tough sell, and many experts were skeptical about claims that climate might change as rapidly as was claimed. Some respectable scholars were even confidently warning of global cooling and an imminent new ice age. In 1974, *Time* magazine headlined "Another Ice Age?," arguing that such a prospect was the likely interpretation of the "bizarre and unpredictable weather pattern of the past several years." But just the following year, Wallace Broecker published what now looks like a prophetic paper: "Climatic Change: Are We on the Brink of a Pronounced Global Warming?" His position would receive support from the records of previous climate changes preserved in Greenland's ancient ice cores, which showed just how thoroughly matters could alter in just a decade or two—a revolutionary insight at the time.[4]

From 1990, the United Nations–linked Intergovernmental Panel on Climate Change (IPCC) issued the first of several surveys of accumulating evidence, concluding that warming was happening and that human actions were chiefly responsible. Subsequent observations have largely confirmed that analysis, as temperatures have risen around the globe; nineteen of the twenty hottest years ever recorded all occurred in the early part of this century. July 2019 was the hottest month globally since measurements began, and in Europe, the winter of 2019–2020 was by far the hottest on record. Moreover, a substantial scientific consensus came to believe that those warming trends were human-caused, or anthropogenic, rather than deriving from "normal" fluctuations, due perhaps to solar activity. Many nations acknowledged the need to curb emissions, and in 1992 the United Nations adopted its Framework Convention on Climate Change. In 2015, a conference held in Paris agreed on a common goal of ensuring that global temperatures would not rise by more than two degrees Celsius above preindustrial levels, and ideally by no more than a degree and a half.[5]

Those recommendations met widespread opposition in many countries. The primary objection was that effective responses to the climate issue demanded revolutionary changes to every aspect of life, including virtually all social and economic arrangements, with an aggressive expansion of government intervention that was quite unacceptable to conservatives. Also, critics of that climate science approach were quick to point to claims of the scale or severity of warming that could be presented as exaggerated or misleading. Only gradually, during the 2010s, did the scientific consensus achieve anything like mainstream status within media coverage and political discourse.[6]

Once that recognition was achieved, the main issue was to decide how much worse matters might become, and how soon. As we have seen, international conferences initially operated on the assumption that a two-degree rise in temperature might be manageable, a number originally proposed during the mid-1970s. But on closer examination, even that seems perilously high. Although the numbers may seem small to nonspecialists, even a difference of a degree or so Celsius can drastically alter an environmental system, as was amply demonstrated during the Little Ice Age. Soon scientists were projecting a possible global temperature rise of four or even five degrees Celsius (seven to nine degrees Fahrenheit) during the twenty-first century, which would be devastating. Some projections for the end of the century are still more terrifying.[7]

Meanwhile, efforts to control emissions lagged badly. Journalist Elizabeth Kolbert points out that just between 2010 and 2020, more CO_2 was emitted than in the whole of human history up to 1963. Put another way, more than half the carbon dioxide in the atmosphere has been put there since Hansen's presentation in 1988. Over the past two centuries, atmospheric levels of carbon dioxide have risen from about 280 parts per million (ppm) to 300 ppm in the early 1950s, and today to almost 420 ppm. A two-degree temperature rise would correspond to a figure of 450 ppm, and 500 would be likely by 2060 at the latest. If those numbers mean little on their own, they also correlate with significant rises in sea levels, and 500 ppm could mean a sea rise of over a hundred feet. Projecting what the planet's land surfaces would be like following such a rise gives a picture of a totally alien world, in which so many familiar cities, regions, and whole nations will largely have vanished.[8]

Possible Futures

Successive reports by the IPCC and other bodies paint an appalling picture of coastal flooding, unprecedented superstorms, droughts, heatwaves, and wildfires, and all on a scale scarcely imaginable in terms of past human experience. Within the United States, a megadrought that has blighted southwestern regions since the start of the century is the second-driest such period since the year 800. Predictions for the middle and long term are grim. Within a decade or two, we could imagine the Arctic Ocean ice free in summers. By midcentury, higher temperatures could mean rising sea levels and spreading deserts, as well as falling supplies of food and drinkable water. The worst effects would strike the global South, across Africa, Asia, and Latin America. By some predictions, perhaps half a billion people live in coastal areas that would potentially become uninhabitable, and they would need to be relocated. As the seas rise, freshwater becomes salinated, and ever larger areas of the world become subject to water stress. Both in seas and in lakes, fishing industries will be severely affected. Even projecting a temperature increase of a degree and a half Celsius would probably double the frequency of extreme El Niños. Changes in rainy seasons compound the effects of higher temperatures on agricultural productivity, which would be further threatened by extreme and unpredictable weather patterns. Facing the loss of fertile lands, we become wearily accustomed to the technical language of aridization, and its most extreme form, desertification. Perhaps 40 percent of the land on which Africans currently grow maize could be lost. If the harm to humans is not enough, animals would suffer horribly from the loss of habitats, and mass extinctions would be certain.[9]

All those visions are of course projections of *possible* futures, and the realities may well fall short of current scenarios, but they are at least firmly rooted in testable evidence. More speculative, but well within the bounds of possibility, are massive collapses in ice sheets in Greenland or the Antarctic, which would cause even higher rises in sea level. Also controversial are apparent changes in the "great conveyor" currents in the Atlantic, which keep northern lands such as the British Isles relatively warm, far more so than other territories on the same latitude, such as Labrador. According to some theories, current climate changes might weaken that current, causing incalculable damage to those coastal lands. In that case, global warming might result in drastic cooling in particular regions. At some points, even words like "cataclysm" become inadequate to describe consequences. Originating in Britain, a militant and disruptive group that campaigns vigorously against climate change has adopted the evocative title Extinction Rebellion. The stakes are indeed very high.[10]

Such analyses commonly invoke the four apocalyptic horsemen we have encountered previously in this book: famine, plague, death, and war. A Western world that had long assumed that plagues and pestilences were extinct on their own territories received a ghastly shock in 2020 with the COVID-19 pandemic, and the prospects for similar events in the future remain high. Past precedent suggests that changes in the habitats of wild creatures would also result in the movement of pests and parasites, resulting in the outbreak of new diseases that would assail animal herds as well as human populations—panzootics as well as pandemics. Many experts fear the emergence of new zoonotic ailments, which spread from animals to humans. All those trends would mean intensified conflict and war and forced mass migrations. As David Wallace-Wells notes, "The vision is a bleak one, often pieced together from perennial eschatological imagery inherited from existing apocalyptic texts like the Book of Revelation, the inescapable sourcebook for Western anxiety about the end of the world." That ancient script is so deeply entrenched in our culture and consciousness.[11]

Salvaging a Future?

Even if the worst visions came to pass, apocalyptic changes would not come overnight, and the effects would be very mixed. Some regions would actively benefit—for instance, from the expansion of navigable sea routes into the Arctic, or the extension of growing seasons in northern lands such as Canada and Siberia. Also, human populations are by no means passive victims of global assaults, and societies cope as best they can, depending on the means they have at their disposal at particular times. The best-situated nations are what are sometimes termed the "WEIRD" societies—Western, educated, industrial, rich, and democratic. Such nations in Europe and North America have long experience in preventing floods through seawalls. When we look at the modern Netherlands, we are seeing a landscape that was largely won from the sea, defended from the sea's return, and used to form the basis of immensely successful agriculture and commerce. A quarter of the Netherlands already lies below sea level as it exists presently. Many adaptations are possible, and urban infrastructures can be radically reimagined. Ever since the first cities in ancient Mesopotamia, civilizations have depended on applying human ingenuity to exploit the environment and to fend off its worst assaults. Human beings are good at dealing with disasters; if they were not, their civilizations would not have lasted as long as they have. As Germaine Greer observed, "Perhaps catastrophe is the natural human environment, and even though we spend a good deal of energy trying to get away from it, we are programmed for survival amid catastrophe."[12]

Even apart from emissions control, it is also possible to imagine near-future societies deploying new technologies to limit or reverse global trends. As the menace of carbon products has become starker, the suggested means of combatting them have proliferated, to include various forms of carbon capture, sequestration, or storage. Once a power plant produces carbon dioxide, for instance, it can be pumped deep underground in a process of sequestration. Ironically, much of the technological expertise developed by the fracking industry over the past quarter century can usefully be applied to such pumping. Some scientists place their hopes in titanic schemes of geoengineering, using tiny reflecting particles to reflect sunlight back into space before it hits the planet and warms it. We could even imagine a kind of giant sunshade in a stable orbit between the Earth and the Moon. All these speculative ideas are controversial (to say the least), and conceivably some or all could have side effects quite as bad as the harms they were designed to fight. But the proposals reinforce the point that humans will not respond to the warming issue with simple resignation. Adaptations are possible.

Poor and Rich

But not all societies have the luxury of this kind of wealth, and others are much more at the mercy of climate change. The societies least able to cope or adapt are in precisely the tropical or global South regions facing sudden and severe temperature increases. In terms of the direct effects on human populations, warming would have its most extensive impact on the tropics, that is, those areas between the latitudes of roughly 23 degrees north of the Equator and 23 degrees south (the Equator itself is 0 degrees, of course). That region includes most of Africa and Southeast Asia, and large portions of India and Latin America. Within a few decades, between 1 and 3 billion people would find themselves in conditions too warm for comfortable survival, outside the ecological niche in which most humans have survived for the past few millennia. By a cruel irony, the countries most likely to face existential dangers are precisely those that have contributed least to emissions and done least to create the larger problem.[13]

The word "tropical" is not presently used much in political analysis, because it has become associated with semi-joking visions of exotic tourism: clothing, hats, and drinks are all sold as tropical. But used according to strict geographical criteria, the word is valuable, and it may be ready for a renaissance, demarcating the harshest effects of the incipient climate crisis. When policymakers forecast the future prospects of particular nations in any context whatever, they need to begin with a basic geographical question: what is its latitude? They need to distinguish carefully between the temperate zones—those areas between the tropics and the polar circles—and the truly tropical. Temperate countries are by no means immune from disasters, especially as such a large proportion of their populations live in coastal regions and port cities. But they still are nothing like as endangered as the tropical nations. Nigeria, for instance, is roughly located between 5 and 14 degrees north of the Equator. Uganda lies between the Equator and 5 degrees north; the Philippines are between 5 and 20 degrees north; Brazil stretches from the Equator to 30 degrees south. As I will suggest, latitude will also be a critical factor in shaping the future of all the world's religions.

People, Fertility, and Faiths

The direct effects of climate change are bad enough in their own right, but to fully understand the likely impact of warming, we have to consider some other trends that have no obvious or direct connection with climate. Demography is critical, in vastly increasing the proportion of the world's population living within those imperiled tropical zones. That context affects the likelihood of conflict, and specifically conflict framed in religious terms.

Fertility is commonly measured by counting the number of children that a typical woman will bear during her lifetime. This total fertility rate, or TFR, is by no means a perfect measure, but it is a good general standard. If that fertility rate is 2.1, then a society will remain demographically stable, neither growing nor shrinking in numbers over time. If the figure is significantly higher—say, 5 or 6—then population will grow rapidly, and the overall population profile will lean towards the younger end of the spectrum. A TFR below 2.1, a sub-replacement figure, produces a declining population, and an older one. Since the mid-twentieth century, sub-replacement fertility has become the norm in much of the world, initially in Europe, subsequently in much of East Asia and Latin America, and more recently in the United States. Very high fertility survives in Africa, in much of the Middle East, and in South Asia. The cumulative effect of those changes is the dramatic increase of African and other high-fertility populations as a relative proportion of the world's people. Africans made up 10 percent of the world's people in 1960 as against 17 percent today and a likely 25 percent by 2050. If we frame this trend in broader terms of planetary geography, then the world's most explosive population growth is heavily concentrated in the tropics, those regions facing the deadliest assaults from warming.[14]

That demographic trend has other implications that are highly relevant to shaping responses to crisis. One involves the age structure of societies, and the very high proportion of teenagers and young adults found in high-fertility societies. That so-called youth bulge is often associated with political and social instability, especially when poor societies find it impossible to find productive employment for so many of their younger citizens arriving annually on the job market. In the worst-case scenario, that demographic imbalance can spark communal violence. Furthermore, high-fertility societies also tend to be more religious in outlook and behavior. To oversimplify a complex story, fertility rates correlate closely to levels of religiosity, and changes in one phenomenon are reflected in the other. The low-fertility societies of Europe include some of the world's least religious societies, while religion remains very strong and socially dominant in the high-fertility nations, overwhelmingly so in Africa and much of the Middle East. However humorous the intent of his remark, novelist John Updike was stating a significant truth when he wrote, "I don't think God plays well in Sweden. God sticks pretty close to the Equator."[15]

The regions that stand to lose most directly and harshly from global warming include the world's most fragile states, those with a high potential for state breakdown or failure and for communal conflict. In demographic terms, these regions are also by far the youngest and fastest-growing. Those swelling billions of people include the populations most deeply immersed in religious thought and practice, of whatever faith tradition, and they are likely to interpret problems or disasters in supernatural terms, or at least to acknowledge a spiritual dimension to such issues.

Looking at the likely prospects for such nations, it is hard not to discern analogies to some of the historical societies we have observed in earlier chapters, notably the European worlds of the later Middle Ages or the early modern period. In particular, we look at periods where climate changes were very long-term, spread over decades or centuries, as in the fourteenth or seventeenth centuries, as opposed to shorter crises such as that of the early 1740s. Obviously we can draw no precise analogies between such very different communities in distinct eras, but we can legitimately point to broad similarities between historical experience and present-day conditions. If the real-world physical consequences of warming can be predicted with fair confidence, what about the possible religious outcomes?

Past, Present, Future

In 2011, a large-scale study by a group of researchers from Columbia University offered startling evidence of the linkage between quite sudden climate change and armed conflict. In particular, they showed a strong correlation between El Niño events and outbreaks of revolution and civil wars within tropical nations. A historically strong El Niño in 1982–1983 contributed to escalating savage and long-lasting violence as far afield as Peru and Sudan. Between the 1970s and 1990s, other El Niños had disastrous impacts on Central America, Central Africa, and Southeast Asia. Some of those struggles, but by no means all, were expressed in terms of religious ideologies and conflicts. Other regions of the world were affected by these natural phenomena, notably Australia, but the country's wealth and the resilience of its state apparatus largely immunized Australians from violence and disorder. Although that particular study focused on El Niño effects, such research suggests the intimate connection between long-term climate change and political violence, and especially points to the main geographical areas that will be worst affected.[16]

The Middle East offers another example of the intimate linkage between climate stress and violence. Between 1998 and 2012, the Levant suffered a drought that was the worst in the region in nine hundred years—at least since the time when the Crusaders first took Jerusalem. The chronology of that situation naturally makes us think of the surging discontent that culminated in the Arab Spring democratization movement of 2011, and the subsequent civil war that largely destroyed the nation of Syria over the following decade. No observer attributed those outcomes to the drought alone in any simplistic sense. But across the region, the water crisis ravaged rural communities, forcing hundreds of thousands off their lands and driving them to seek refuge in cities. Just in the first decade of the century, Syria's urban population grew by 50 percent. Lacking state-supplied facilities for welfare, education, and health care provision, many of those migrants turned to religious institutions, which were commonly of Islamist leanings. Beyond the simple demographics, economic pressure aggravated tensions between communities and faith groups. When open conflict did erupt, it was not explicitly religious in its character. Even so, it transformed long-established religious patterns in the region, putting great stress on the region's minorities.[17]

Let us imagine a world in which such conditions of drought and water stress do not just occur sporadically but become a new normal, and indeed, at a level far worse than anything we have known in recent decades. That would bring some or all of the consequences suggested in the various projections of the near future: drought, plague, famine, and savage confrontations over scarce remaining resources. How would the likely reactions compare with those we have seen in historical contexts? We can imagine an era of mass migrations driven by climate and resulting conflicts, of fleeing—indeed, this is already in evidence. But surely we also are likely to see a revival of intercommunal religious strife and mass persecution.

One near-certain parallel to earlier societies is the quest for the malefactors who are causing the various assaults. In most African societies, witchcraft is a deeply established cultural reality, one that has not vanished with modernization and the growth of cities. In recent decades, witch-hunts and persecutions have been just as likely to erupt in sprawling cities and shantytowns as in villages. Although the phenomenon is less often acknowledged in Asian societies, they too are prone to witch-hunts, especially in the Indian subcontinent and in Indonesia. There is no reason to believe that such paranoia would be any less in a decade or two, particularly if economic circumstances are as badly affected as is commonly believed.[18]

Historical precedent also suggests that threatened societies are extremely fertile in generating conspiracy theories of many and wondrous kinds in order to identify and punish suspected perpetrators, whether those are understood as secular or supernatural. Across Africa, both Muslims and Christians already deploy a rich array of conspiracy theories about the other side, ranging from broad global plots to very specific plans to advance the interests of one faith at the expense of the other. Those conspiracies exist as potential sources of discord, ready to be brought out in full force at times of aggravated tension. In India, similar theorizing is commonplace among extremist Hindu activists, who target the country's very large Muslim minority, which is over 200 million strong. Looking at a map of the worst areas for such tensions offers a sobering message about the exposure of those communities to environmental stresses, present and future. In her book *The Tenth Parallel*, journalist Eliza Griswold portrayed the chief interfaith battlefronts running across Africa and Asia, the fault line that coincides quite neatly with latitude 10 degrees north of the Equator, and well within that tropical region. Within Africa, that line roughly demarcates Christianity and Islam, and that borderland often features in news stories of terrorism and mayhem.[19]

Scapegoating and conspiracy-mongering cause riots, persecutions, pogroms, and local civil wars. On a larger and more systematic scale, communal tensions contribute to the rise of militias, movements, and parties, which become revolutionary challenges to states. Commonly, those groups define themselves in religious terms and justify themselves by attacking not just rival faith communities but also other members of the same faith who are seen as deviant or less committed. Attitudes and actions that would once have been unthinkable gain mass support at a time of hunger, social stress, and political breakdown.

Nigerian Collisions

Some tropical regions, especially in Africa, are uniquely stressed and already perilous. If no part of that continent can be exempted from the long-term threats, some are more imperiled than others. Those areas of greatest concern include some of the continent's wealthiest and most economically significant regions, and at the same time key areas of religious growth, innovation, and rivalry.

The land of Nigeria offers a telling example. Nigeria's present population is about 200 million, a figure that might well grow to over 400 million by 2050, by which point it would be almost as populous as the United States. The country's economic resources are enormous. In 2020, a *Newsweek* cover story offered the startling (and somewhat exaggerated) headline "Black China: Africa's First Superpower Is Coming Sooner Than You Think." In religious terms too, Nigeria is an emerging superpower. The country is evenly matched between religious communities, Muslims and Christians, each of which constitutes around 100 million people. By 2050, each faith might count as many as 200 million believers, placing the country as at once one of the world's largest Christian countries and also among the largest Muslim powers. All sections of society are profoundly religious in outlook and practice, and that faith division is at every stage critical for defining identity. But the dangers and weaknesses that Nigeria faces are daunting, including deep and systematic corruption and acute divisions between those two great faith communities. The confrontation between Muslims and Christians has often produced rioting, religious cleansing, and terrorism. Over the last decade the ferocious Islamist movement Boko Haram has spread its power over much of the country's north, in those regions on or just north of the tenth parallel.[20]

Ecological changes due to warming threaten to intensify all these issues. In the country's north and center, the main peril stems from lack of water and the spread of deserts. Damage to fishing resources and to drinking water endanger the livelihood of many millions. Threats to potable water are all the more serious in societies prone to infectious diseases, and the risk of sweeping new pandemics is high. Normally in such circumstances rural people flee ruined areas to seek some kind of salvation in major cities, which in such crises often witness explosive population growth. In Nigeria, the obvious destination would be Lagos, a city of some 25 million presently (and growing fast), and the heart of the country's economic power. But in this case, any such urban movement would be a dubious proposition. As is common around the world, major cities tend to develop on the seacoast or on major rivers, which makes them peculiarly sensitive to climate change. Lagos itself takes its name from the Portuguese word for "lakes" or "calm water," suggesting its original ecological context. The city is desperately vulnerable to flooding and storm surges, which will become far worse in coming decades, to the point of making the city close to uninhabitable. Not only do such changes undermine any aspirations to become the next China, they raise questions about how long the country can prevent religious-based internal wars and rebellions that could create a failed state on a terrifying scale.[21]

The Sahel

Another area facing acute difficulties in the near future is the Sahel region of northern Africa. This enormous semi-arid belt of land just south of the Sahara Desert runs for over 3,300 miles from the Atlantic Ocean to the Red Sea. The western Sahel includes most or all of the modern nations of Niger, Mali, Mauretania, and Burkina Faso. Together, those four nations cover an area of 1.5 million square miles, almost half the size of the continental United States.

The western Sahel has always possessed a delicate ecological balance, and under the best circumstances it has been the setting for flourishing trading societies and wealthy kingdoms. But in recent years, warming temperatures have become a very present and palpable reality, rather than some distant or theoretical prospect. A historic drought in 2010 caused a harrowing famine, and many millions remain in conditions of food insecurity. Rain patterns have become erratic and unpredictable, and when the rains do come, they have arrived as torrents that flatten crops. By midcentury, temperatures in the region will rise by a bare minimum of 1.6 degrees Celsius, or almost three degrees Fahrenheit, while rainfall would decline by 10 percent. In some nightmare scenarios, temperatures in the western Sahel could rise by a crushing six degrees Celsius, or more than ten degrees Fahrenheit, an increase that would pose grave risks to continued human habitation.[22]

But accounts of ecological change rarely pay enough attention to the effects on the human societies and cultures affected. For one thing, those nations have among the highest fertility rates on the planet, with three of the four having TFRs around 6 (Mauretania's is significantly lower). In consequence, all have grown very rapidly in size in modern times, and will continue to do so. Roughly, the populations are doubling every quarter century or so. In 1980, the four nations combined had a population of 22 million, as against 66 million today, and by some estimates the projected figure for 2050 is 170 million. But even if it was somewhat less than that, the implications are still sobering. That growth involves headlong urbanization. Presently little known to the outside world, the cities of Bamako, Ouagadougou, and Niamey should by 2050 be very sizable urban centers, each with populations of at least several million. That population growth drives demand for food and encourages farmers to expand arable cultivation at the expense of the very large number of pastoralists, whose environmental footprint is usually much lighter. That exacerbates historical rivalries between farmers and herders, with great potential for armed violence. Even without any change in the climate, population growth inevitably stresses local resources, and the environmental threats immeasurably escalate those dangers. Unsurprisingly, given the region's extreme poverty, political structures are very weak.[23]

New Wars of Faith?

These countries are extremely religious in orientation, with very high levels of practice and belief. Islam dominates in the region, claiming the adherence of 99 percent of the people of Niger and Mauretania, and 94 percent of Malians; Burkina Faso, meanwhile, has a sizable Christian minority, of perhaps 30 percent. In recent years, popular rivalries and discontent have usually been channeled into radical Islamist movements, which pose a lethal threat to public security and have effectively removed whole areas from state control. The most successful and visible jihadi groups are violent, confrontational, and rigidly theocratic, with a vigorous apocalyptic strain.[24]

As we have often witnessed in earlier centuries, struggles in one country tend inevitably to spill across frontiers to affect neighboring lands. That might involve one state intervening to take advantage of unrest in a bordering country, or else insurgent movements spreading their ideology farther afield. That process has become vastly easier with modern technological developments and the easy spread of global movements of all kinds. The Islamist militants of the western Sahel are now affiliated with global franchises, either al-Qaeda or the Islamic State. After the Islamic State movement was defeated in the Levant in 2019, its leadership announced that its major efforts would in the future be concentrated in the western Sahel, in a theater of guerrilla struggle that some commentators have ominously termed "Africanistan."[25]

Beyond the obvious perils, that extremism involves a transformational religious revolution within North African Islam, which was traditionally dominated by the Sufi orders and beliefs. Sufi Islam emphasizes the power of charismatic holy figures, whose shrines and tombs attract fervent pilgrimage, and the whole system emphasizes obtaining healing and other benefits through supernatural means. Scholars of religion often draw obvious analogies between that Sufi system and the Catholic Christianity of medieval or early modern Europe, and as in earlier times, the older model confronts a radically different interpretation of the faith. In the European context, parts of the old order survived because they were incorporated into the practice of a reforming Catholic Church operating in close alliance with strong states. Nothing like that situation exists in the world of African Islam, to the point that we must wonder how much longer that traditional world of ritual, shrines, and sanctity can endure. Jihadis target Sufi shrines for demolition and attack communities in a modern version of the iconoclasm that was so marked a feature of sixteenth-century Europe. As climate-induced stresses grow, that Islamic "Reformation" threatens to achieve total victory. Or to use another analogy, those sects are pushing to their natural conclusion the radical arguments made by Ibn Taymiyyah in the desperate years around 1320.[26]

Over the coming decades, these regions face grim prospects. As conflicts emerge, the terror movements will target Christian minorities in Burkina Faso and neighboring nations. Furthermore, conflicts and guerrilla warfare will themselves aggravate economic decline by crippling agriculture and driving people off the lands into the relative safety of cities. As conditions deteriorate, many people from these countries will be forced to move far afield simply to ensure survival for their families. We could easily be looking at tens of millions of migrants.

Africa's Great Lakes

West Africa is only one of many regions that stands directly in harm's way, and it is by no means the only one with a potentially explosive religious brew. Another sensitive area of potential change is the central and eastern portions of Africa, and particularly a group of seven bodies of water known as the Great Lakes. Most celebrated are such continental treasures as Lakes Victoria, Tanganyika, and Nyasa. Some of these drain into the Congo River to the west, and others into the Nile, which runs over 4,000 miles to the Mediterranean. Those water systems are essential for the continued flourishing of some of the world's most populous and most rapidly growing nations. By 2050, a billion Africans will probably be living in just those areas directly dependent on the Nile. Adding the larger Great Lakes region would raise this dependent population by some hundreds of millions more, accounting for around a fifth of the world's people.[27]

As in the Sahel, the Nile Valley and Great Lakes countries are also deeply religious, with the presence of two thriving and fast-expanding world faiths. Taken together, these lands account for a large share of the numerical growth of both Christianity and Islam worldwide over the past century. Christian numbers have surged spectacularly in countries such as Uganda, Kenya, and the Democratic Republic of Congo, just as Muslim populations have swelled in Egypt and Sudan. To varying degrees, all countries in the region have mixed populations of Christians, Muslims, and (sometimes) animists, and most have experienced tensions between majority and minority communities.

In ecological terms, the Nile and Great Lakes regions are very sensitive areas, and explosive population growth makes the situation much worse. At the heart of the story is water. Agriculture is critically dependent on water resources, booming cities need water to drink, and many millions of ordinary people find a livelihood in fishing. Water resources will be profoundly stressed anyway, even before we take account of climate change and temperature rises. Since 2000, Lake Tanganyika has recorded ever-warmer surface temperatures, with grave effects on biodiversity and fish yields. Worst-case scenarios portray this lake and its neighbors as facing terminal crisis by midcentury. Over decades, whole areas could become arid, uninhabitable wastelands, and the deserts are already spreading. The larger region includes some of the world's poorest nations, and poverty and resource conflicts have contributed mightily to religious and ethnic struggles. Environmental issues (including the effects of El Niño) played a toxic role in the Rwandan genocide of the 1990s.[28]

Social or environmental collapse will not come overnight, but it is not hard to contemplate the structural impact of diminishing resources. In multiple nations, we would expect violent tugs-of-war over the remaining fertile lands and water supplies, with intercommunal raiding. Long historical precedent suggests that such apocalyptic transformations will spawn social conflicts, together with the scapegoating and persecutions of unpopular minorities. That is likely to mean the targeting of religious groups such as Egypt's Copts or Kenya's Muslims. Across the region, environmental crisis threatens to provoke calamitous waves of religious wars and persecutions and pogroms. Christians and Muslims alike would suffer appallingly, as religious civil wars leave a pernicious legacy of failed states. Africa's future really is written in water.

Latitudes of Faith

The prospective crises would assuredly not be confined to Africa, nor would the religious consequences. In Latin America, I have mentioned the striking linkage between the effects of the mega El Niño of the early 1980s and the upsurge of civil wars and guerrilla struggles in Central America and especially in the Andes. Peasants already living close to the margin of survival now faced severe drought conditions, water shortages, and crop failures, and many turned to revolutionary activism. Other civilians fled to the cities, further driving uncontrolled urbanization, and that in turn placed intense stress on water resources. Although that particular series of crises passed, droughts have continued to afflict the continent, and future warming would be likely to stir new and more potent conflicts.[29]

Those climate-driven disasters had clear religious outcomes. Some of the insurgent movements, like Peru's Shining Path, had a strongly millenarian and utopian cast, although they phrased their appeal in Marxist terms. But more directly, the disruption of rural societies across the region opened a wide door to the then-new Pentecostal and evangelical churches, which acquired a special foothold in the burgeoning cities. Much of the success of these churches reflected their vital role in supplying essential services to those recent migrants to the cities. The years immediately following the migrations marked a critical turning point in the Pentecostal growth that has been such a salient feature of modern Latin American history. That experience indicates once more the possible religious outcomes of a modern climate crisis, and suggests possible futures.[30]

Asian Crises

Some of the world's most endangered regions lie in Asia, especially in countries most affected by the vagaries of El Niño systems. At urgent risk of catastrophic floods are some of China's most vital commercial hubs, including Guangzhou and other manufacturing cities of the Pearl River Delta, and even Shanghai. Yet China, at least as much as Europe, has the wealth and technological capacity to avert or seriously delay the outright destruction of its population centers. Other nations are far less fortunate. One whole country facing obliteration is Bangladesh, which currently has 165 million people living in a very low-lying terrain. Predominantly Islamic in its faith, Bangladesh has in recent years been troubled by the rise of jihadi extremism, which would grow as the country faced the prospect of inundation. A quarter of Vietnam's 80 million people live on land that could be inundated by 2050, and that includes most of Ho Chi Minh City, the former Saigon.[31]

Other gravely endangered countries include the very populous lands of Indonesia, with 270 million people, and the Philippines, with 110 million. By 2050, the two nations could have a combined population approaching half a billion. Both countries are extremely vulnerable to a convergence of climate hazards. Manila stands high on most lists of the megacities most endangered by the multifaceted consequences of warming, from threats to the supply of power and potable water to ruinous typhoons, superstorms, and floods. The Indonesian national capital, Jakarta, is a city of some 10 million, but the government is so concerned about subsidence and flooding that it is currently proposing to create a whole new capital on a fresh site. Jakarta is already slowly sinking, and its northern part could be wholly submerged by 2050.[32]

In religious terms, the two countries represent a kind of mirror image. Indonesia has by a considerable margin the world's largest Islamic population, although the country has a Christian minority of some 10 percent. The Philippines is overwhelmingly Christian, one of the world's largest Catholic nations. Here too we find a sizable minority, as some 10 percent of the people are Muslim. Both nations have long and bloody histories of interfaith terrorism and violence. Although Indonesian Islam is traditionally tolerant, interfaith relations have broken down during times of severe economic crisis, when Islamic militias and mobs have targeted Christian communities. As in much of Africa, the most visible and uncompromising Islamist sects stand at odds with traditional forms of Islam, which they view with what Christians might characterize as a kind of Reformation zeal. Also as in Africa, it is all but certain that growing environmental threats, with all their predictable consequences, would lead directly to greatly enhanced intergroup tensions and violence.[33]

Christianity and Islam are by no means the only faiths whose great centers of strength face ecological failure. The same is true of Buddhist lands, and a great city like Bangkok—with a metropolitan population of 15 million—is at serious risk of succumbing to flooding within a few decades. Thailand is a profoundly Buddhist society, and in recent years Buddhist nations such as Myanmar and Sri Lanka have spawned violent extremist sects that attack and scapegoat minorities. Developing environmental catastrophes will incite similar movements across the region.

Fleeing

From the point of view of the global North, such conflicts in tropical regions have often been viewed distantly, at best as problems demanding charitable outreach or relief. Western nations could afford to ignore even the most severe African crises, as notoriously occurred during the Rwandan massacres of 1994 and the ensuing cataclysm that killed millions in Congo/Zaire over the following decade. But matters will be very different in our near future because of the role of mass migrations on an unprecedented scale. If and when tropical lands succumb to ruin—when the deserts spread and the cities sink—their former residents will not simply remain in place to die. They will move, in their hundreds of millions.

In our own time, many impoverished Africans have been emboldened to move north to Mediterranean lands and to seek succor in wealthy Europe. Already, the western Sahel occupies center stage in European discussions of their ongoing migrant crisis, both as a source of migration and as the critical transit point for so many people. Many arrive by boat across the Mediterranean, and the resulting loss of human life is fearsome. Over the past decade, the number killed in such crossings has at the worst points reached an annual total as high as 3,000. The situation is even grimmer than the notorious desert borderlands between the United States and Mexico.[34]

Migrants and refugees from those regions will increasingly carry their ideas and beliefs, their visions and dreams, far beyond the region, to Europe and worldwide. Already, population movements have had a very sizable religious impact on the global North, through the spread of Islam across Europe, and at the same time the global diffusion of African patterns of Christian belief and practice. The impact of these trends is all the greater at a time of secularization in all the advanced nations, which serve as hosts to those immigrants. Global South patterns increasingly join the religious mainstream of the North and will eventually dominate it. At the least, newer waves of religious refugees and exiles will continue and accelerate those trends, and we know they will bring their memories of parched ground, failing cities, and dying landscapes. What remains to be seen is just how novel and radical will be the beliefs of those refugees from apocalypse, who import beliefs and ideas forged in the ongoing struggles.

New Visions

We can confidently predict that ecological strains will provoke conflict, and on a scale that threatens the survival of states. But past precedent also suggests that such tumultuous times will also produce other manifestations in the form of new religious movements or revivals within existing faiths.

The degree or scale of any such innovations would of course be related to the extent of the climate's impact in particular societies, with the wealthy (and temperate) world being affected very differently from the increasingly torrid poor regions. At least for some decades to come, societies of the global North will suffer far less immediate effects from warming dangers than will the tropics, and what we might call apocalyptic pressures will be consequently less. Also, state mechanisms there are much better able to cope and respond to dangers. But even in the more developed countries, climate concerns have played a growing role in forming religious agendas. In the past quarter century, such issues have inspired many theologians and ethicists, and emerging green approaches have often looked to the insights and experience of primal and indigenous societies. From the Christian perspective, the most visible expression of theological rethinking came in 2015, when Pope Francis made environmental and climate threats a central theme of his encyclical *Laudato Si*. Such an emphasis was natural given the heavy and ever-growing concentration of Catholic numbers within the tropics, in nations such as Brazil and the Philippines, and in much of Black Africa.[35]

In North America, a new outlook has been evident in many Christian churches, even or especially some of the most politically conservative. The Evangelical Environmental Network was founded as early as 1993, and scientists of Christian faith have been holding workshops and conferences since the start of the century. In 2000 and 2001, bitter debates over US ratification of the Kyoto climate protocol showed just how broad the interfaith coalition was on green issues. In 2006, a large group of Christian thinkers and church leaders, many of distinctly conservative political bent, signed the Evangelical Climate Initiative, and other statements have followed. Climate concerns have been reflected in a sizable outpouring of books and articles in denominational magazines using the language of Christian stewardship, of Creation Care. Jews too have expressed their commitment through groups such as the Jewish Climate Action Network.[36]

Across the spectrum, most such manifestations to date have tended to be at the level of leaders, intellectuals, and bureaucrats rather than grassroots activists, but at that level too, networks have been emerging. What we can scarcely guess at present is how such stirrings might develop as climate shifts have their effects—not just in North America or Europe directly, but through media reports of far worse cataclysms around the world. Creation Care issues will become ever more central to the theologies and the worship of churches and synagogues.

In earlier years, we might well have expected an outpouring of concern to lead to an upsurge in New Age–oriented movements, sects, or even cults dedicated to the protection or worship of the Earth and environment. That would perhaps be associated with a decisive shift to the feminine in its emphasis, perhaps a new stress on Mother Earth. Such an outcome may yet occur in the global North, although new and fringe religious movements have done quite poorly in recent decades and are far smaller and less obvious a part of the cultural mainstream than they were in, say, the 1970s. Matters might change swiftly under the influence of events. A society constantly rent by extreme forest fires or dustbowl conditions, where famous cities are sinking under the waves, offers ample opportunities for preachers and prophets of all shades.[37]

Healing the World

Prospects for religious innovation are much stronger in the global South, in areas that assuredly will face the wrath of Nature at its most unbridled.

Africa itself offers a strong precedent for likely futures. One of the central facts of twentieth-century religious history was the phenomenal growth of Christianity on that continent, from some 10 million adherents in 1900 to 360 million by 2000. In that process, the First World War era was a decisive landmark, not just because of the disruption caused by war itself but, much more centrally, because of the influenza pandemic of 1918, which killed millions on this continent alone. Seeing that European and colonial authorities had no valid response to that situation, Africans listened avidly to prophets or charismatic leaders who offered the prospect of healing. Most of these were Christian, although hewing more closely to native healing traditions than missionary churches might have liked. Many offered their protection against the witches and sorcerers who, when left unchecked, inflicted so much damage on believers and their property. A few of the emerging prophets made messianic claims that discomforted Europeans. Out of that upsurge came many new churches and congregations, which over the past century have repeatedly split and re-formed. But the spiritual descendants of that earlier crisis now number at least in the tens of millions. Many of those adherents have joined the African diaspora around the world, and their churches can today be found across Europe and North America.[38]

Might that experience provide any kind of template for our near future? We can plausibly imagine a world of 2040 (say) in which large sections of the tropics would be suffering from the cumulative disasters and dysfunctions outlined above. Imagine Manila or Lagos or Mumbai under constant threat of annihilation, a world in which ever more deadly pestilences arise with numbing frequency. In such circumstances, we would expect a powerful thirst for religious explanations of the disasters, and a fresh openness to apocalyptic and millenarian preaching. As in 1741, the evidence for God's furious judgment would be plain to see, as would the utter inadequacy of human solutions. So what messages will those humbled sinners be willing to accept?

And There Was No More Sea

The exact form that any such spiritual explosion might take would be conditioned by local circumstances and traditions. Societies with a Christian foundation would respond to certain images and messages, Muslims or Buddhists or Hindus differently. As I have suggested, rigorous and puritanical Islamist sects have exercised their appeal in both Africa and Asia, and that would continue to grow. But Christianity also has some powerful weapons in its own spiritual arsenal, by far the greatest of which is the offer of healing and miracle that is such a mainstay of all thriving churches across the denominational spectrum. Miracle crusades and healing-oriented revivals are a fundamental part of African urban life, and equivalents can readily be found in Asian cities with large Christian populations, in southern India or Southeast Asia. Within Islam, in contrast, it is precisely those newer and puritanical currents that look most harshly on the older Sufi world of charismatic miracle workers and their healing shrines. Besides healing of individual bodies, African Christians enthusiastically engage in ritual acts of blessing and purging, of exorcism and spiritual warfare, which could easily be deployed in circumstances of drought or environmental decline.

The scriptural context is relevant. Both the Quran and the Christian Bible were compiled in ecologically delicate Middle Eastern lands that were thoroughly familiar with problems of drought, famine, plague, and natural disaster. The Quran mentions these sporadically, as tests facing believers or as means of punishing the wicked. But the detailed consciousness of environment and landscape is much more evident in the Bible, especially the Old Testament, and indeed informs much of the text. The Bible regularly frames God's promises in terms of restored and flowing rivers, of landscapes wounded and healed. Old and New Testament alike use storms and wild seas as symbols of the evil natural forces that are miraculously controlled by holy people. Jesus is so powerful, we hear, that even the wind and waves obey him. The foundational myth of Judaism (and Christianity) tells of passing through deadly waters in which God's enemies drown.

I have remarked how precisely texts such as Revelation serve to describe environmental crises and to elevate them to a cosmic dimension. It is almost too easy to compile relevant passages that would interpret worldly disasters in this way, to offer meaning and solace at a time when natural systems are imploding—and, beyond that, to present visions of a millennial or messianic age. In the closing pages of the Christian Bible, the visionary of Revelation promises his hearers a glorious future when "there was no more sea," and that much-wished consummation heralds the coming of New Jerusalem. The time may yet come when believers would so dread the rising seas that they would grasp desperately at promises that those lethal dangers might cease or even vanish altogether. That biblical narrative is also fundamentally concerned with escape and exodus, migration and exile, all the forms of fleeing that will be very familiar to this near-future world. In recent decades, Christian churches and congregations have deployed these scriptural resources to frame and comprehend migrations and to shape practical responses to serving migrating communities. Those efforts will become ever more central in a near future world in chaotic motion.[39]

Just how sweeping any such emerging religious movement might be is beyond any reasonable attempt at prediction. We can be sure that an audience for such messages will exist, and that all manner of prophets and would-be messiahs will seek to win them over. We cannot possibly know what success they will enjoy, or how far the response could be contained within the bounds of known denominations or faiths.

Scholars have often noticed growing trends of secularization and religious decline, initially in Europe, and then increasingly around the world. As global wealth and development have grown and women have become more educated and independent, changes in attitudes toward family and morality have undermined many of the functions traditionally accorded to churches and religious institutions. Societies around the world show ever larger proportions of people who refuse to identify with religious faiths, and outright atheism has become an ever more common intellectual stance. Extrapolating these trends, some credible experts have forecast the end of religion within a century or two, a near-literal death of God.

However well grounded in present realities, such predictions look tenuous in the context of the conditions that much of the world will unquestionably be entering in coming decades. The most vulnerable parts of the planet are already suffused in faith, and those religious beliefs and values can only grow in the face of worldly disaster. At the same time, the residents of those countries represent an ever-growing share of the planet's population. Albeit for the worst and grimmest reasons, religious faith of a distinctly non-modern and non-progressive kind is set to reassert itself worldwide. God is far from dead, and He may yet return with faces that are comforting to his followers, but which outsiders might find stern and even terrifying.

Conclusion

My own interest in the topics of this book dates back a good many years. In fact, it predates the emergence of the modern field of climate history, or the identification of global warming as an incipient menace. In saying that, I am claiming no status as a prodigy, still less a prophet. Rather, in my teenage years, I read a great deal of speculative fiction, science fiction, in which themes of climate change and cataclysm have long percolated, at least since the latter years of the nineteenth century. We can debate how accurate the scientific analyses or predictions were in many of these works—in many cases, the level of accurate knowledge was minimal—but those works had the inordinate advantage of thinking through the human and cultural consequences of catastrophe, commonly speculating about religious dimensions. Obviously, some works succeeded better than others in that regard, but the essential project was critically important. If we are foretelling that the world will be assailed by lethal menaces, then we cannot fail to go on to imagine what the political or cultural consequences would or should be.[1]

In 1965, I devoured J. G. Ballard's then-recent novel *The Drowned World* (1962), which has come to be regarded as a classic of modern British literature. The book imagines a world in 2145 when global temperatures have soared, the glaciers have melted, and what civilization does survive chiefly exists in the Arctic and Antarctic. Once-temperate lands such as Britain have been engulfed by rising seas and have succumbed to tropical conditions. A scientific expedition to a jungle-like London finds a world reverting to something like the age of dinosaurs:

> All the way down the creek, perched in the windows of the office blocks and department stores, the iguanas watched them go past, their hard frozen heads jerking stiffly. . . . Without the reptiles, the lagoons and the creeks of office blocks half-submerged in the immense heat would have had a strange dream-like beauty, but the iguanas and basilisks brought the fantasy down to earth. As their seats in the one-time board-rooms indicated, the reptiles had taken over the city. Once again they were the dominant form of life.

The point of the story is not merely to describe exotic locales, still less to offer mythical battles against monster reptiles, but rather to imagine how human consciousness changes in that radically changed environment: Ballard was the great explorer of inner space. Moral dilemmas abound through his vision. Even if it is feasible, should humans in that future age drain the lagoons at the center of London to explore the sunken buildings? Must they accept the new drowned world? If climate changes reshape the world so thoroughly as to make, in effect, a new kind of humanity, what will those future generations think and feel? How different will they be from us in their basic assumptions? What kind of faith, or faiths, could exist in a drowned world?

In retrospect, *The Drowned World* looks like an amazingly prophetic work, almost a literary representation of the worst nightmares of esteemed scientific groups such as the Intergovernmental Panel on Climate Change. Today, it is commonly cited as a foundation text of a burgeoning genre of novels that explore the consequences of global warming, which over the past decade has come to be known as climate fiction, or cli-fi. But at the time, Ballard's work was part of a larger range of books that contemplated various types of catastrophe, whether inflicted by nuclear weapons, asteroids, or mysterious plagues. Ballard himself wrote other novels about planetary ruin arising from various causes—from a great drought, or still more fantastic menaces. The point was not to analyze the threat, or indeed to single out any particular danger, but to imagine the outcomes for humanity and for human societies.

In such speculations, religion has often played a critical role. The future of post-calamity faith has been imagined in very different guises, both favorable and negative. Some stories envisage new orders of Christian monks rebuilding civilization after a collapse, lantern-bearers through a new dark age. Commonly, writers draw analogies from Europe's history after the fall of Rome, wondering what future generations might fetishize or even worship from the bygone glories of the lost society.

Others portray harsh and irrational sects emerging in reaction to the collapse of the world order: they might be violently puritanical, judgmental, and oppressive, something like the real-life Islamic State of recent memory. Some of these imagined groups of zealots might be homicidal, even cannibalistic. To what extremes might survivors be driven?

However we judge individual contributions, the great value of such efforts is that they recognize how vital religion is likely to be in a disintegrating society as political structures fall and people confront what seems like the uncontrollable fury of nature. But in envisaging such futures, we have another resource beyond the imagination of particular writers, and that is the very substantial record of past times. We know how past societies have responded to extreme climate-related crises, which on occasion seemed so severe as to threaten obliteration. We can trace the range of likely options that those religious forms may take, and we understand the conditions—economic, political, technological—that determine when one historical path is taken rather than another. We can never be sure that our deductions from past experience will guide us to an accurate forecast of future developments, but they are of some value.

By far the greatest reason for exploring the impact of climate change on past societies is to understand those communities themselves, to add an essential and often undervalued element to how we write history. That is true especially in matters of religion, where we can see just how pervasively climate factors have created the kinds of faith that we know so well today. But in constructing that history, we are also doing what we can—however tentatively—to understand our possible futures.

Notes

Chapter 1

1. Jonathan Edwards, *The Works of Jonathan Edwards: Sermons and Discourses, 1739–1742,* ed. Harry S. Stout and Nathan O. Hatch, with Kyle P. Farley (New Haven, CT: Yale University Press, 2003); "Shrieks and cries" is quoted from Wilson H. Kimnach, Caleb J. D. Maskell, and Kenneth P. Minkema, eds., *Jonathan Edwards's Sinners in the Hands of an Angry God: A Casebook* (New Haven, CT: Yale University Press, 2010), 1.
2. Thomas S. Kidd, *The Great Awakening: The Roots of Evangelical Christianity in Colonial America* (New Haven, CT: Yale University Press, 2007).
3. Christof Mauch and Christian Pfister, eds., *Natural Disasters, Cultural Responses* (Lanham, MD: Lexington Books, 2009); John L. Brooke, *Climate Change and the Course of Global History: A Rough Journey* (New York: Cambridge University Press, 2014); Gerrit Jasper Schenk, ed., *Historical Disaster Experiences: Towards a Comparative and Transcultural History of Disasters Across Asia and Europe* (Cham, Switzerland: Springer, 2017); Benjamin Lieberman and Elizabeth Gordon, *Climate Change in Human History: Prehistory to the Present* (New York: Bloomsbury Academic, 2018); Daniel R. Headrick, *Humans Versus Nature: A Global Environmental History* (New York: Oxford University Press, 2020).
4. John L. Brooke, *Climate Change and the Course of Global History* (New York: Cambridge University Press, 2014).
5. Ellsworth Huntington, *Civilization and Climate* (New Haven, CT: Yale University Press, 1915).
6. I discuss these ideas at length in *Crucible of Faith* (New York: Basic Books, 2017).
7. For the concept of punctuated equilibrium in understanding historical change, see Peter Der Manuelian and Thomas Schneider, eds., *Towards a New History for the Egyptian Old Kingdom* (Leiden: Brill, 2015).
8. For the event of 43 BCE, see Katherine Kornei, "Ancient Rome Was Teetering. Then a Volcano Erupted 6,000 Miles Away," *New York Times*, June 22, 2020. "The sun gave forth its light" is from Procopius, *History of the Wars*, IV, xiv (Loeb Classics). For the sixth-century crisis, see William Rosen, *Justinian's Flea: Plague, Empire and the Birth of Europe* (London: Cape, 2007); Michael McCormick et al., "Climate Change During and After the Roman Empire: Reconstructing the Past from Scientific and Historical Evidence," *Journal of Interdisciplinary History* 43.2 (2012): 169–220; Sarah Zielinski, "Sixth-Century Misery Tied to Not One, but Two, Volcanic Eruptions," *Smithsonian Magazine,* July 8, 2015, at https://www.smithsonianmag.com/science-nature/sixth-century-misery-tied-not-one-two-volcanic-eruptions-180955858; Kyle Harper, *The Fate of Rome: Climate, Disease, and the End of an Empire* (Princeton, NJ: Princeton

University Press, 2017); Timothy P. Newfield, "The Climate Downturn of 536–50," in Sam White, Christian Pfister, and Franz Mauelshagen, eds., *The Palgrave Handbook of Climate History* (London: Palgrave, 2018), 447–493; Ulf Büntgen et al., "Cooling and Societal Change During the Late Antique Little Ice Age from 536 to Around 660 AD," *Nature Geoscience* 9 (2016): 231–236. It should be said that the scale of impact of the sixth-century plague in the Near East has been questioned: Lee Mordechai, Merle Eisenberg, Timothy P. Newfield, Adam Izdebski, Janet E. Kay, and Hendrik Poinar, "The Justinianic Plague: An Inconsequential Pandemic?," *Proceedings of the National Academy of Sciences of the United States of America* 116.51 (2019): 25546–25554. For other factors in this era, see Matthew S. Lachniet and Juan Pablo Bernal-Uruchurtu, "AD 550–600 Collapse at Teotihuacan: Testing a Climate Forcing from a 2400-Year Mesoamerican Rainfall Reconstruction," in Harvey Weiss, ed., *Megadrought and Collapse: From Early Agriculture to Angkor* (New York: Oxford University Press, 2017). For the post-1815 crisis, see Chapter 8. Stuart W. Manning and David A. Sewell, "Volcanoes and History," in John Grattan and Robin Torrence, eds., *Natural Disasters and Cultural Change* (London: Routledge, 2003), 264–291.

9. Brian Fagan, *The Little Ice Age: How Climate Made History, 1300–1850* (New York: Basic Books, 2000); Geoffrey Parker, *Global Crisis: War, Climate Change and Catastrophe in the Seventeenth Century* (New Haven, CT: Yale University Press, 2013); Richard Grove and George Adamson, *El Niño in World History* (London: Palgrave Macmillan, 2018); Philipp Blom, *Nature's Mutiny: How the Little Ice Age of the Long Seventeenth Century Transformed the West and Shaped the Present* (New York: W. W. Norton, 2019).
10. Peter Garnsey, *Famine and Food Supply in the Graeco-Roman World: Responses to Risk and Crisis* (New York: Cambridge University Press, 1988); Evan D. G. Fraser and Andrew Rimas, *Empires of Food: Feast, Famine, and the Rise and Fall of Civilizations* (New York: Free Press, 2010).
11. Throughout this book, I will be using John Walter, Roger Schofield, and Andrew B. Appleby, eds., *Famine, Disease and the Social Order in Early Modern Society* (Cambridge: Cambridge University Press, 1989); and Guido Alfani and Cormac Ó Gráda, eds., *Famine in European History* (Cambridge: Cambridge University Press, 2017). See also Cormac Ó Gráda, *Famine: A Short History* (Princeton, NJ: Princeton University Press, 2009).

    Cold alone was not the driver of crisis. Critiquing modern interpretations of "climate shocks," William M. Cavert points out that contemporary discussions of extremely cold conditions of themselves rarely produced fearful or negative reactions from observers. The problem was that such cold was infallibly linked to the other harms described here, including above all famine and disease. See William M. Cavert, "Winter and Discontent in Early Modern England," in Sara Miglietti and John Morgan, eds., *Governing the Environment in the Early Modern World* (New York: Routledge/Taylor & Francis, 2018).
12. Martin Wainwright, "Village Skull Finds Deepen Mystery of Roundheads," *Guardian*, August 25, 2007.
13. William H. McNeill, *Plagues and Peoples* (Garden City, NY: Anchor Press, 1976); J. N. Hays, *The Burdens of Disease: Epidemics and Human Response in Western*

History, revised edition (Piscataway, NJ: Rutgers University Press, 2010); Irwin W. Sherman, *The Power of Plagues*, second edition (Washington, DC: ASM Press, 2017); Anthony McMichael, *Climate Change and the Health of Nations: Famines, Fevers, and the Fate of Populations* (New York: Oxford University Press, 2017); Joshua S. Loomis, *Epidemics: The Impact of Germs and Their Power over Humanity* (Santa Barbara, CA: Praeger, 2018); Frank M. Snowden, *Epidemics and Society: From the Black Death to the Present* (New Haven, CT: Yale University Press, 2019); Elizabeth Kolbert, "Pandemics and the Shape of Human History," *New Yorker,* March 31, 2020, at https://www.newyorker.com/magazine/2020/04/06/pandemics-and-the-shape-of-human-history.

14. Richard Grove and George Adamson, "El Niño Events and the History of Epidemic Disease Incidence," in Richard Grove and George Adamson, *El Niño in World History* (London: Palgrave Macmillan, 2018), 159–178. For the Chinese experience, see Timothy Brook, *The Troubled Empire: China in the Yuan and Ming Dynasties* (Cambridge, MA: Belknap Press of Harvard University Press, 2010); Huidong Tian, Chuan Yan, Lei Xu, Ulf Büntgen, Nils C. Stenseth, and Zhibin Zhang, "Scale-Dependent Climatic Drivers of Human Epidemics in Ancient China," *Proceedings of the National Academy of Sciences of the United States of America* 114.49 (2017): 12970–12975. There is possible evidence of an influenza epidemic as early as 1510, but the undisputed example occurs at the end of the 1550s: J. K. Taubenberger and D. M. Morens, "Pandemic Influenza—Including a Risk Assessment of H5N1," *Revue Scientifique et Technique* 28 (2009): 187–202.
15. John D. Post, *Food Shortage, Climatic Variability, and Epidemic Disease in Pre-industrial Europe: The Mortality Peak in the Early 1740s* (Ithaca, NY: Cornell University Press, 1985); Richard Adler and Elise Mara, *Typhoid Fever: A History* (Jefferson, NC: McFarland, 2016).
16. Clive A. Spinage, *Cattle Plague: A History* (New York: Kluwer/Plenum, 2003); Sam White, "A Model Disaster," in Nukhet Varlik, ed., *Plague and Contagion in the Islamic Mediterranean* (n.p.: Arc Humanities Press, 2017), 57–90. See Chapters 4 and 7 for European panzootics. For the close evolutionary connections between diseases affecting humans and animals, see Timothy P. Newfield, "Human-Bovine Plagues in the Early Middle Ages," *Journal of Interdisciplinary History* 46.1 (2015): 1–38.
17. Hubert H. Lamb, *Historic Storms of the North Sea, British Isles and Northwest Europe* (New York: Cambridge University Press, 1991); Jan Golinski, *British Weather and the Climate of Enlightenment* (Chicago: University of Chicago Press, 2007); David Brennan, "Medieval Witch Hunts Influenced by Climate Change," *Scientific American,* November 3, 2014.
18. Sam White, *The Climate of Rebellion in the Early Modern Ottoman Empire* (New York: Cambridge University Press, 2011).
19. Arnaud Blin, *War and Religion: Europe and the Mediterranean from the First Through the Twenty-first Centuries* (Oakland: University of California Press, 2019).
20. The Adam Smith quotation is much used, but see, for instance, "Adam Smith Would Not Be Optimistic in Today's Economic World," *Daily Telegraph*, September 6, 2009. For the substantial literature on social and environmental collapse, see, for instance,

Jared Diamond, *Collapse: How Societies Choose to Fail or Succeed* (New York: Penguin Books, 2004); Glenn M. Schwartz and John J. Nichols, eds., *After Collapse: The Regeneration of Complex Societies* (Tucson: University of Arizona Press, 2006); Patricia A. McAnany and Norman Yoffee, eds., *Questioning Collapse: Human Resilience, Ecological Vulnerability, and the Aftermath of Empire* (New York: Cambridge University Press, 2009); Jago Cooper and Payson Sheets, eds., *Surviving Sudden Environmental Change: Answers from Archaeology* (Boulder: University of Colorado Press, 2012); Karl W. Butzer and Georgina H. Endfield, eds., "Critical Perspectives on Historical Collapse: Special Feature," *Proceedings of the National Academy of Sciences of the United States of America* 109.10 (2012): 3628–3681; Ronald K. Faulseit, ed., *Beyond Collapse: Archaeological Perspectives on Resilience, Revitalization, and Transformation in Complex Societies* (Carbondale: Southern Illinois University Press, 2015); Guy D. Middleton, *Understanding Collapse: Ancient History and Modern Myths* (New York: Cambridge University Press, 2017); Scott A. J. Johnson, *Why Did Ancient Civilizations Fail?* (New York: Routledge, 2017).

21. The general crisis at the end of the Mediterranean Bronze Age has attracted a large literature. See Eric H. Cline, *1177 B.C.: The Year Civilization Collapsed* (Princeton, NJ: Princeton University Press, 2014); Daniel Kaniewski and Elise Van Campo, "3.2 ka BP Megadrought and the Late Bronze Age Collapse," in Harvey Weiss, ed., *Megadrought and Collapse: From Early Agriculture to Angkor* (New York: Oxford University Press, 2017). From many other ancient examples, see Harvey Weiss, "4.2 ka BP Megadrought and the Akkadian Collapse," in Weiss, ed., *Megadrought and Collapse.*

22. For Maya classic civilization, see Richardson B. Gill, *The Great Maya Droughts: Water, Life, and Death* (Albuquerque: University of New Mexico Press, 2000); David Webster, *The Fall of the Ancient Maya: Solving the Mystery of the Maya Collapse* (London: Thames and Hudson, 2002); Gerald H. Haug et al., "Climate and the Collapse of Maya Civilization," *Science* 299 (March 14, 2003): 1731–1735; Douglas J. Kennett et al., "Development and Disintegration of Maya Political Systems in Response to Climate Change," *Science* 338 (November 9, 2012): 788–791; Douglas J. Kennett and David A. Hodell, "AD 750–1100 Climate Change and Critical Transitions in Classic Maya Sociopolitical Networks," in Weiss, ed., *Megadrought and Collapse.* For the Maya cave evidence, see Will Hunt, *Underground: A Human History of the Worlds Beneath Our Feet* (New York: Random House, 2019). For "disaster scholarship," see Kevin Rozario, *The Culture of Calamity: Disaster and the Making of Modern America* (Chicago: University of Chicago Press, 2007); Christof Mauch and Christian Pfister, eds., *Natural Disasters, Cultural Responses: Case Studies Toward a Global Environmental History* (Lanham, MD: Lexington Books, 2009); Lucy Jones, *The Big Ones: How Natural Disasters Have Shaped Us (and What We Can Do About Them)* (New York: Doubleday, 2018); Cynthia Kierner, *Inventing Disaster: The Culture of Calamity from Jamestown to Johnstown* (Chapel Hill: University of North Carolina Press, 2019).

23. Jonathan Porter, *Imperial China, 1350–1900* (Lanham, MD: Rowman and Littlefield, 2016); Jiang Yonglin, *The Mandate of Heaven and the Great Ming Code* (Seattle: University of Washington Press, 2011).

24. Quoted from Sophocles, *Oedipus Tyrannus*, at http://www.perseus.tufts.edu/hopper/text?doc=Perseus%3Atext%3A1999.01.0192%3Acard%3D14.
25. Philip Jenkins, *Laying Down the Sword* (San Francisco: HarperOne, 2011); Peter J. Thuesen, *Tornado God: American Religion and Violent Weather* (New York: Oxford University Press, 2020). During the severe climate crisis of the late 1670s, Puritan minister John Flavel offered an extensive exposition of the whole providential world view in his *Divine Conduct, Or, The Mysterie of Providence Wherein the Being and Efficacy of Providence Is Asserted and Vindicated* (London, 1678).
26. Robert Warren Anderson, Noel D. Johnson, and Mark Koyama, "Jewish Persecutions and Weather Shocks: 1100–1800," *Economic Journal* 127 (2017): 924–958. For the close relationship between climate change and armed conflict, see Murat Iyigun, Nathan Nunn, and Nancy Qian, *Winter Is Coming: The Long-Run Effects of Climate Change on Conflict, 1400–1900* (Bonn, Germany: Institute of Labor Economics, 2017).
27. See, for instance, Carlo Cipolla, *Faith, Reason, and the Plague* (New York: W. W. Norton, 1981).
28. Daniel Defoe, *History of the Plague in London, 1665: To Which Is Added the Great Fire of London, 1666* (London: G. Bell and Sons, 1908), 255–256.
29. Psalm 148:8. Increase Mather, *The Voice of God, in Stormy Winds. Considered, in Two Sermons, Occasioned by the Dreadful and Unparallel'd Storm, in the European Nations* (Boston: Printed by T. Green for Nicholas Buttolph, 1704).
30. For the emergence of apocalyptic, see Jenkins, *Crucible of Faith*; Robert E. Bjork, ed., *Catastrophes and the Apocalyptic in the Middle Ages and Renaissance* (Turnhout: Brepols, 2019); Colin McAllister, *The Cambridge Companion to Apocalyptic Literature* (Cambridge: Cambridge University Press, 2020).
31. Bernard McGinn, *Visions of the End: Apocalyptic Traditions in the Middle Ages*, new edition (New York: Columbia University Press, 1998); Jennifer Spinks and Charles Zika, eds., *Disaster, Death, and the Emotions in the Shadow of the Apocalypse, 1400–1700* (London: Palgrave Macmillan, 2016).
32. Rodney Stark, *The Rise of Christianity* (Princeton, NJ: Princeton University Press, 1996); Kyle Harper, *The Fate of Rome: Climate, Disease, and the End of an Empire* (Princeton, NJ: Princeton University Press, 2017).
33. Alex Ross, "The Past and the Future of the Earth's Oldest Trees," *New Yorker*, January 13, 2020, at https://www.newyorker.com/magazine/2020/01/20/the-past-and-the-future-of-the-earths-oldest-trees; Jie Fei, Jie Zhou and Yongjian Hou, "Circa A.D. 626 Volcanic Eruption, Climatic Cooling, and the Collapse of the Eastern Turkic Empire," *Climatic Change* 81 (2007): 469–475; A. Shapur Shahbazi, "Sasanian Dynasty," *Encyclopedia Iranica*, 2005, http://www.iranicaonline.org/articles/sasanian-dynasty; Philip Jenkins, *Jesus Wars* (San Francisco: HarperOne, 2010).
34. Harper, *The Fate of Rome.*
35. Parker, *Global Crisis.*
36. Gerald Harriss, *Shaping the Nation: England, 1360–1461* (Oxford: Oxford University Press, 2005); Chantal Camenisch et al., "The 1430s: A Cold Period of Extraordinary Internal Climate Variability During the Early Spörer Minimum with Social and Economic Impacts in North-Western and Central Europe," *Climate of the Past* 12

(2016): 2107–2126; Axel Bojanowski, "Klimakatastrophe im Mittelalter Europas härtestes Jahrzehnt," *Spiegel*, December 28, 2016.

For the 1465 event, see Martin Bauch, "The Day the Sun Turned Blue: A Volcanic Eruption in the Early 1460s and Its Possible Climatic Impact—A Natural Disaster Perceived Globally in the Late Middle Ages?," in Gerrit Jasper Schenk, ed., *Historical Disaster Experiences: Towards a Comparative and Transcultural History of Disasters Across Asia and Europe* (Cham, Switzerland: Springer, 2017), 107–138.

For extreme conditions in the Americas in that period, see John S. Cable, *Megadrought in the Carolinas* (Tuscaloosa: University of Alabama Press, 2020).

37. Walter, Schofield, and Appleby, eds., *Famine, Disease and the Social Order in Early Modern Society*.
38. Emmanuel Le Roy Ladurie, *Histoire du climat depuis l'an Mil* (Paris: Flammarion, 1967); and also *Histoire humaine et comparée du climat,* 3 vols. (Paris: Fayard, 2004–2009); Emmanuel Le Roy Ladurie, "The Birth of Climate History," in Claus Leggewie and Franz Mauelshagen, eds., *Climate Change and Cultural Transition in Europe* (Leiden: Brill, 2018), 197–216. For Hubert H. Lamb, see his *Climate: Present, Past and Future,* Volume 2: *Climatic History and the Future* (London: Methuen, 1977); *Weather, Climate and Human Affairs* (London: Routledge, 1988); *Climate, History and the Modern World* (New York: Routledge, 1995); and *The Changing Climate* (New York: Routledge, 2011). Also, "History of the Climatic Research Unit," http://www.cru.uea.ac.uk/web/cru/about-cru/history. See also Robert Rotberg and Theodore Rabb, eds., *Climate and History: Studies in Interdisciplinary History* (Princeton, NJ: Princeton University Press, 1981); H. Flohn and R. Fantechi, *The Climate of Europe: Past, Present and Future* (Dordrecht: Reidel, 1984); Christian Pfister, *Das Klima der Schweiz von 1525–1860 und seine Bedeutung in der Geschichte von Bevölkerung und Landwirtschaft* (Bern, Switzerland: Haupt, 1984); Peter Brimblecombe and Christian Pfister, eds., *The Silent Countdown: Essays in European Environmental History* (Berlin: Springer-Verlag, 1990); Rudolf Brazdil and Oldrich Kotyza, *History of Weather and Climate in the Czech Lands* (Zurich: Geographisches Institut, Eidgenössische Technische Hochschule, 1995); Christian Pfister, *Wetternachhersage. 500 Jahre Klimavariationen und Naturkatastrophen (1496–1995)* (Bern, Switzerland: Haupt, 1999); P. D. Jones, A. E. J. Ogilvie, T. D. Davies, and K. R. Briffas, *History and Climate: Memories of the Future* (New York: Springer, 2001); József Laszlovszky and Péter Szabó, eds., *People and Nature in Historical Perspective* (Budapest: Central European University, Dept. of Medieval Studies and Archaeolingua, 2003); Neville Brown, *History and Climate Change: A Eurocentric Perspective* (New York: Routledge, 2005); Rüdiger Glaser, *Klimageschichte Mitteleuropas: 1200 Jahre Wetter, Klima, Katastrophen,* second edition (Darmstadt: Primus-Verlag, 2008); Sam White, Christian Pfister, and Franz Mauelshagen, eds., *The Palgrave Handbook of Climate History* (London: Palgrave, 2018).
39. Geoffrey Parker, *Global Crisis*; Kyle Harper, *The Fate of Rome*; Blom, *Nature's Mutiny*. From many other recent examples, see Ted Steinberg, *Down to Earth: Nature's Role in American History,* third edition (New York: Oxford University Press, 2013); Ronald D. Gerste, *Wie das Wetter Geschichte macht: Katastrophen und Klimawandel von der*

Antike bis heute, second edition (Stuttgart: Klett-Cotta, 2015); Anya Zilberstein, *A Temperate Empire: Making Climate Change in Early America* (New York: Oxford University Press, 2016); Luis Alberto Arrioja Díaz and Armando Alberola Romá, eds., *Clima, Desastres y Convulsiones sociales en España e Hispanoamérica, siglos XVII–XX* (Zamora, Mexico: El Colegio de Michoacán, 2016); Sam White, *A Cold Welcome: The Little Ice Age and Europe's Encounter with North America* (Cambridge, MA: Harvard University Press, 2017); Dagomar Degroot, *The Frigid Golden Age: Climate Change, The Little Ice Age, and the Dutch Republic, 1560–1720* (Cambridge: Cambridge University Press, 2018).

Brian Fagan's books include *Floods, Famines, and Emperors: El Niño and the Fate of Civilizations* (New York: Basic Books, 1999); *The Little Ice Age: How Climate Made History, 1300–1850* (New York: Basic Books, 2000); *The Long Summer: How Climate Changed Civilization* (New York: Basic Books, 2003); *The Great Warming: Climate Change and the Rise and Fall of Civilization* (New York: Bloomsbury Press, 2008).

40. J. Donald Hughes, *An Environmental History of the World* (New York: Routledge, 2001); Clive Ponting, *A New Green History of the World: The Environment and the Collapse of Great Civilizations*, revised edition (New York: Penguin Books, 2007); Edmund Burke III and Kenneth Pomeranz, eds., *The Environment and World History* (Berkeley: University of California Press, 2009); Wolfgang Behringer, *A Cultural History of Climate* (Malden, MA: Polity Press, 2010); Anthony N. Penna, *The Human Footprint: A Global Environmental History*, second edition (Malden, MA: Wiley Blackwell, 2015).

Chapter 2

1. John Evelen, *The Diaries of John Evelyn* (London: M. Walter Dunne, 1901), 2:192; Philip Eden, *Great British Weather Disasters* (London: Continuum, 2008); For Einsiedeln, see Bradley S. Klapper, "Ancient Weather Records Provide Clues to the Present and Future," *Los Angeles Times*, September 16, 2007.
2. John L. Brooke, *Climate Change and the Course of Global History: A Rough Journey* (New York: Cambridge University Press, 2014); Colin P. Summerhayes, *Earth's Climate Evolution* (Hoboken, NJ: Wiley Blackwell, 2015); Benjamin Lieberman and Elizabeth Gordon, *Climate Change in Human History: Prehistory to the Present* (New York: Bloomsbury Academic, 2018).
3. Hubert H. Lamb, "The Early Medieval Warm Epoch and Its Sequel," *Palaeogeography, Palaeoclimatology, Palaeoecology* 1 (1965): 13–37.
4. Dagomar Degroot, "Climate Change and Society in the 15th to 18th Centuries," *WIREs Climate Change* 9.4 (2017), https://onlinelibrary.wiley.com/doi/full/10.1002/wcc.518.
5. See especially Chapter 6 for the precise terminal dates of the "seventeenth-century crisis."
6. See, for instance, Gavin Schmidt, "Medieval Warmth and English Wine," *Real Climate* (blog), July 12, 2006, http://www.realclimate.org/index.php/archives/2006/07/medieval- warmth-and-english-wine.

7. For challenges to the standard climate science model, see Willie Wei-Hock Soon and Steven H. Yaskell, *The Maunder Minimum and the Variable Sun-Earth Connection* (River Edge, NJ: World Scientific, 2003); Marc Morano, *The Politically Incorrect Guide to Climate Change* (Washington, DC: Regnery, 2018). For Climategate, see James Lawrence Powell, *The Inquisition of Climate Science* (New York: Columbia University Press, 2011).
8. Hans Renssen, "The Role of Forcing and Internal Dynamics in Explaining the 'Medieval Climate Anomaly,'" *Climate Dynamics* 39.12 (2012): 2847–2866.
9. Michael E. Mann, *The Hockey Stick and the Climate Wars* (New York: Columbia University Press, 2012).
10. For challenges to the concept of the Little Ice Age, see, for instance, Morgan Kelly and Cormac Ó Gráda, "The Myth of Europe's Little Ice Age," Vox EU, March 28, 2015, at https://voxeu.org/article/myth-europe-s-little-ice-age; Kevin Krajick, "The Climate Epochs That Weren't," Earth Institute, Columbia University, July 24, 2019, at https://blogs.ei.columbia.edu/2019/07/24/climate-epochs-that-werent; Raphael Neukom, Nathan Steiger, Juan José Gómez-Navarro, Jianghao Wang, and Johannes P. Werner, "No Evidence for Globally Coherent Warm and Cold Periods over the Preindustrial Common Era," *Nature* 571 (2019): 550–554; S. Lüning, L. Schulte, S. Garcés-Pastor, I. B. Danladi, and M. Gałka, "The Medieval Climate Anomaly in the Mediterranean Region," *Paleoceanography and Paleoclimatology* 34.10 (2019): 1625–1649; Brian Handwerk, "Modern Climate Change Is the Only Worldwide Warming Event of the Past 2,000 Years," *Smithsonian Magazine*, July 24, 2019, at https://www.smithsonianmag.com/science-nature/modern-climate-change-only-worldwide-warming-event-past-2000-years-180972719.
11. Alf Hornborg and Carole L. Crumley, eds., *The World System and the Earth System: Global Socioenvironmental Change and Sustainability Since the Neolithic* (New York: Routledge, 2006).
12. Drew T. Shindell, Gavin A. Schmidt, Ron L. Miller, and Michael E. Mann, "Volcanic and Solar Forcing of Climate Change During the Preindustrial Era," *Journal of Climate* 16.24 (2003): 4094–4107; Friedhelm Steinhilber and Jürg Beer, "Solar Activity—The Past 1200 Years," *PAGES News* 19.1 (2011): 5–6; Arnab Rai Choudhuri, *Nature's Third Cycle: A Story of Sunspots* (Oxford: Oxford University Press, 2015); M. G. Ogurtsov, "The Spörer Minimum Was Deep," *Advances in Space Research* 64.5 (2019): 1112–1116.
13. Marie-Antoinette Melieres and Chloe Marechal, *Climate Change: Past, Present, and Future* (Chichester, UK: John Wiley and Sons, 2015).
14. Jelle Zeilinga de Boer and Donald Theodore Sanders, *Volcanoes in Human History: The Far-Reaching Effects of Major Eruptions* (Princeton, NJ: Princeton University Press, 2001); Clive Oppenheimer, *Eruptions That Shook the World* (Cambridge: Cambridge University Press, 2011).
15. Oregon State University offers good online resources on the study of volcanoes. See, for instance, "Largest Eruptions Since 1400 AD," http://volcano.oregonstate.edu/book/export/html/227. The Paektu volcano is also known as Changbai or Báitóushān. Precise dates offered for the Paektu event vary by some decades. Gina L. Barnes and Tsutoma

Soda, eds., *TephroArchaeology in the North Pacific* (Summertown, UK: Archaeopress, 2019); Donald R. Prothero, *When Humans Nearly Vanished: The Catastrophic Explosion of the Toba Volcano* (Washington, DC: Smithsonian Books, 2018).

16. Martin Bauch, "The Day the Sun Turned Blue: A Volcanic Eruption in the Early 1460s and Its Possible Climatic Impact—A Natural Disaster Perceived Globally in the Late Middle Ages?," in Gerrit Jasper Schenk, ed., *Historical Disaster Experiences: Towards a Comparative and Transcultural History of Disasters Across Asia and Europe* (Cham, Switzerland: Springer, 2017), 107–138; Zaria Gorvett, "The Massive Volcano That Scientists Can't Find," BBC, July 3, 2017, at https://www.bbc.com/future/article/20170630-the-massive-volcano-that-scientists-cant-find; A. Guevara-Murua, C. A. Williams, E. J. Hendy, A. C. Rust, and K. V. Cashman, "Observations of a Stratospheric Aerosol Veil from a Tropical Volcanic Eruption in December 1808: Is This the Unknown ~1809 Eruption?," *Climate of the Past* 10.5 (2014): 1707–1722. That large eruptions occurred in the 1450s and 1460s is quite certain, but their exact dating and sequence are controversial. See Jihong Cole-Dai et al., "Two Likely Stratospheric Volcanic Eruptions in the 1450s C.E. Found in a Bipolar, Subannually Dated 800-Year Ice Core Record," *Journal of Geophysical Research* 118 (2013): 7459–7466.
17. Bruce M. S. Campbell, "Global Climates, the 1257 Mega-Eruption of Samalas Volcano, Indonesia, and the English Food Crisis of 1258," *Transactions of the Royal Historical Society* 27 (2017): 87–121.
18. Sébastien Guillet et al., "Climatic and Societal Impacts of a 'Forgotten' Cluster of Volcanic Eruptions in 1108–1110 CE," *Scientific Reports* 10 (2020); Cormac Ó Gráda, *Famine: A Short History* (Princeton, NJ: Princeton University Press, 2009).
19. See Chapter 5 for the impact of these eruptions.
20. Richard Grove and George Adamson, *El Niño in World History* (London: Palgrave Macmillan, 2018); Brian Fagan, *Floods, Famines, and Emperors: El Niño and the Fate of Civilizations* (New York: Basic Books, 1999).
21. Grove and Adamson, *El Niño in World History*; Patrick D. Nunn, *Climate, Environment and Society in the Pacific During the Last Millennium* (Amsterdam: Elsevier, 2007).
22. Lisa Cox, "Indian Ocean System That Drives Extreme Weather in Australia Likely to Worsen with Global Heating," *Guardian*, March 9, 2020.
23. Grove and Adamson, *El Niño in World History*; Harvey Weiss, ed., *Megadrought and Collapse: From Early Agriculture to Angkor* (New York: Oxford University Press, 2017).
24. For "the Earth's largest and most important climate phenomenon," see Brendan M. Buckley et al., "Monsoon Extremes and Society over the Past Millennium on Mainland Southeast Asia," *Quaternary Science Reviews* 95.1 (2014): 1–19.
25. Geoffrey Parker, *Global Crisis: War, Climate Change and Catastrophe in the Seventeenth Century* (New Haven, CT: Yale University Press, 2013), 10–17.
26. Bill McGuire, *Waking the Giant: How a Changing Climate Triggers Earthquakes, Tsunamis, and Volcanoes* (New York: Oxford University Press, 2011); Alan Buis, "Can Climate Affect Earthquakes, or Are the Connections Shaky?," NASA, October 29, 2019, at https://climate.nasa.gov/news/2926/can-climate-affect-earthquakes-or-are-the-connections-shaky; Jelle Zeilinga de Boer and Donald Theodore Sanders,

Earthquakes in Human History: The Far-Reaching Effects of Seismic Disruptions (Princeton, NJ: Princeton University Press, 2004).

27. William W. Hay, *Experimenting on a Small Planet*, second edition (Cham, Switzerland: Springer, 2016); H. Guðlaugsdóttir et al., "The Influence of Volcanic Eruptions on Weather Regimes over the North Atlantic Simulated by ECHAM5/MPI-OM Ensemble Runs from 800 to 2000 CE," *Atmospheric Research* 213 (2018): 211–223.
28. Sean D. Birkel, Paul A. Mayewski, Kirk A. Maasch, Andrei V. Kurbatov, and Bradfield Lyon, "Evidence for a Volcanic Underpinning of the Atlantic Multidecadal Oscillation," *Climate and Atmospheric Science* 1 (2018), at https://www.nature.com/articles/s41612-018-0036-6.
29. Rosanne D'Arrigo et al., "The Anomalous Winter of 1783–1784: Was the Laki Eruption or an Analog of the 2009–2010 Winter to Blame?," *Geophysical Research Letters* 38.5 (2011).
30. Michael E Mann, "Little Ice Age," in Michael C. MacCracken and John S. Perry, eds., *Encyclopedia of Global Environmental Change* (Chichester, UK: John Wiley and Sons, 2002), I:504–509; Valérie Trouet et al., "Persistent Positive North Atlantic Oscillation Mode Dominated the Medieval Climate Anomaly," *Science* 324 (2009): 74–80; James Scourse, Valerie Trouet, and Christoph Raible, "The Medieval Climate Anomaly and the Little Ice Age: Testing the NAO Hypothesis," paper presented at EGU General Assembly 2010, Vienna, Austria, 2010, p. 9179; Elena A. Ilyashuk et al., "The Little Ice Age Signature in a 700-Year High-Resolution Chironomid Record of Summer Temperatures in the Central Eastern Alps," *Climate Dynamics* 52 (2019): 6953–6967.
31. I will discuss these themes in Chapter 9.

Chapter 3

1. Lindy Grant, *Abbot Suger of St. Denis: Church and State in Early Twelfth-Century France* (New York: Routledge, 1998).
2. Throughout this chapter, I am using Miri Rubin and Walter P. Simons, eds., *Cambridge History of Christianity: Christianity in Western Europe, c. 1000–c. 1500* (Cambridge: Cambridge University Press, 2009); John H. Arnold, ed., *The Oxford Handbook of Medieval Christianity* (Oxford: Oxford University Press, 2014); Kevin Madigan, *Medieval Christianity* (New Haven, CT: Yale University Press, 2015); Chris Wickham, *Medieval Europe* (New Haven, CT: Yale University Press, 2016); R. N. Swanson, *The Twelfth-Century Renaissance* (Manchester: Manchester University Press, 1999).
3. Malcolm K. Hughes and Henry F. Diaz, eds., *The Medieval Warm Period* (Dordrecht: Springer, 1994); John Aberth, *An Environmental History of the Middle Ages: The Crucible of Nature* (New York: Routledge, 2012); John L. Brooke, *Climate Change and the Course of Global History: A Rough Journey* (New York: Cambridge University Press, 2014).
4. H. Goosse et al., "The Origin of the European Medieval Warm Period," *Climate of the Past* 2 (2006): 99–113; Brian Fagan, *The Great Warming: Climate Change and the*

Rise and Fall of Civilization (New York: Bloomsbury, 2008); Nora Schultz, "Natural Mechanism for Medieval Warming Discovered," *New Scientist*, April 2, 2009; Christian Rohr, Chantal Camenisch, and Kathleen Pribyl, "European Middle Ages," in Sam White, Christian Pfister, and Franz Mauelshagen, eds., *The Palgrave Handbook of Climate History* (London: Palgrave, 2018), 247–263.

5. Josiah C. Russell, *Medieval Demography* (New York: AMS Press, 1987); William Chester Jordan, *Europe in the High Middle Ages* (New York: Viking, 2003).
6. Guido Alfani and Cormac Ó Gráda, eds., *Famine in European History* (Cambridge: Cambridge University Press, 2017).
7. R. I. Moore, *The Formation of a Persecuting Society: Power and Deviance in Western Europe, 950–1250* (Oxford: Blackwell, 1987); Timothy S. Miller and John W. Nesbitt, *Walking Corpses: Leprosy in Byzantium and the Medieval West* (Ithaca, NY: Cornell University Press, 2014); Elma Brenner, "Leprosy and Identity in the Middle Ages," in Mark Jackson, ed., *The Routledge History of Disease* (London: Routledge, 2016).
8. Peter Frankopan, *The Silk Roads* (New York: Alfred A. Knopf, 2016); Alfred W. Crosby, *Ecological Imperialism: The Biological Expansion of Europe, 900–1900* (New York: Cambridge University Press, 1986); Liang Emlyn Yang, Hans-Rudolf Bork, Xiuqi Fang and Steffen Mischke, eds., *Socio-Environmental Dynamics along the Historical Silk Road* (Cham, Switzerland: Springer, 2019).
9. Paul Bairoch, *The Population of European Cities from 800 to 1850* (Geneva: Université de Genève, 1988).
10. Edward Miller, Cynthia Postan, and M. M. Postan, eds., *The Cambridge Economic History of Europe from the Decline of the Roman Empire*, volume 2 (Cambridge: Cambridge University Press, 1987).
11. Christopher Tyerman, *Fighting for Christendom: Holy War and the Crusades* (New York: Oxford University Press, 2004).
12. Jordan, *Europe in the High Middle Ages;* David Crouch, *The Chivalric Turn: Conduct and Hegemony in Europe Before 1300* (New York: Oxford University Press, 2019).
13. Ronald B. Begley and Joseph W. Koterski, *Medieval Education* (New York: Fordham University Press, 2009).
14. Nicola Coldstream, *Medieval Architecture* (Oxford: Oxford University Press, 2002).
15. Alain Erlande-Brandenburg, *The Cathedral: The Social and Architectural Dynamics of Construction* (New York: Cambridge University Press, 1994).
16. Quoted in Peter Simpson, *England in the Middle Ages: The Normans 1066–1154* (Xlibris, 2019).
17. Frances Gies and Joseph Gies, *Cathedral, Forge, and Waterwheel: Technology and Invention in the Middle Ages* (New York: HarperCollins, 1994); Henrietta Leyser, *Hermits and the New Monasticism: A Study of Religious Communities in Western Europe, 1000–1150* (New York: St. Martin's Press, 1984); Alison I. Beach and Isabelle Cochelin, eds., *The Cambridge History of Medieval Monasticism in the Latin West* (Cambridge: Cambridge University Press, 2020). For the military orders, see Jonathan Riley-Smith, *The Crusades*, third edition (London: Bloomsbury Academic, 2014).
18. Emilia Jamroziak, *The Cistercian Order in Medieval Europe, 1090–1500* (New York: Routledge, 2013).

19. Bradley R. Franco and Beth A. Mulvaney, eds., *The World of St. Francis of Assisi* (Leiden: Brill, 2015).
20. H. E. J. Cowdrey, *Popes and Church Reform in the 11th Century* (Burlington, VT: Ashgate, 2000); Constance Hoffman Berman, ed., *Medieval Religion: New Approaches* (London: Routledge, 2005); Thomas F. X. Noble and Julia M. H. Smith, eds., *Cambridge History of Christianity: Early Medieval Christianity, c. 600–c. 1100* (Cambridge: Cambridge University Press, 2008); Sandra Visser and Thomas Williams, *Anselm* (New York: Oxford University Press, 2009); Horst Fuhrmann, *Papst Gregor VII. und das Zeitalter der Reform* (Wiesbaden: Harrassowitz Verlag, 2016).
21. Wilfried Hartmann and Kenneth Pennington, eds., *The History of Medieval Canon Law in the Classical Period, 1140–1234: From Gratian to the Decretals of Pope Gregory IX* (Washington, DC: Catholic University of America Press, 2008).
22. James M. Powell, *Innocent III: Vicar of Christ or Lord of the World?*, second edition (Washington, DC: Catholic University of America Press, 1994).
23. R. N. Swanson, ed., *The Church and Mary* (Woodbridge, UK: Boydell Press, 2004); Miri Rubin, *Mother of God: A History of the Virgin Mary* (New Haven, CT: Yale University Press, 2009).
24. Malcolm Lambert, *Medieval Heresy: Popular Movements from Bogomil to Hus* (New York: Holmes and Meier, 1976); R. I. Moore, *The Formation of a Persecuting Society: Power and Deviance in Western Europe, 950–1250* (New York: Blackwell, 1987); Peter Biller and Anne Hudson, eds., *Heresy and Literacy, 1000–1530* (Cambridge: Cambridge University Press, 1996); Malcolm Barber, *The Cathars: Dualist Heretics in Languedoc in the High Middle Ages* (New York: Longman, 2000); Michael Frassetto, ed., *Heresy and the Persecuting Society in the Middle Ages: Essays on the Work of R. I. Moore* (Leiden: Brill, 2006); Louisa A. Burnham, *Medieval Heresy: The Church's Struggle for Orthodoxy and Survival* (London: I. B. Tauris, 2008); Philip Jenkins, *The Many Faces of Christ* (New York: Basic Books, 2015); John H. Arnold and Peter Biller, *Heresy and Inquisition in France, 1200–1300* (Manchester, UK: Manchester University Press, 2016).
25. Mark Gregory Pegg, *A Most Holy War: The Albigensian Crusade and the Battle for Christendom* (New York: Oxford University Press, 2008).
26. Amira K. Bennison, *The Great Caliphs: The Golden Age of the 'Abbasid Empire* (New Haven, CT: Yale University Press, 2009).
27. Roni Ellenblum, *The Collapse of the Eastern Mediterranean: Climate Change and the Decline of the East, 950–1072* (New York: Cambridge University Press, 2012); Sarah Kate Raphael, *Climate and Political Climate: Environmental Disasters in the Medieval Levant* (Leiden: Brill, 2013).
28. Henri Stierlin, *Islam: From Baghdad to Cordoba* (Hong Kong: Taschen, 2009); Brian A. Catlos, *Kingdoms of Faith: A New History of Islamic Spain* (London: Hurst, 2018).
29. Peter Adamson and Matteo Di Giovanni, eds., *Interpreting Averroes* (New York: Cambridge University Press, 2019).
30. Catlos, *Kingdoms of Faith*.
31. Bryan Walsh, "How Climate Change Drove the Rise of Genghis Khan," *Time*, March 10, 2014, at https://time.com/18147/climate-change-genghis-khan-mongolia.

32. Eugene N. Anderson, *The East Asian World-System: Climate and Dynastic Change* (Cham, Switzerland: Springer, 2019); Qing Yan, Zhongshi Zhang, Huijun Wang, and Dabang Jiang, "Simulated Warm Periods of Climate over China During the Last Two Millennia: The Sui-Tang Warm Period Versus The Song-Yuan Warm Period," *Journal of Geophysical Research* (2015), at https://agupubs.onlinelibrary.wiley.com/doi/full/10.1002/2014JD022941; Stephen Chen, "Mother Nature vs. the Mongol Hordes: Did Climate Change Keep Genghis Khan at Bay and the Southern Song Dynasty in Power?," SCMP, November 5, 2015, at https://www.scmp.com/tech/science-research/article/1875612/mother-nature-vs-mongol-hordes-did-climate-change-keep-genghis.
33. Victor Cunrui Xiong and Kenneth J. Hammond, eds., *Routledge Handbook of Imperial Chinese History* (New York: Routledge, 2019). Of course, even the long centuries of the Song dynasty had their disasters and blunders. See Ling Zhang, *The River, the Plain, and the State: An Environmental Drama in Northern Song China, 1048–1128* (Cambridge: Cambridge University Press, 2015).
34. Sem Vermeersch, *The Power of the Buddhas: The Politics of Buddhism During the Koryŏ Dynasty (918–1392)* (Cambridge, MA: Harvard University Press, 2008); Mario Poceski, ed., *The Wiley Blackwell Companion to East and Inner Asian Buddhism* (Malden, MA: Wiley Blackwell, 2014); Michael J. Seth, *A Concise History of Korea: From Antiquity to the Present,* second edition (Lanham, MD: Rowman and Littlefield, 2016). For the wider networks in this era, see Sujung Kim, *Shinra Myōjin and Buddhist Networks of the East Asian "Mediterranean"* (Honolulu: University of Hawaiʻi Press, 2020).
35. For the cultural achievement of the era, see Ive Covaci, ed., *Kamakura: Realism and Spirituality in the Sculpture of Japan* (New Haven, CT: Yale University Press, 2016).
36. Thomas P. Kasulis, *Engaging Japanese Philosophy* (Honolulu: University of Hawaiʻi Press, 2018).
37. For Nichiren, see Donald S. Lopez Jr. and Jacqueline I. Stone, *Two Buddhas Seated Side by Side* (Princeton, NJ: Princeton University Press, 2019); Soho Machida, *Renegade Monk: Hōnen and Japanese Pure Land Buddhism* (Berkeley: University of California Press, 1999).
38. Steven Heine, *Dōgen and Sōtō Zen* (New York: Oxford University Press, 2015).
39. For the wide degree of local independence, see, for instance, Janet R. Goodwin and Joan R. Piggott, eds., *Land, Power, and the Sacred: The Estate System in Medieval Japan* (Honolulu: University of Hawaiʻi Press, 2018).

Chapter 4

1. The era's disasters, climatic and otherwise, were popularized for a modern audience in Barbara Tuchman, *A Distant Mirror: The Calamitous Fourteenth Century* (New York: Alfred A. Knopf, 1978); William Chester Jordan, *The Great Famine: Northern Europe in the Early Fourteenth Century* (Princeton, NJ: Princeton University Press, 1996); Philip Slavin, "The Crisis of the Fourteenth Century Reassessed: Between Ecology and Institutions—Evidence from England (1310–1350)," paper presented

at the meeting of the Economic History Association, 2010, available at https://www.medievalists.net/2011/10/the-crisis-of-the-fourteenth-century-reassessed-between-ecology-and-institutions-%E2%80%93-evidence-from-england-1310-1350; John Aberth, *An Environmental History of the Middle Ages: The Crucible of Nature* (New York: Routledge, 2012); William Rosen, *The Third Horseman: A Story of Weather, War, and the Famine History Forgot* (New York: Viking, 2014); Bruce M. S. Campbell, *The Great Transition: Climate, Disease and Society in the Late-Medieval World* (New York: Cambridge University Press, 2016).

2. Miri Rubin and Walter P. Simons, eds., *Cambridge History of Christianity: Christianity in Western Europe, c. 1000–c. 1500* (Cambridge: Cambridge University Press, 2009); Kevin Madigan, *Medieval Christianity* (New Haven, CT: Yale University Press, 2015); Chris Wickham, *Medieval Europe* (New Haven, CT: Yale University Press, 2016); Charles F. Briggs, *The Body Broken: Late Medieval and Renaissance Europe, 1300–1525,* second edition (New York: Routledge, 2020).
3. Brian Fagan, *The Little Ice Age: How Climate Made History, 1300–1850* (New York: Basic Books, 2000); J. M. Grove, "The Onset of the Little Ice Age," in P. D. Jones, A. E. J. Ogilvie, T. D. Davies, and K. R. Briffas, *History and Climate: Memories of the Future* (New York: Springer, 2001), 153–186; Michael E. Mann, "Little Ice Age," in Michael C. MacCracken and John S. Perry, eds., *Encyclopedia of Global Environmental Change* (Chichester, UK: John Wiley and Sons, 2002), I:504–509; John L. Brooke, *Climate Change and the Course of Global History: A Rough Journey* (New York: Cambridge University Press, 2014); Richard Grove and George Adamson, *El Niño in World History* (London: Palgrave Macmillan, 2018), 49–79; Christian Rohr, Chantal Camenisch, and Kathleen Pribyl, "European Middle Ages," in Sam White, Christian Pfister, and Franz Mauelshagen, eds., *The Palgrave Handbook of Climate History* (London: Palgrave, 2018), 247–263.
4. Christian Jörg, *Teure, Hunger, großes Sterba: hungersnot und Versorgungskrisen in der Stadt des Reichs während des 15. Jahrhunderts* (Stuttgart: Hiersemann, 2008); Chantal Camenisch, *Endlose Kälte. Witterungsverlauf und Getreidepreise in den Burgundischen Niederlanden im 15. Jahrhundert* (Basel: Schwabe, 2015); Chantal Camenisch et al., "The 1430s: A Cold Period of Extraordinary Internal Climate Variability During the Early Spörer Minimum with Social and Economic Impacts in North-Western and Central Europe," *Climate of the Past* 12 (2016): 2107–2126.
5. Morgan Kelly and Cormac Ó Gráda, "The Myth of Europe's Little Ice Age," Vox EU, March 28, 2015, at https://voxeu.org/article/myth-europe-s-little-ice-age; Kevin Krajick, "The Climate Epochs That Weren't," Earth Institute, Columbia University, July 24, 2019, at https://blogs.ei.columbia.edu/2019/07/24/climate-epochs-that-werent; Brian Handwerk, "Modern Climate Change Is the Only Worldwide Warming Event of the Past 2,000 Years," *Smithsonian Magazine*, July 24, 2019, at https://www.smithsonianmag.com/science-nature/modern-climate-change-only-worldwide-warming-event-past-2000-years-180972719.
6. William Farr, "The Influence of Scarcities and the High Price of Wheat on the Mortality of the People of England," *Journal of the Statistical Society of London* 9 (1846): 161; Dalya Alberge, "Mass Grave in London Reveals How Volcano Caused

Global Catastrophe," *Guardian*, August 5, 2012, at https://www.theguardian.com/uk/2012/aug/05/medieval-volcano-disaster-london-graves; George Saliba, "Cultural Implications of Natural Disasters: Historical Reports of the Volcano Eruption of July, 1256 CE," in Gerrit Jasper Schenk, ed., *Historical Disaster Experiences: Towards a Comparative and Transcultural History of Disasters Across Asia and Europe* (Cham, Switzerland: Springer, 2017), 139–154; Dale Gnidovec, "Geology: Sulfur-Rich Volcanic Eruption in Indonesia in 1257 Cooled Northern Europe for Years," *Columbus Dispatch*, August 13, 2017, at https://www.dispatch.com/news/20170813/geology-sulfur-rich-volcanic-eruption-in-indonesia-in-1257-cooled-northern-europe-for-years.

7. Cormac Ó Gráda, *Famine: A Short History* (Princeton, NJ: Princeton University Press, 2009).
8. Andrew H. Chen, *Flagellant Confraternities and Italian Art, 1260–1610* (Amsterdam: Amsterdam University Press, 2018).
9. "Produced no grain or fruits" is from Farr, "The Influence of Scarcities and the High Price of Wheat on the Mortality of the People of England," 161. For droughts, see Benjamin I. Cook, Kevin J. Anchukaitis, Ramzi Touchan, David M. Meko, and Edward R. Cook, "Spatiotemporal Drought Variability in the Mediterranean over the Last 900 Years," *Journal of Geophysical Research* 121.5 (2016): 2060–2074.

   For the New World, see Timothy A. Kohler, Mark D. Varien, and Aaron M. Wright, eds., *Leaving Mesa Verde: Peril and Change in the Thirteenth-Century Southwest* (Tucson: University of Arizona Press, 2010); Barbara J. Mills and Severin Fowles, eds., *The Oxford Handbook of Southwest Archaeology* (New York: Oxford University Press, 2017); David W. Stahle, Dorian J. Burnette, Daniel Griffin, and Edward R. Cook, "Thirteenth Century AD: Implications of Seasonal and Annual Moisture Reconstructions for Mesa Verde, Colorado," in Harvey Weiss, ed., *Megadrought and Collapse: From Early Agriculture to Angkor* (New York: Oxford University Press, 2017); Grove and Adamson, *El Niño in World History*, 54–56. For the kachina cult, see E. Charles Adams, *The Origin and Development of the Pueblo Katsina Cult* (Tucson: University of Arizona Press. 1991); D. M. Glowacki and Scott Van Keuren, eds., *Religious Transformation in the Late Pre-Hispanic Pueblo World* (Tucson: University of Arizona Press, 2012). Compare Michael W. Binford et al., "Climate Variation and the Rise and Fall of an Andean Civilization," *Quaternary Research* 47.2 (March 1997): 235–248; Benjamin I. Cook, "Pan-Continental Droughts in North America over the Last Millennium," *Journal of Climate* 27.1 (2014): 383–397.
10. Rosen, *The Third Horseman.*
11. Campbell, *The Great Transition.*
12. I draw heavily here on Rosen, *The Third Horseman.* See also Mauricio Lima, "Climate Change and the Population Collapse During the 'Great Famine' in Pre-Industrial Europe," *Ecology and Evolution* 4.3 (February 2014): 284–291; Philip Slavin, "The 1310s Event," in Sam White, Christian Pfister, and Franz Mauelshagen, eds., *The Palgrave Handbook of Climate History* (London: Palgrave, 2018), 495–515. For animal diseases, see Timothy P. Newfield, "A Cattle Panzootic in Early Fourteenth-Century Europe," *Agricultural History Review* 57.2 (2009): 155–190; Philip Slavin, "The Great

Bovine Pestilence and Its Economic and Environmental Consequences in England and Wales, 1318–50," *Economic History Review* 65.4 (2012): 1239–1266; Philip Slavin, "Flogging a Dead Cow: Coping with Animal Panzootic on the Eve of the Black Death," in A. T. Brown, Andy Burn, and Rob Doherty, eds., *Crises in Economic and Social History: A Comparative Perspective* (Woodbridge, UK: Boydell Press, 2015).

13. Quoted from "Famine of 1315," Internet Medieval Source Book, at https://sourcebooks.fordham.edu/source/famin1315a.asp. Michael Prestwich, *Plantagenet England, 1225–1360,* new edition (Oxford: Oxford University Press, 2007); Kathleen Pribyl, *Farming, Famine and Plague: The Impact of Climate in Late Medieval England* (Cham, Switzerland: Springer, 2017).
14. Farr, "The Influence of Scarcities and the High Price of Wheat on the Mortality of the People of England," 162; "New Drought Atlas Maps 2,000 Years of Climate in Europe: Completes the First Big-Picture View Across Northern Hemisphere," Earth Institute, Columbia University, November 6, 2015, at https://www.earth.columbia.edu/articles/view/3264; P. S. Langeslag, "Weathering the Storm: Adverse Climates in Medieval Literature," in Adeline Johns-Putra, ed., *Climate and Literature* (Cambridge: Cambridge University Press, 2019), 76–91.
15. John Kelly, *The Great Mortality: An Intimate History of the Black Death, the Most Devastating Plague of All Time* (New York: Harper, 2005); Timothy Brook, *The Troubled Empire: China in the Yuan and Ming Dynasties* (Cambridge, MA: Belknap Press of Harvard University Press, 2010); Campbell, *The Great Transition;* Pribyl, *Farming, Famine and Plague.* The quotation is from Allen James Fromherz, *Ibn Khaldun* (Edinburgh: Edinburgh University Press, 2011), 51.
16. Alvin Powell, "Did Famine Worsen the Black Death?," *Harvard Gazette,* January 5, 2016, at https://news.harvard.edu/gazette/story/2016/01/did-famine-worsen-the-black-death.
17. Campbell, *The Great Transition, 247.*
18. Prestwich, *Plantagenet England, 1225–1360*; Kathryn Warner, *Edward II: The Unconventional King* (Stroud, UK: Amerley, 2014); Justine Firnhaber-Baker and Dirk Schoenaers, eds., *The Routledge History Handbook of Medieval Revolt* (New York: Routledge, 2017). For crises at this time in Spain and Portugal, Peter Linehan, *At the Edge of Reformation: Iberia Before the Black Death* (Oxford: Oxford University Press, 2019).
19. Caroline Finkel, *Osman's Dream: The History of the Ottoman Empire* (New York: Basic Books, 2007).
20. Miri Rubin, *Gentile Tales: The Narrative Assault on Late Medieval Jews* (Philadelphia: University of Pennsylvania Press, 2004).
21. Jochen Burgtorf, Paul Crawford, and Helen Nicholson, eds., *The Debate on the Trial of the Templars, 1307–1314* (Burlington, VT: Ashgate, 2010); Dan Jones, *The Templars* (New York: Viking, 2017).
22. This era, and the continuing persecution of Albigensians, forms the subject of Emmanuel LeRoy Ladurie, *Montaillou* (New York: G. Braziller, 1978).
23. Quoted in Malcolm Barber, "Lepers, Jews and Moslems," *History* 66 (1981): 1–17; Bernard Gui, *The Inquisitor's Guide: A Medieval Manual on Heretics*, ed. Janet Shirley (Welwyn Garden City, UK: Ravenhall Books, 2006).

24. Evans-Pritchard is quoted from Antonius C. G. M. Robben, eds., *Death, Mourning, and Burial* (Hoboken, NJ: John Wiley and Sons, 2017), 89. For developing ideas of witchcraft, see Alan C. Kors and Edward Peters, eds., *Witchcraft in Europe, 400–1700: A Documentary History,* second edition (Philadelphia: University of Pennsylvania Press, 2001); David J. Collins, ed., *The Cambridge History of Magic and Witchcraft in the West* (Cambridge: Cambridge University Press, 2015); Ronald Hutton, *The Witch* (New Haven, CT: Yale University Press, 2017). I particularly draw on the diverse and wide-ranging essays in Brian P. Levack, ed., *The Oxford Handbook of Witchcraft in Early Modern Europe and Colonial America* (Oxford: Oxford University Press, 2013), which together offer a comprehensive survey of the topic.
25. Dante, *Inferno,* 20.123.
26. Sebastian Zanke, *Johannes XXII, Avignon und Europa* (Leiden: Brill, 2013); Joëlle Rollo-Koster, *Avignon and Its Papacy, 1309–1417: Popes, Institutions, and Society* (New York: Rowman and Littlefield, 2017).
27. Kors and Peters, eds., *Witchcraft in Europe, 400–1700,* 118–120.
28. For *Super illius specula,* see James Joseph Walsh, *The Popes and Science* (New York: Fordham University Press, 1908), 415; Edward Peters, *The Magician, the Witch, and the Law* (Philadelphia: University of Pennsylvania Press, 1978).
29. Kathrin Utz Tremp, *Von der Häresie zur Hexerei: "wirkliche" und imaginäre Sekten im Spätmittelalter* (Hannover, Germany: Hahnsche Buchhandlung, 2008); Andrew Colin Gow, Robert B. Desjardins, and François V. Pageau, eds., *The Arras Witch Treatises* (University Park: Pennsylvania State University Press, 2016); Louise Nyholm Kallestrup and Raisa Maria Toivo, eds., *Contesting Orthodoxy in Medieval and Early Modern Europe: Heresy, Magic and Witchcraft* (London: Palgrave Macmillan, 2017).
30. Irene Bueno, *Defining Heresy: Inquisition, Theology, and Papal Policy in the Time of Jacques Fournier* (Leiden: Brill, 2015).
31. Maeve Brigid Callan, *The Templars, the Witch, and the Wild Irish: Vengeance and Heresy in Medieval Ireland* (Ithaca, NY: Cornell University Press, 2015); L. S. Davidson and J. O. Ward, eds., *The Sorcery Trial of Alice Kyteler: A Contemporary Account (1324)* (New York: Medieval and Renaissance Texts and Studies, 1993).
32. Michael D. Bailey and Edward Peters, "A Sabbat of Demonologists: Basel, 1431–1440," *The Historian* 65.6 (2003): 1375–1395; Richard Kieckhefer, "Mythologies of Witchcraft in the Fifteenth Century," *Magic, Ritual, and Witchcraft* 1.1 (2006): 79–108; Michael D. Bailey, *Battling Demons: Witchcraft, Heresy, and Reform in the Late Middle Ages* (University Park: Pennsylvania State University Press, 2010); Hans Peter Broedel, "Fifteenth-Century Witch Beliefs," in Brian P. Levack, ed., *The Oxford Handbook of Witchcraft in Early Modern Europe and Colonial America* (Oxford: Oxford University Press, 2013).
33. From a vast literature, see David Nirenberg, *Anti-Judaism: The Western Tradition* (New York: W. W. Norton, 2013).
34. Malcolm Barber, "The Pastoureaux of 1320," *Journal of Ecclesiastical History* 32.2 (1981): 143–166; Christopher Tyerman, *Fighting for Christendom: Holy War and the Crusades* (New York: Oxford University Press, 2004).

35. Tzafrir Barzilay, "Well-Poisoning Accusations in Medieval Europe: 1250–1500," Ph.D. dissertation, Columbia University, 2017; Magda Teter, *Blood Libel: On the Trail of an Antisemitic Myth* (Cambridge, MA: Harvard University Press, 2020).
36. John Friedman, Jean Connell Hoff, and Robert Chazan, eds., *The Trial of the Talmud, Paris, 1240* (Toronto: Pontifical Institute of Mediaeval Studies, 2012).
37. Samuel K. Cohn Jr., "The Black Death and the Burning of Jews," *Past and Present* 196 (2007): 3–36; "The Black Death and the Jews, 1348–1349 CE," Internet Medieval Source Book, at https://sourcebooks.fordham.edu/jewish/1348-jewsblackdeath.asp; Cohn, "The Black Death and the Burning of Jews."
38. Lukas Clemens and Christoph Cluse, eds., *The Jews of Europe Around 1400* (Wiesbaden: Harrassowitz Verlag, 2018).
39. Gordon Leff, *Heresy in the Later Middle Ages: The Relation of Heterodoxy to Dissent, c. 1250–c. 1450* (New York: Barnes and Noble, 1967); Walter L. Wakefield and Austin P. Evans, *Heresies of the High Middle Ages* (New York: Columbia University Press, 1969); Malcolm Lambert, *Medieval Heresy: Popular Movements from Bogomil to Hus* (New York: Holmes and Meier, 1976); René Weis, *The Yellow Cross: The Story of the Last Cathars, 1290–1329* (New York: Alfred A. Knopf, 2001).
40. "Who is, after Christ" is from "Petrus Iohannis Olivi: Selections from the Apocalypse Commentary," at https://www2.kenyon.edu/projects/margin/olivi.htm; David Burr, *The Spiritual Franciscans: From Protest to Persecution in the Century After Saint Francis* (University Park: Pennsylvania State University Press, 2001); Rosalind B. Brooke, *The Image of St. Francis: Responses to Sainthood in the Thirteenth Century* (Cambridge: Cambridge University Press, 2006); Jerry B. Pierce, *Poverty, Heresy, and the Apocalypse: The Order of Apostles and Social Change in Medieval Italy, 1260–1307* (New York: Continuum, 2012).
41. Jennifer Kolpacoff Deane, *A History of Medieval Heresy and Inquisition* (Lanham, MD: Rowman and Littlefield, 2011); Walter Simons, *Cities of Ladies: Beguine Communities in the Medieval Low Countries, 1200–1565* (Philadelphia: University of Pennsylvania Press, 2001); Louisa A. Burnham, *So Great a Light, So Great a Smoke: The Beguin Heretics of Languedoc* (Ithaca, NY: Cornell University Press, 2008); Miri Rubin, ed., *Medieval Christianity in Practice* (Princeton, NJ: Princeton University Press, 2009); Irene Bueno, *Defining Heresy: Inquisition, Theology, and Papal Policy in the Time of Jacques Fournier* (Leiden: Brill, 2015). See also Ernest W. McDonnell, *The Beguines and Beghards in Medieval Culture: With Special Emphasis on the Belgian Scene* (New York: Octagon Books, 1969).
42. "Abominable sect" is from "Council of Vienne 1311–1312 AD," at https://www.papalencyclicals.net/councils/ecum15.htm. "Their erroneous opinions" is quoted from "Bernard Gui: Inquisitor's Manual," Internet Medieval Source Book, at https://sourcebooks.fordham.edu/source/bernardgui-inq.asp; Bernard Gui, *The Inquisitor's Guide: A Medieval Manual on Heretics*, ed. Janet Shirley (Welwyn Garden City, UK: Ravenhall Books, 2006).
43. In modern times, the conflict supplies the background to Umberto Eco's celebrated 1980 novel, *The Name of the Rose*; see James Hitchcock, "War of the Rose: The Historical Context of *The Name of the Rose*," *Crisis Magazine*, January 1, 1987; Patrick Nold, *Pope John XXII and His Franciscan Cardinal* (Oxford: Clarendon, 2003); Sylvain

Parent, *Dans les abysses de l'infidélité: les procès contre les ennemis de l'Église en Italie au temps de Jean XXII (1316–1334)* (Rome: École française de Rome, 2014).

44. Burr, *The Spiritual Franciscans.*
45. "Many articles considered heretical" and "the carnal church" are from "Bernard Gui: Inquisitor's Manual." Richard Kieckhefer, *Repression of Heresy in Medieval Germany* (Philadelphia: University of Pennsylvania Press, 1979); Bernard McGinn, *Visions of the End: Apocalyptic Traditions in the Middle Ages*, new edition (New York: Columbia University Press, 1998); Burr, *The Spiritual Franciscans*; Bueno, *Defining Heresy*; Nelly Ficzel, *Der Papst als Antichrist: Kirchenkritik und Apokalyptik im 13. und frühen 14. Jahrhundert* (Leiden: Brill, 2018).
46. Robert E. Lerner, *The Heresy of the Free Spirit in the Later Middle Ages* (Berkeley: University of California Press, 1972); Raoul Vaneigem, *The Movement of the Free Spirit* (Cambridge, MA: MIT Press, 1994).
47. Bernard McGinn, ed., *Meister Eckhart and the Beguine Mystics: Hadewijch of Brabant, Mechthild of Magdeburg, and Marguerite Porete* (New York: Continuum, 1994); Sean L. Field, *The Beguine, The Angel, and the Inquisitor: The Trials of Marguerite Porete and Guiard of Cressonessart* (Notre Dame, IN: University of Notre Dame Press, 2012); "Council of Vienne 1311–1312 AD," at https://www.papalencyclicals.net/councils/ecum15.htm.
48. Philip Jenkins, *The Lost History of Christianity* (San Francisco: HarperOne, 2008); Sarah Kate Raphael, *Climate and Political Climate: Environmental Disasters in the Medieval Levant* (Leiden: Brill, 2013).
49. Yossef Rapoport and Shahab Ahmed, eds., *Ibn Taymiyya and His Times* (Karachi: Oxford University Press Pakistan, 2010).
50. B. T. A. Evetts, *The Churches and Monasteries of Egypt and Some Neighbouring Countries* (Oxford: Clarendon Press, 1895), 340. Jenkins, *The Lost History of Christianity.* See also Syrinx von Hees, "The Great Fire in Cairo in 1321," in Gerrit Jasper Schenk, ed., *Historical Disaster Experiences: Towards a Comparative and Transcultural History of Disasters Across Asia and Europe* (Cham, Switzerland: Springer, 2017), 307–326.
51. The following discussion is drawn from Jenkins, *The Lost History of Christianity.*
52. Brook, *The Troubled Empire.*
53. Grove and Adamson, *El Niño in World History.*
54. Roland Fletcher, Brendan M. Buckley, Christopher Potter, and Shi-yu Simon Wang, "Fourteenth to Sixteenth Centuries AD: The Case of Angkor and Monsoon Extremes in Mainland Southeast Asia," in Harvey Weiss, ed., *Megadrought and Collapse: From Early Agriculture to Angkor* (New York: Oxford University Press, 2017), 275–313.
55. Quotations are from Timothy Brook, "Nine Sloughs: Profiling the Climate History of the Yuan and Ming Dynasties, 1260–1644," *Journal of Chinese History* 1.1 (2017): 27–58.
56. Brook, *The Troubled Empire.*
57. Jenkins, *The Lost History of Christianity.*
58. "John of Montecorvino," *Catholic Encyclopedia*, http://www.newadvent.org/cathen/08474a.htm.
59. "Manicheism in China," *Encyclopedia Iranica*, http://www.iranicaonline.org/articles/manicheism-v-in-china-1.

Chapter 5

1. Throughout this chapter, I have used Diarmaid MacCulloch, *The Reformation* (New York: Viking, 2004); Patrick Collinson, *The Reformation* (New York: Modern Library, 2004); Carlos M. N. Eire, *Reformations: The Early Modern World, 1450–1650* (New Haven, CT: Yale University Press, 2016), and the diverse essays in Ulinka Rublack, ed., *The Oxford Handbook of the Protestant Reformations* (New York: Oxford University Press, 2017).
2. R. Po-chia Hsia, ed., *Cambridge History of Christianity: Reform and Expansion, 1500–1660* (Cambridge: Cambridge University Press, 2006); Ulinka Rublack, *Reformation Europe*, second edition (New York: Cambridge University Press, 2017).
3. Oliver Wetter et al., "The Year-Long Unprecedented European Heat and Drought of 1540—A Worst Case," *Climatic Change* 125 (2014): 340–363; Christian Pfister, "The Black Swan of 1540: Aspects of a European Megadrought," in Claus Leggewie and Franz Mauelshagen, eds., *Climate Change and Cultural Transition in Europe* (Leiden: Brill, 2018), 156–194; Axel Bojanowski, "Wetterdaten enthüllen Europas größte Naturkatastrophe," *Spiegel*, July 2, 2014; William C. Innes, *Social Concern in Calvin's Geneva* (Eugene, OR: Wipf and Stock, 1983).
4. Christian Pfister et al., "Early Modern Europe," in Sam White, Christian Pfister, and Franz Mauelshagen, eds., *The Palgrave Handbook of Climate History* (London: Palgrave, 2018), 265–295.
5. Tim Ball, "Climate Change, Baltic Herring and the Reformation?," Watts Up with That?, July 18, 2015, at https://wattsupwiththat.com/2015/07/18/climate-change-baltic-herring-and-the-reformation.
6. Henry Heller, "Famine, Revolt and Heresy at Meaux: 1521–1525," in Erik A. Heinrichs, ed., *Plague, Print, and the Reformation: The German Reform of Healing, 1473–1573* (London: Routledge, 2017); Mohamed Mezzine, "Political Power and Social-Religious Networks in Sixteenth-Century Fes," in Tsugitaka Sato, ed., *Islamic Urbanism in Human History* (London: Kegan Paul, 1996), 107–141; Andrew Cunningham and Ole Peter Grell, *The Four Horsemen of the Apocalypse: Religion, War, Famine and Death in Reformation Europe* (Cambridge: Cambridge University Press, 2000).
7. George Huntston Williams, *The Radical Reformation* (Philadelphia: Westminster Press, 1962); Michael G. Baylor, ed., *The Radical Reformation* (New York: Cambridge University Press, 1991); Curtis V. Bostick, *The Antichrist and the Lollards: Apocalypticism in Late Medieval and Reformation England* (Leiden: Brill, 1998).
8. W. G. Hoskins, "Harvest Fluctuations and English Economic History, 1480–1619," *Agricultural History Review* 12.1 (1964): 28–46; Christian Pfister, Rudolf Brázdil, and Rüdiger Glaser, eds., *Climatic Variability in Sixteenth-Century Europe and Its Social Dimension* (Dordrecht: Springer, 1999); Philipp Blom, *Nature's Mutiny: How the Little Ice Age of the Long Seventeenth Century Transformed the West and Shaped the Present* (New York: W. W. Norton, 2019).
9. Blom, *Nature's Mutiny;* Sam White, *A Cold Welcome: The Little Ice Age and Europe's Encounter with North America* (Cambridge, MA: Harvard University Press, 2017);

Lowell Duckert, "The Climate of Shakespeare: Four (or More) Forecasts," in Adeline Johns-Putra, ed., *Climate and Literature* (Cambridge: Cambridge University Press, 2019), 76–91. I will often here draw on evidence from the American Southwest and northern Mexico, a region that has been very well studied archaeologically. Since the 1980s, this distinctive ecological region has usefully been called "Aridoamerica" because of its extreme dryness.

10. Alfred W. Crosby, *The Columbian Exchange: Biological and Cultural Consequences of 1492* (Westport, CT: Greenwood, 1972); Noble David Cook, *Demographic Collapse: Indian Peru, 1520–1620* (New York: Cambridge University Press, 1981); Elinor G. K. Melville, *A Plague of Sheep: Environmental Consequences of the Conquest of Mexico* (New York: Cambridge University Press, 1994); Noble David Cook, *Born to Die: Disease and the New World Conquest, 1492–1650* (New York: Cambridge University Press, 1998); William F. Ruddiman, *Plows, Plagues, and Petroleum: How Humans Took Control of Climate* (Princeton, NJ: Princeton University Press, 2005); Simon L. Lewis and Mark A. Maslin, *The Human Planet: How We Created the Anthropocene* (New Haven, CT: Yale University Press, 2018).
11. Geoffrey Parker, *Global Crisis: War, Climate Change and Catastrophe in the Seventeenth Century* (New Haven, CT: Yale University Press, 2013); Blom, *Nature's Mutiny*; Rüdiger Glaser, *Klimageschichte Mitteleuropas: 1200 Jahre Wetter, Klima, Katastrophen,* second edition (Darmstadt: Primus-Verlag, 2008); Christian Pfister, Rudolf Brázdil, Jürg Luterbacher, Astrid E. J. Ogilvie, and Sam White, "Early Modern Europe," in Sam White, Christian Pfister, and Franz Mauelshagen, eds., *The Palgrave Handbook of Climate History* (London: Palgrave, 2018), 265–295; Jennifer Spinks and Charles Zika, eds., *Disaster, Death and the Emotions in the Shadow of the Apocalypse, 1400–1700* (London: Palgrave Macmillan, 2016); Murat Iyigun, Nathan Nunn, and Nancy Qian, *Winter Is Coming: The Long-Run Effects of Climate Change on Conflict, 1400–1900* (Bonn, Germany: Institute of Labor Economics, 2017).
12. William Farr, "The Influence of Scarcities and the High Price of Wheat on the Mortality of the People of England," *Journal of the Statistical Society of London* 9 (1846): 158–174; Yves-Marie Bercé, *History of Peasant Revolts: The Social Origins of Rebellion in Early Modern France* (Ithaca, NY: Cornell University Press, 1990).
13. Charles Creighton, *History of Epidemics in Britain,* 2 vols. (Cambridge: Cambridge University Press, 1891–1894); Andrew Cunningham and Ole Peter Grell, *The Four Horsemen of the Apocalypse: Religion, War, Famine and Death in Reformation Europe* (Cambridge: Cambridge University Press, 2000).
14. Mezzine, "Political Power and Social-Religious Networks in Sixteenth-Century Fes"; Carlo M. Cipolla, *Fighting the Plague in Seventeenth-Century Italy* (Madison: University of Wisconsin Press, 1981); Guido Alfani, "Plague in Seventeenth-Century Europe and the Decline of Italy: An Epidemiological Hypothesis," *European Review of Economic History* 17.4 (2013): 408–430; Nükhet Varlik, *Plague and Empire in the Early Modern Mediterranean World: The Ottoman Experience, 1347–1600* (New York: Cambridge University Press, 2015); Matthew Kroenig, "Pandemics Can Fast Forward the Rise and Fall of Great Powers," *National Interest,* March 23, 2020, at https://nationalinterest.org/blog/buzz/

pandemics-can-fast-forward-rise-and-fall-great-powers-136417. For influenza, see "The Threat of Pandemic Influenza: Are We Ready? Workshop Summary," at https://www.ncbi.nlm.nih.gov/books/NBK22148.

15. *Midsummer Night's Dream,* act 2, scene 1; Peter Clark, ed., *The European Crisis of the 1590s* (London: Unwin Hyman, 1985); Susan Brigden, *New Worlds, Lost Worlds: The Rule of the Tudors, 1485–1603* (New York: Viking, 2001); Geoffrey Parker, "History and Climate: The Crisis of the 1590s Reconsidered," in Claus Leggewie and Franz Mauelshagen, eds., *Climate Change and Cultural Transition in Europe* (Leiden: Brill, 2018), 119–155.
16. Sam White, "A Model Disaster," in Nukhet Varlik, ed., *Plague and Contagion in the Islamic Mediterranean* (n.p.: Arc Humanities Press, 2017), 57–90; Richard Grove and George Adamson, *El Niño in World History* (London: Palgrave Macmillan, 2018), 60–61.
17. Maureen Perrie, ed., *The Cambridge History of Russia,* volume 1 (Cambridge: Cambridge University Press, 2006).
18. Perrie, ed., *The Cambridge History of Russia,* volume 1; Sam White, *The Climate of Rebellion in the Early Modern Ottoman Empire* (New York: Cambridge University Press, 2011).
19. Timothy Brook, *The Troubled Empire: China in the Yuan and Ming Dynasties* (Cambridge, MA: Belknap Press of Harvard University Press, 2010); Parker, *Global Crisis.*
20. Johannes Dillinger, "Organized Arson as a Political Crime: The Construction of a Terrorist Menace in the Early Modern Period," *Crime History and Societies* 10.1 (2006): 101–121; Christian Pfister, "When Europe Was Burning: The Multi-Season Mega-Drought of 1540 and Arsonist Paranoia," in Gerrit Jasper Schenk, ed., *Historical Disaster Experiences: Towards a Comparative and Transcultural History of Disasters Across Asia and Europe* (Cham, Switzerland: Springer, 2017), 155–185. For the Anabaptist threat, see Gary K. Waite, *Eradicating the Devil's Minions: Anabaptists and Witches in Reformation Europe, 1525–1600* (Toronto: University of Toronto Press, 2007); Kat Hill, *Baptism, Brotherhood, and Belief in Reformation Germany: Anabaptism and Lutheranism, 1525–1585* (Oxford: Oxford University Press, 2015); Ambrosius Trota, *Der Mordtbrenner Zaichen vnnd Losunge, Etwa bey Dreyhundert vnnd Viertzig außgeschickt* (Melchior Kriegstein, 1540), at https://digital.slub-dresden.de/werkansicht/dlf/281659/1.
21. Magda Teter, *Sinners on Trial: Jews and Sacrilege After the Reformation* (Cambridge, MA: Harvard University Press, 2011).
22. See especially the essays in Brian P. Levack, ed., *The Oxford Handbook of Witchcraft in Early Modern Europe and Colonial America* (Oxford: Oxford University Press, 2013). See also Alan C. Kors and Edward Peters, eds., *Witchcraft in Europe, 400–1700: A Documentary History,* second edition (Philadelphia: University of Pennsylvania Press, 2001); David J. Collins, ed., *The Cambridge History of Magic and Witchcraft in the West: From Antiquity to the Present* (Cambridge: Cambridge University Press, 2015); Ronald Hutton, *The Witch* (New Haven, CT: Yale University Press, 2017).
23. See, for instance, the dates chosen in Erik Midelfort's classic *Witch Hunting in Southern Germany, 1562–1684* (Palo Alto, CA: Stanford University Press, 1972);

Wolfgang Behringer, "Climatic Change and Witch-Hunting: The Impact of the Little Ice Age on Mentalities," *Climatic Change* 1.1 (1999): 335–351.

24. Stuart Clark, *Thinking with Demons: The Idea of Witchcraft in Early Modern Europe* (New York: Oxford University Press, 1997); Robin Briggs, *The Witches of Lorraine* (Oxford: Oxford University Press, 2007); Virginia Krause, *Witchcraft, Demonology, and Confession in Early Modern France* (New York: Cambridge University Press, 2015); Brian P. Levack, *The Witch-Hunt in Early Modern Europe*, fourth edition (New York: Routledge, 2016). For England, see Peter Elmer, *Witchcraft, Witch-Hunting, and Politics in Early Modern England* (Oxford: Oxford University Press, 2016).
25. Gustav Henningsen, *The Witches' Advocate: Basque Witchcraft and the Spanish Inquisition, 1609–1614* (Reno: University of Nevada Press, 1980); Johannes Dillinger, *"Evil People": A Comparative Study of Witch Hunts in Swabian Austria and the Electorate of Trier* (Charlottesville: University of Virginia Press, 2009).
26. Lyndal Roper, *Witch Craze: Terror and Fantasy in Baroque Germany* (New Haven, CT: Yale University Press, 2004); Jonathan B. Durrant, *Witchcraft, Gender, and Society in Early Modern Germany* (Leiden: Brill, 2007); Laura Kounine, *Imagining the Witch: Emotions, Gender, and Selfhood in Early Modern Germany* (Oxford: Oxford University Press, 2018).
27. Gerhild Scholz Williams, ed., *On the Inconstancy of Witches: Pierre de Lancre's Tableau de l'inconstance des mauvais anges et demons (1612)* (Tempe: Arizona Center for Medieval and Renaissance Studies, 2006); Jean Bodin, *De la démonomanie des sorciers*, ed. Virginia Krause, Christian Martin, and Eric MacPhail (Geneva: Droz, 2016); Howell A. Lloyd, *Jean Bodin: This Pre-Eminent Man of France* (Oxford: Oxford University Press, 2017); Jan Machielsen, ed., *The Science of Demons: Early Modern Authors Facing Witchcraft and the Devil* (London: Routledge, 2020). For frauds, see James Shapiro, *The Year of Lear* (New York: Simon and Schuster, 2015).
28. For the wide cultural dissemination of these ideas, see Charles Zika, *The Appearance of Witchcraft: Print and Visual Culture in Sixteenth-Century Europe* (New York: Routledge, 2007); John Callow, *Embracing the Darkness: A Cultural History of Witchcraft* (London: I. B. Tauris, 2018).
29. Rublack, *Reformation Europe*.
30. James B. Wood, *The King's Army: Warfare, Soldiers, and Society During the Wars of Religion in France, 1562–1576* (New York: Cambridge University Press, 1996); Philip Benedict, Guido Marnef, Henk van Nierop, and Marc Venard, eds., *Reformation, Revolt and Civil War in France and the Netherlands, 1555–1585* (Amsterdam: Royal Netherlands Academy of Arts and Sciences, 1999); Jan Glete, *War and the State in Early Modern Europe: Spain, the Dutch Republic and Sweden as Fiscal-Military States, 1500–1660* (New York: Routledge, 2002); Mack P. Holt, ed., *Renaissance and Reformation France, 1500–1648* (New York: Oxford University Press, 2002); Arlette Jouanna, *The Saint Bartholomew's Day Massacre: The Mysteries of a Crime of State (24 August 1572)* (Manchester, UK: Manchester University Press, 2013); Wayne P. Te Brake, *Religious War and Religious Peace in Early Modern Europe* (Cambridge: Cambridge University Press, 2017).

31. Philip Benedict, *Rouen During the Wars of Religion* (Cambridge: Cambridge University Press, 1981); Mack P. Holt, *The French Wars of Religion, 1562–1629*, second edition (New York: Cambridge University Press, 2005); R. J. Knecht, *The French Wars of Religion, 1559–1598* (London: Longman, 2010).
32. Luc Racaut, *Hatred in Print: Catholic Propaganda and Protestant Identity During the French Wars of Religion* (Burlington, VT: Ashgate, 2002). For visual commemorations of bloodshed and carnage, see Philip Benedict, *Graphic History: The Wars, Massacres and Troubles of Tortorel and Perrissin*, revised edition (Geneva: Librairie Droz, 2007). For "Liever Turks dan Paaps," see, for instance, the medal at https://commons.wikimedia.org/wiki/File:3_Geuzenpenning,_halve_maan.jpg.
33. Diarmaid MacCulloch, *The Reformation* (New York: Viking, 2004); Irena Backus and Philip Benedict, eds., *Calvin and His Influence, 1509–2009* (New York: Oxford University Press, 2011); D. G. Hart, *Calvinism: A History* (New Haven, CT: Yale University Press, 2013); Jon Balserak, *John Calvin as Sixteenth-Century Prophet* (Oxford: Oxford University Press, 2014); James Simpson, *Permanent Revolution: The Reformation and the Illiberal Roots of Liberalism* (Cambridge, MA: Belknap Press of Harvard University Press, 2019); Brian C. Brewer and David M. Whitford, eds., *Calvin and the Early Reformation* (Leiden: Brill, 2020).
34. Carlos M. N. Eire, *Reformations: The Early Modern World, 1450–1650* (New Haven, CT: Yale University Press, 2016); Rublack, ed., *The Oxford Handbook of the Protestant Reformations*.
35. Eamon Duffy, *The Stripping of the Altars: Traditional Religion in England, c. 1400–c. 1580*, second edition (New Haven, CT: Yale University Press, 2005).
36. Carlos M. N. Eire, *War Against the Idols* (Cambridge: Cambridge University Press, 1989); Lee Palmer Wanderl, *Voracious Idols and Violent Hands* (Cambridge: Cambridge University Press, 1995); Virginia Chieffo Raguin, ed., *Art, Piety and Destruction in the Christian West, 1500–1700* (Burlington, VT: Ashgate, 2010); James Noyes, *The Politics of Iconoclasm: Religion, Violence and the Culture of Image-Breaking in Christianity and Islam* (London: I. B. Tauris, 2013); Margaret Aston, *Broken Idols of the English Reformation* (Cambridge: Cambridge University Press, 2016).
37. Nikki Shepardson, *Burning Zeal: The Rhetoric of Martyrdom and the Protestant Community in Reformation France, 1520–1570* (Bethlehem, PA: Lehigh University Press, 2007). For the role of Calvinist networks in political conspiracy, see Philip Benedict, *Season of Conspiracy: Calvin, the French Reformed Churches, and Protestant Plotting in the Reign of Francis II (1559–60)* (Philadelphia: American Philosophical Society Press, 2020).
38. I draw heavily here on Philip Benedict, *Christ's Churches Purely Reformed: A Social History of Calvinism* (New Haven, CT: Yale University Press, 2002); Graeme Murdock, *Calvinism on the Frontier, 1600–1660* (Oxford: Clarendon, 2000); Pál Ács, *Reformations in Hungary in the Age of the Ottoman Conquest* (Göttingen: Vandenhoeck and Ruprecht, 2019).
39. Benedict, *Christ's Churches Purely Reformed*; Susan Brigden, *New Worlds, Lost Worlds: The Rule of the Tudors, 1485–1603* (New York: Viking, 2001); Alec Ryrie, *The Age of Reformation: The Tudor and Stewart Realms, 1485–1603*, second edition

(New York: Routledge, 2017); David D. Hall, *The Puritans: A Transatlantic History* (Princeton, NJ: Princeton University Press, 2019).

40. Herbert Darling Foster, "The Political Theories of Calvinists Before the Puritan Exodus to America," *American Historical Review* 21.3 (1916): 481–503.
41. Roger A. Mason and Martin S. Smith, *A Dialogue on the Law of Kingship Among the Scots* (Burlington, VT: Ashgate, 2004); Roger Mason and Caroline Erskine, eds., *George Buchanan: Political Thought in Early Modern Britain and Europe* (Burlington, VT: Ashgate, 2012); Cesare Cuttica, "Tyrannicide and Political Authority in the Long Sixteenth Century," in Henrik Lagerlund and Benjamin Hill, eds., *Routledge Companion to Sixteenth-Century Philosophy* (New York: Routledge, 2017).
42. "If the people rise up" is quoted in Dagomar Degroot, *The Frigid Golden Age: Climate Change, the Little Ice Age, and the Dutch Republic, 1560–1720* (Cambridge: Cambridge University Press, 2018), 162; K. W. Swart, *William of Orange and the Revolt of the Netherlands, 1572–84* (Burlington, VT: Ashgate, 2003).
43. James Tracy, *The Founding of the Dutch Republic: War, Finance, and Politics in Holland, 1572–1588* (Oxford: Oxford University Press, 2008); Peter Arnade, *Beggars, Iconoclasts, and Civic Patriots: The Political Culture of the Dutch Revolt* (Ithaca, NY: Cornell University Press, 2008); Marjolein 't Hart, *The Dutch Wars of Independence: Warfare and Commerce in the Netherlands, 1570–1680* (New York: Routledge, 2014).
44. Jonathan Israel, *The Dutch Republic: Its Rise, Greatness, and Fall, 1477–1806* (Oxford: Clarendon Press, 1995); Helmer J. Helmers and Geert H. Janssen, eds., *The Cambridge Companion to the Dutch Golden Age* (Cambridge: Cambridge University Press, 2018).
45. Degroot, *The Frigid Golden Age.*
46. Geoffrey Parker, *The Army of Flanders and the Spanish Road, 1567–1659*, second edition (Cambridge: Cambridge University Press, 2004).
47. Michael A. Mullett, *The Catholic Reformation* (New York: Routledge, 1999); R. Po-chia Hsia, *The World of Catholic Renewal, 1540–1770,* second edition (New York: Cambridge University Press, 2005); Alexandra Bamji, Geert H. Janssen, and Mary Laven, eds., *The Ashgate Research Companion to the Counter-Reformation* (Burlington, VT: Ashgate, 2013).
48. Joachim Whaley, *Germany and the Holy Roman Empire*, 2 vols. (Oxford: Oxford University Press, 2013).
49. Felicity Heal, *Reformation in Britain and Ireland* (Oxford: Oxford University Press, 2003); Éamonn Ó Ciardha and Micheál Ó Siochrú, eds., *The Plantation of Ulster: Ideology and Practice* (Manchester, UK: Manchester University Press, 2012).

Chapter 6

1. Gary S. De Krey, *Restoration and Revolution in Britain: A Political History of the Era of Charles II and the Glorious Revolution* (New York: Palgrave Macmillan, 2007).
2. Anne Somerset, *The Affair of the Poisons: Murder, Infanticide and Satanism at the Court of Louis XIV* (London: Weidenfeld and Nicolson, 2003); Josephine Wilkinson, *Louis XIV: The Power and the Glory* (New York: Pegasus Books, 2019).

3. Merry E. Wiesner-Hanks, *Early Modern Europe, 1450–1789*, second edition (Cambridge: Cambridge University Press, 2013).
4. Geoffrey Parker, *Global Crisis: War, Climate Change and Catastrophe in the Seventeenth Century* (New Haven, CT: Yale University Press, 2013).
5. Philipp Blom, *Nature's Mutiny: How the Little Ice Age of the Long Seventeenth Century Transformed the West and Shaped the Present* (New York: W. W. Norton, 2019).
6. Parker does indeed quote Madame de Sévigné's observation, together with others concerning bitter conditions at the end of the century and beyond. S. Pain, "The Winter of Incomparable Cold," *New Scientist*, February 7, 2009, 46–47.
7. Wiesner-Hanks, *Early Modern Europe, 1450–1789*.
8. "Largest Eruptions Since 1400 AD," at http://volcano.oregonstate.edu/book/export/html/227; Jürg Luterbacher, "The Late Maunder Minimum (1675–1715)—Climax of the Little Ice Age in Europe," in P. D. Jones, A. E. J. Ogilvie, T. D. Davies, and K. R. Briffas, eds., *History and Climate: Memories of the Future* (New York: Springer, 2001); Stefan Brönnimann, *Climatic Changes Since 1700* (Cham, Switzerland: Springer, 2015); Richard Grove and George Adamson, *El Niño in World History* (London: Palgrave Macmillan, 2018), 65–68; Sid Perkins, "How a Volcanic Eruption Helped Create Modern Scotland," *Science*, December 5, 2019, at https://www.sciencemag.org/news/2019/12/how-volcanic-eruption-helped-create-modern-scotland.
9. Brian Fagan, *The Little Ice Age: How Climate Made History, 1300–1850* (New York: Basic Books, 2000), 49–50, 118–119.
10. Blom, *Nature's Mutiny*, 185–252. Purcell is quoted in Christopher D'Addario and Matthew C. Augustine, eds., *Texts and Readers in the Age of Marvell* (Manchester, UK: Manchester University Press, 2018).
11. John Evelyn, *The Diary of John Evelyn*, ed. Austin Dobson (Cambridge: Cambridge University Press, 2015), 3:121.
12. John Walter, Roger Schofield, and Andrew B. Appleby, eds., *Famine, Disease and the Social Order in Early Modern Society* (Cambridge: Cambridge University Press, 1989); W. G. Hoskins, "Harvest Fluctuations and English Economic History, 1620–1759," *Agricultural History Review* 16.1 (1968): 15–31.
13. Mary J. Dobson, *Contours of Death and Disease in Early Modern England* (Cambridge: Cambridge University Press, 1997); E. A. Wrigley and Roger Schofield, *The Population History of England, 1541–1871* (London: Edward Arnold, 1981). For droughts, see Rudolf Brázdil et al., "Documentary Data and the Study of Past Droughts," *Climate of the Past* 14 (2018): 1915–1960.
14. Dobson, *Contours of Death and Disease*. See especially her chronology of epidemic disease and mortality, 383–449: the discussion of the years 1678–1683 is taken from 415–419. For European pandemics, see J. K. Taubenberger and D. M. Morens, "Pandemic Influenza—Including a Risk Assessment of H5N1," *Revue Scientifique et Technique* 28 (2009): 187–202; Pavla Jirkova, "Plague Year 1680 in Central Europe," in A. T. Brown, Andy Burn, and Rob Doherty, eds., *Crises in Economic and Social History: A Comparative Perspective* (Woodbridge, UK: Boydell Press, 2015). For Persia, see Andrew Newman, *Safavid Iran* (New York: Bloomsbury, 2006), 94.

15. Fagan, *Little Ice Age*, 105. Clive A. Spinage, *Cattle Plague: A History* (New York: Kluwer/Plenum, 2003); Karen Ordahl Kupperman, "The Puzzle of American Climate in the Early Colonial Period," *American Historical Review* 87 (1982): 1262–1289; and also Kupperman, "Climate and Mastery of the Wilderness in Seventeenth-Century New England," Colonial Society of Massachusetts, at https://www.colonialsociety.org/node/1742. For Sewall, see *Diary of Samuel Sewall* (Boston: Massachusetts Historical Society, 1878), 5:479. For Scotland, see Rosanne D'Arrigo et al., "Complexity in Crisis: The Volcanic Cold Pulse of the 1690s and the Consequences of Scotland's Failure to Cope," *Journal of Volcanology and Geothermal Research* 389 (2020).
16. Frank Tallett, *War and Society in Early Modern Europe: 1495–1715* (London: Routledge, 1997); Mark Kishlansky, *The Penguin History of Britain: A Monarchy Transformed*, sixth edition (London: Penguin, 1997); Julian Hoppit, *A Land of Liberty? England, 1689–1727* (Oxford: Clarendon Press, 2000); Tim Harris, *Revolution: The Great Crisis of the British Monarchy, 1685–1720* (London: Allen Lane, 2006); James B. Collins, *The State in Early Modern France*, second edition (New York: Cambridge University Press, 2009). For the English political crisis, see Geoffrey Holmes, "The Sacheverell Riots: The Crowd and the Church in Early Eighteenth-Century London," *Past and Present* 72 (1976): 55–85.
17. Michael Davies and W. R. Owens, eds., *The Oxford Handbook of John Bunyan* (Oxford: Oxford University Press, 2018).
18. Ronald Stoyan, *Atlas of Great Comets* (Cambridge: Cambridge University Press, 2015).
19. For "The Devil, the Turk, and the Comet," see Edwin Emerson, *Comet Lore: Halley's Comet in History and Astronomy* (New York: Schilling Press, 1910); Robert Law, *Memorialls: Or, The Memorable Things That Fell Out Within This Island of Brittain from 1638 to 1684* (Edinburgh: A. Constable, 1818), 170.
20. Bayle is quoted from *Various Thoughts on the Occasion of a Comet, by Pierre Bayle*, ed. Robert C. Bartlett (Albany: State University of New York Press, 2000), 13. Blom, *Nature's Mutiny*, 188; Pierre Bayle, *Miscellaneous Reflections, Occasion'd by the Comet Which Appear'd in December 1680: . . . Written to a Doctor of the Sorbon, by Mr. Bayle. Translated from the French. To Which Is Added, the Author's Life*, 2 vols. (London: Printed for J. Morphew, 1708). For Evelyn, see *Diary and Correspondence of John Evelyn, F.R.S.* (London: H. G. Bohn, 1862), 2:163.
21. Roy Porter, *Enlightenment: Britain and the Creation of the Modern World*, new edition (London: Allen Lane, 2001); Warren Johnston, *Revelation Restored: The Apocalypse in Later Seventeenth-Century England* (Woodbridge, UK: Boydell Press, 2011); Douglas Hedley and David Leech, eds., *Revisioning Cambridge Platonism* (Cham, Switzerland: Springer, 2019); Henry More, *A Plain and Continued Exposition of the Several Prophecies or Divine Visions of the Prophet Daniel Which Have or May Concern the People of God, Whether Jew or Christian* (London, 1681).
22. Johannes Kelpius, *The Diarium of Magister Johannes Kelpius*, ed. Julius F. Sachse (University Park: Pennsylvania State University Press, 2012).
23. Martin Gierl, *Pietismus und Aufklärung: theologische Polemik und die Kommunikationsreform der Wissenschaft am Ende des 17. Jahrhunderts* (Göttingen:

Vandenhoeck and Ruprecht, 1997); Douglas H. Shantz, *An Introduction to German Pietism: Protestant Renewal at the Dawn of Modern Europe* (Baltimore: Johns Hopkins University Press, 2013); Ulrich L. Lehner, Richard A. Muller, and A. G. Roeber, eds., *The Oxford Handbook of Early Modern Theology, 1600–1800* (New York: Oxford University Press, 2016); Jonathan Strom, *German Pietism and the Problem of Conversion* (University Park: Pennsylvania State University Press, 2018).

24. Lucinda Martin, "Female Reformers as the Gatekeepers of Pietism," *Monatshefte* 95.1 (2003): 33–58; Jonathan Strom, ed., *Pietism and Community in Europe and North America, 1650–1850* (Leiden: Brill, 2010).
25. Jonathan Barry, *Witchcraft and Demonology in South-West England, 1640–1789* (Basingstoke, UK: Palgrave Macmillan, 2012).
26. Per Sörlin, *"Wicked Arts": Witchcraft and Magic Trials in Southern Sweden, 1635–1754* (Leiden: Brill, 1998).
27. Brian P. Levack, ed., *The Oxford Handbook of Witchcraft in Early Modern Europe and Colonial America* (Oxford: Oxford University Press, 2013). For the larger contexts of the Salem affair, see Ben Hughes, *Apocalypse 1692: Empire, Slavery, and the Great Port Royal Earthquake* (Yardley, PA: Westholme, 2017).
28. For the Sadducees, see Acts 23:8. Joseph Glanvill, *Saducismus Triumphatus, Or, Full and Plain Evidence Concerning Witches and Apparitions in Two Parts: The First Treating of Their Possibility, the Second of Their Real Existence* (London: Printed for J. Collins and S. Lownds, 1681); Cotton Mather, *The Wonders of the Invisible World* (Boston: Benjamin Harris, 1693).
29. Philip Benedict, *The Faith and Fortunes of France's Huguenots, 1600–85* (Aldershot, UK: Ashgate, 2001); Diarmaid MacCulloch, *The Reformation* (New York: Viking, 2004); Carlos M. N. Eire, *Reformations: The Early Modern World, 1450–1650* (New Haven, CT: Yale University Press, 2016).
30. Benedict, *The Faith and Fortunes of France's Huguenots*; Geoffrey Treasure, *The Huguenots* (New Haven, CT: Yale University Press, 2013); Joseph Bergin, *The Politics of Religion in Early Modern France* (New Haven, CT: Yale University Press, 2014); Josephine Wilkinson, *Louis XIV: The Power and the Glory* (New York: Pegasus Books, 2019).
31. For "missionary dragoons," see, for instance, *Le Dragon Missionaire, Or, The Dragoon Turn'd Apostle: Being a Dialaogue Between a French Protestant-Gentleman, and a French Dragoon, Wherein the New-Way of Convverting Hereticks by Dragoons Is Very Lively and Truly Represented* (London, 1686); W. Gregory Monahan, *Let God Arise: The War and Rebellion of the Camisards* (Oxford: Oxford University Press, 2014); Carolyn Chappell Lougee, *Facing the Revocation: Huguenot Families, Faith, and the King's Will* (New York: Oxford University Press, 2016).
32. "Squalled most hideously" is from John Miller, *After the Civil Wars: English Politics and Government in the Reign of Charles II* (London: Routledge, 2014), 75; Mark Knights, *Politics and Opinion in Crisis, 1678–81* (New York: Cambridge University Press, 1994); David Lemmings and Claire Walker, eds., *Moral Panics, the Media and the Law in Early Modern England* (New York: Palgrave Macmillan, 2009); Peter Hinds, *The Horrid Popish Plot: Roger L'Estrange and the Circulation of Political Discourse in*

Late Seventeenth-Century London (New York: Oxford University Press, 2010); Janet Clare, ed., *From Republic to Restoration: Legacies and Departures* (Manchester, UK: Manchester University Press, 2018).

33. Grant Tapsell, *The Personal Rule of Charles II, 1681–85* (Woodbridge, UK: Boydell Press, 2007).
34. David L. Smith, *A History of the Modern British Isles, 1603–1707* (Oxford: Blackwell, 1998); Allan I. MacInnes, *The British Revolution, 1629–1660* (London: Palgrave Macmillan, 2005); Michael Braddick, *God's Fury, England's Fire* (London: Penguin, 2009).
35. Cadoc Leighton, "Apocalyptic and History Among the Later Covenanters," *Archivium Hibernicum* 68 (2015): 312–332; Allan I. MacInnes, *A History of Scotland* (London: Red Globe Press, 2019).
36. Geoffrey Holmes, *The Making of a Great Power: Late Stuart and Early Georgian Britain, 1660–1722* (New York: Longman, 1993); James B. Collins, *The State in Early Modern France,* second edition (New York: Cambridge University Press, 2009); Cesare Cuttica and Glenn Burgess, eds., *Monarchism and Absolutism in Early Modern Europe* (London: Routledge, 2015).
37. Robert Warren Anderson, Noel D. Johnson, and Mark Koyama, "Jewish Persecutions and Weather Shocks: 1100–1800," *Economic Journal* 127 (2017): 924–958.
38. Joachim Whaley, *Germany and the Holy Roman Empire*, 2 vols. (Oxford: Oxford University Press, 2013).
39. David Onnekink, *War and Religion After Westphalia, 1648–1713* (London: Routledge, 2016); N. F. Dreisziger, *Church and Society in Hungary and the Hungarian Diaspora* (Toronto: University of Toronto Press, 2016); A. Wess Mitchell, *The Grand Strategy of the Habsburg Empire* (Princeton, NJ: Princeton University Press, 2018).
40. Josephine Wilkinson, *Louis XIV: The Power and the Glory* (New York: Pegasus Books, 2019).
41. Andrew Wheatcroft, *The Enemy at the Gate: Habsburgs, Ottomans and the Battle for Europe* (New York: Basic Books, 2009).
42. Wheatcroft, *The Enemy at the Gate*; Parker, *Global Crisis*, 209.
43. Increase Mather, *An Essay for the Recording of Illustrious Providences: Wherein, An Account Is Given of Many Remarkable and Very Memorable Events, Which Have Happened in This Last Age; Especially in New-England* (Boston, 1684); Cotton Mather, *Brontologia Sacra: The Voice of the Glorious God in the Thunder* (London: John Astwood, 1695).
44. Samuel G. Drake, ed., *The History of King Philip's War by the Rev. Increase Mather, D.D. Also, A History of the Same War, by the Rev. Cotton Mather,* D.D. (Albany, NY: Printed for the editor, 1862); Lisa Brooks, *Our Beloved Kin: A New History of King Philip's War* (New Haven, CT: Yale University Press, 2018). For Bacon's Rebellion, see Stephen Saunders Webb, *1676, The End of American Independence* (New York: Knopf, 1984); James D. Rice, *Tales from a Revolution: Bacon's Rebellion and the Transformation of Early America* (New York: Oxford University Press, 2012). "Hailstorms, floods, dry spells, and hurricanes" is from "Bacon's Rebellion," National Park Service, https://www.nps.gov/jame/learn/historyculture/bacons-rebellion.htm.

45. David J. Weber, ed., *What Caused the Pueblo Revolt of 1680?* (Boston: Bedford/ St. Martin's, 1999). Charles Wilson Hackett, ed., *Historical Documents Relating to New Mexico, Nueva Vizacaya and Approaches Thereto in 1773,* 3 vols. (Washington, DC: Carnegie Institute of Washington, 1923–1937).
46. David Roberts, *The Pueblo Revolt: The Secret Rebellion That Drove the Spaniards Out of the Southwest* (New York: Simon and Schuster, 2004); Michael V. Wilcox, *The Pueblo Revolt and the Mythology of Conquest* (Berkeley: University of California Press, 2009).
47. Jerry H. Bentley, Sanjay Subrahmanyam, and Merry E. Wiesner-Hanks, eds., *The Cambridge World History,* Volume 6, *The Construction of a Global World, 1400–1800 CE* (Cambridge: Cambridge University Press, 2015).
48. M. Boucher, *French Speakers at the Cape in the First Hundred Years of Dutch East India Company Rule,* second edition (Pretoria: University of South Africa, 1983).
49. Jon Butler, *The Huguenots in America: A Refugee People in New World Society* (Cambridge, MA: Harvard University Press, 1992); Bertrand Van Ruymbeke and Randy J. Sparks, eds., *Memory and Identity: The Huguenots in France and the Atlantic Diaspora* (Columbia: University of South Carolina Press, 2003); Catharine Randall, *From a Far Country: Camisards and Huguenots in the Atlantic World* (Athens: University of Georgia Press, 2009).
50. Laura Brennan, *The Duke of Monmouth: Life and Rebellion* (Havertown, PA: Pen and Sword History, 2018).
51. Andrew R. Murphy, *William Penn: A Life* (New York: Oxford University Press, 2019).
52. William I. Hull, *William Penn and the Dutch Quaker Migration to Pennsylvania* (Swarthmore, PA: Swarthmore College, 1935); Philip S. Klein and Ari Hoogenboom, *A History of Pennsylvania,* second edition (University Park: Pennsylvania State University Press, 1980); Randall M. Miller and William A. Pencak, *Pennsylvania: A History of the Commonwealth* (University Park: Pennsylvania State University Press, 2002).
53. David Hackett Fischer, *Albion's Seed: Four British Folkways in America* (New York: Oxford University Press, 1989); Thomas S. Kidd and Barry Hankins, *Baptists in America* (New York: Oxford University Press, 2015).
54. William Harrison Taylor, *Unity in Christ and Country: American Presbyterians in the Revolutionary Era, 1758–1801* (Tuscaloosa: University of Alabama Press, 2017).
55. Stephanie Grauman Wolf, *Urban Village: Population, Community, and Family Structure in Germantown, Pennsylvania, 1683–1800* (Princeton, NJ: Princeton University Press, 1976); Miller and Pencak, *Pennsylvania.*
56. Kelpius, *Diarium*; Patrick M. Erben, *A Harmony of the Spirits: Translation and the Language of Community in Early Pennsylvania* (Chapel Hill: University of North Carolina Press, 2013).
57. John D. Roth, ed., *Letters of the Amish Division: A Sourcebook* (Goshen, IN: Mennonite Historical Society, 1993).

Chapter 7

1. "The great crowds of these orthodox, letter-learned, and regular Pharisees" is quoted from Gilbert Tennent, *The Danger of an Unconverted Ministry* (Philadelphia: Benjamin

Franklin, 1740), 4; Jonathan Edwards, *The Works of Jonathan Edwards: Sermons and Discourses, 1739–1742,* ed. Harry S. Stout and Nathan O. Hatch with Kyle P. Farley (New Haven, CT: Yale University Press, 2003); George M. Marsden, *Jonathan Edwards* (New Haven, CT: Yale University Press, 2003); Thomas S. Kidd, *The Great Awakening: The Roots of Evangelical Christianity in Colonial America* (New Haven, CT: Yale University Press, 2007); Wilson H. Kimnach, Caleb J. D. Maskell, and Kenneth P. Minkema, eds., *Jonathan Edwards's Sinners in the Hands of an Angry God: A Casebook* (New Haven, CT: Yale University Press, 2010); Jonathan M. Yeager, ed., *Early Evangelicalism: A Reader* (New York: Oxford University Press, 2013).

2. Brian Fagan, *The Little Ice Age: How Climate Made History, 1300–1850* (New York: Basic Books, 2000).
3. "Largest Eruptions Since 1400 AD," http://volcano.oregonstate.edu/book/export/html/227. W. G. Hoskins, "Harvest Fluctuations and English Economic History, 1620–1759," *Agricultural History Review* 16.1 (1968): 15–31.
4. Timo Myllyntaus is quoted from "Summer Frost," in Christof Mauch and Christian Pfister, eds., *Natural Disasters, Cultural Responses* (Lanham, MD: Lexington Books, 2009), 77–102. For "the coldest day," see G. T. Gwilliam, "Frost of 1739–40," *Symons's Meteorological Magazine* 20 (1885): 71–73; John D. Post, *Food Shortage, Climatic Variability, and Epidemic Disease in Pre-Industrial Europe: The Mortality Peak in the Early 1740s* (Ithaca, NY: Cornell University Press, 1985), 60–61; "New Drought Atlas Maps 2,000 Years of Climate in Europe: Completes the First Big-Picture View Across Northern Hemisphere," Earth Institute, Columbia University, November 6, 2015, at https://www.earth.columbia.edu/articles/view/3264.
5. John D. Meredith, "The Yaqui Rebellion of 1740: A Jesuit Account and Its Implications," *Ethnohistory* 22.3 (1975): 222–261.
6. Post, *Food Shortage*; John Walter, Roger Schofield, and Andrew B. Appleby, eds., *Famine, Disease and the Social Order in Early Modern Society* (Cambridge: Cambridge University Press, 1989).
7. Mary J. Dobson, *Contours of Death and Disease in Early Modern England* (Cambridge: Cambridge University Press, 1997), 432–434.
8. "Multitudes have perished" is quoted from Charles Creighton, *History of Epidemics in Britain* (Cambridge: Cambridge University Press, 1891–1894), ii:229; David Dickson, *Arctic Ireland: The Extraordinary Story of the Great Frost and Forgotten Famine of 1740–41* (Belfast: White Row Press, 1997); Ian McBride, *Eighteenth-Century Ireland: The Isle of Slaves* (Dublin: Gill and Macmillan, 2009); S. Engler, J. Luterbacher, F. Mauelshagen, and J. Werner, "The Irish Famine of 1740–1741: Causes and Effects," *Climate of the Past* 9 (2013): 1013–1052. The quotation is from Lucy Collins, "The Frosty Winters of Ireland," *Journal of Ecocriticism* 5.2 (2013): 1–11. For the panzootic, see Clive A. Spinage, *Cattle Plague: A History* (New York: Kluwer/Plenum, 2003).
9. Ted Steinberg, *Down to Earth: Nature's Role in American History,* third edition (New York: Oxford University Press, 2013); Thomas L. Purvis, *Colonial America to 1763* (New York: Facts on File, 1993), 1–3.
10. Wilkins Updike and Daniel Goodwin, *A History of the Episcopal Church in Narragansett, Rhode Island: Including a History of Other Episcopal Churches in the State,* second edition (Boston: Merrymount Press, 1907), 186–199, at 199.

11. Joshua Coffin, *A Sketch of the History of Newbury, Newburyport, and West Newbury, from 1635 to 1845* (Boston: Samuel G. Drake, 1845), 209.
12. Hans DePold, "So Cold, the Rich Had to Beg," Bolton (CT) Historical Society, December 1999, at http://www.boltoncthistory.org/socold.html.
13. "Pennsylvania Weather Records, 1644–1835," *Pennsylvania Magazine of History and Biography* 15 (1891): 111–112.
14. DePold, "So Cold, the Rich Had to Beg,"
15. Updike and Goodwin, *A History of the Episcopal Church in Narragansett*, 194.
16. Updike and Goodwin, *A History of the Episcopal Church in Narragansett*, 195.
17. James MacSparran, *America Dissected* (Dublin: S. Powell, 1753).
18. Mark M. Smith, ed., *Stono: Documenting and Interpreting a Southern Slave Revolt* (Columbia: University of South Carolina Press, 2005).
19. Daniel Horsmanden, *The New York Conspiracy Trials of 1741: Daniel Horsmanden's Journal of the Proceedings with Related Documents*, ed. Serena R. Zabin (Boston: Bedford/St. Martins, 2004); Jill Lepore, *New York Burning: Liberty, Slavery, and Conspiracy in Eighteenth-Century Manhattan* (New York: Alfred A. Knopf, 2005).
20. "What then could prompt you" is quoted in Kenneth T. Jackson and David S. Dunbar, eds., *Empire City: New York Through the Centuries* (New York: Columbia University Press, 2002), 66.
21. John Brewer, *The Sinews of Power: War, Money, and the English State, 1688–1783* (Cambridge, MA: Harvard University Press, 1990); James B. Collins, *The State in Early Modern France*, second edition (New York: Cambridge University Press, 2009); Christopher Storrs, ed., *The Fiscal-Military State in Eighteenth-Century Europe* (London: Routledge, 2016).
22. Wilfrid Prest, *Albion Ascendant: English History, 1660–1815* (New York: Oxford University Press, 1998); P. J. Marshall, *A Free Though Conquering People: Eighteenth-Century Britain and Its Empire* (Aldershot, UK: Ashgate, 2003); Hannah Smith, *Georgian Monarchy: Politics and Culture, 1714–1760* (Cambridge: Cambridge University Press, 2006).
23. Catherine-Laurence Maire, *Les convulsionnaires de Saint-Médard: miracles, convulsions et prophéties à Paris au XVIIIe siècle* (Paris: Gallimard, 1985); Peter R. Campbell, *Power and Politics in Old Regime France, 1720–1745* (New York: Routledge, 1996); Brian E. Strayer, *Suffering Saints: Jansenists and Convulsionnaires in France, 1640–1799* (Portland, OR: Sussex Academic Press, 2008); Mita Choudhury, *The Wanton Jesuit and the Wayward Saint: A Tale of Sex, Religion, and Politics in Eighteenth-Century France* (University Park: Pennsylvania State University Press, 2015).
24. William Doyle, ed., *The Oxford Handbook of the Ancien Régime* (Oxford: Oxford University Press, 2012).
25. Paul Langford, *A Polite and Commercial People: England, 1727–1783* (New York: Oxford University Press, 1989); Paul Langford, ed., *The Eighteenth Century: 1688–1815* (New York: Oxford University Press, 2002); Jan Golinski, *British Weather and the Climate of Enlightenment* (Chicago: University of Chicago Press, 2007); Elaine Chalus and Perry Gauci, eds., *Revisiting the Polite and Commercial People* (Oxford: Oxford University Press, 2019).

26. *Miscellaneous Reflections, Occasion'd by the Comet Which Appear'd in December 1680: . . . Written to a Doctor of the Sorbon, by Mr. Bayle* (London: J. Morphew, 1708); A *Dissertation on Comets: Proving That the Vulgar, and Long-Received Notion, That They Either Cause or Foreshew Public Calamities, Is Unphilosophical, Absurd, and Irreligious. Being the Substance of the Celebrated Mr Bayle's Reflections on That Subject, Occasioned by the Great Comet in 1680, and Revived with a View to That Which Has Lately Appeared in a Letter to a Reverend Professor to Which Is Prefixed, The Theory of a Comet, as Given by Sir Isaac Newton and His Followers* (London: Printed for J. Mechell, c. 1750); Anthony Gottlieb, *The Dream of Enlightenment* (New York: Liveright, 2016).
27. Clarke Garrett, *Spirit Possession and Popular Religion: From the Camisards to the Shakers* (Baltimore: Johns Hopkins University Press, 1987); Jim Smyth, *The Making of the United Kingdom, 1660–1800: State, Religion and Identity in Britain and Ireland* (New York: Longman, 2001); Philip Jenkins, "Unenthusiastic About Enthusiasm," *Christian History*, March 2009, at http://www.christianitytoday.com/global/printer.html?/ch/bytopic/movementsdenominationstraditions/unenthusiasticabout.html.
28. Brian P. Levack, ed., *The Oxford Handbook of Witchcraft in Early Modern Europe and Colonial America* (Oxford: Oxford University Press, 2013); Michael Hunter, *The Decline of Magic: Britain in the Enlightenment* (New Haven, CT: Yale University Press, 2020).
29. Owen Davies, "Methodism, the Clergy, and the Popular Belief in Witchcraft and Magic," *History* 82 (1997): 252–265.
30. Thomas S. Kidd, *George Whitefield: America's Spiritual Founding Father* (New Haven, CT: Yale University Press, 2014); Geordan Hammond, *John Wesley in America: Restoring Primitive Christianity* (Oxford: Oxford University Press, 2014).
31. Jonathan Strom, ed., *Pietism and Community in Europe and North America, 1650–1850* (Leiden: Brill, 2010).
32. Milton J. Coalter Jr., *Gilbert Tennent, Son of Thunder* (New York: Greenwood Press, 1986); Jacobus Frelinghuysen, *Forerunner of the Great Awakening: Sermons by Theodorus Jacobus Frelinghuysen (1691–1747)*, ed. Joel R. Beeke (Grand Rapids, MI: W. B. Eerdmans, 2000); *Jonathan Edwards: Writings from the Great Awakening*, ed. Philip F. Gura (New York: Library of America, 2013); Jonathan Edwards, *A Faithful Narrative of the Surprising Work of God in the Conversion of Many Hundred Souls in Northampton* (1737), online text at https://www.jonathan-edwards.org/Narrative.html. C. C. Goen, ed., *Jonathan Edwards: The Great Awakening* (New Haven, CT: Yale University Press, 1972).
33. Kidd, *George Whitefield*; J. D. Dickey, *American Demagogue: The Great Awakening and the Rise and Fall of Populism* (New York: Pegasus Books, 2019).
34. "We went down in the Stream" is from Ellen Douglas Larned, *Historic Gleanings in Windham County, Connecticut* (Providence, RI: Preston and Rounds, 1899), 14–15. "A great and general awakening" is from David Brainerd, referring originally to Yale, but the phenomenon soon spread throughout the region: Jonathan Edwards, *An Account of the Life of the Late Reverend Mr. David Brainerd, Minister of the Gospel, Missionary to the Indians, from the Honourable Society in Scotland, for the Propagation of Christian Knowledge, and Pastor of a Church of Christian Indians in New-Jersey* (Boston: Printed for and sold by D. Henchman, in Cornhill, 1749).

35. "The reverend George Whitefield preached" is from Coffin, *A Sketch of the History of Newbury, Newburyport, and West Newbury*, 209. Isaac Backus, *The Diary of Isaac Backus*, ed. William G. McLoughlin (Providence, RI: Brown University Press, 1979).
36. "A very lamentable decay of religious affections" is from Edwards's much quoted December 1743 letter to Boston minister Thomas Prince, in Jonathan Edwards, *A Narrative of Surprising Conversions* (Lafayette, IN: Sovereign Grace, 2001), 101. See also Douglas Leo Winiarski, *Darkness Falls on the Land of Light: Experiencing Religious Awakenings in Eighteenth-Century New England* (Chapel Hill: University of North Carolina Press, 2017).
37. "Jonathan Edwards: On the Great Awakening," http://www.nhinet.org/ccs/docs/awaken.htm.
38. The anti-revivalist here is Ebenezer Kinnersley, quoted from Kidd and Hankins, *Baptists in America*, 25. Charles Chauncy, *Seasonable Thoughts on the State of Religion in New England* (Boston: Rogers and Fowle, 1743).
39. Edwards, *An Account of the Life of the Late Reverend Mr. David Brainerd.* Dwight is quoted from *The Conquest of Canäan: A Poem, in Eleven Books* (Hartford, CT: Elisha Babcock, 1785); Michael P. Winship, *Hot Protestants: A History of Puritanism in England and America* (New Haven, CT: Yale University Press, 2019).
40. Kidd, *Great Awakening.*
41. Quoted in Frederick Courtney, *The Commemorative Discourses in Observance of the Centennial Year of the Church in the Diocese of Massachusetts: A. D. 1885* (Boston: The Convention, 1885), 28–29.
42. Kidd, *Great Awakening; The Reverend Mr. James Davenport's Confession and Retractations* (Boston: S. Kneeland and T. Green, 1744). For Davenport's "faculties," see Bryan F. LeBeau, *Jonathan Dickinson and the Formative Years of American Presbyterianism* (Louisville: University Press of Kentucky, 1997), 133.
43. Keith Edward Beebe, ed., *The McCulloch Examinations of the Cambuslang Revival (1742)* (Woodbridge, UK: Boydell Press, 2013).
44. T. M. Devine, *To the Ends of the Earth: Scotland's Global Diaspora, 1750–2010* (Washington, DC: Smithsonian Books, 2011); Judith Ridner, *The Scots Irish of Early Pennsylvania* (Philadelphia: Temple University Press, 2018). This story has a personal resonance. I lived for many years in Centre County, PA, the home of Penn State University. The area's first white discoverer and settler was James Potter, whose Scots-Irish family left County Tyrone, in Northern Ireland, precisely in the hunger year of 1741. General Potter was also a pioneer of the Presbyterian churches in that area of Pennsylvania.
45. William G. McLoughlin, *Revivals, Awakening and Reform* (Chicago: University of Chicago Press, 2013).

Chapter 8

1. William K. Klingaman and Nicholas P. Klingaman, *The Year Without Summer: 1816 and the Volcano That Darkened the World and Changed History* (New York: St. Martin's, 2013); Gillen D'Arcy Wood, *Tambora: The Eruption That Changed the*

World (Princeton, NJ: Princeton University Press, 2014); Christian Pfister and Sam White, "A Year Without a Summer 1816," in Sam White, Christian Pfister, and Franz Mauelshagen, eds., *The Palgrave Handbook of Climate History* (London: Palgrave, 2018), 551–561.

2. Bacon is quoted from *The Works of Francis Bacon*, Volume 1 (1884), XXXVIII, "Of Nature in Men." William F. Ruddiman, *Plows, Plagues, and Petroleum: How Humans Took Control of Climate* (Princeton, NJ: Princeton University Press, 2005); Simon L. Lewis and Mark A. Maslin, *The Human Planet: How We Created the Anthropocene* (New Haven, CT: Yale University Press, 2018).
3. For Gilbert White, see *The Natural History and Antiquities of Selborne* (London: George Routledge and Sons, 1891), 281. For the extreme cold at the turn of the century, see Lorin Blodget, *Climatology of the United States* (Lippincott, 1857), 146; G. R. Demaree and A. E. J. Ogilvie, "*Bons Baisers d'Islande*: Climatic, Environmental, and Human Dimensions Impacts of the *Lakagjgar* Eruption (1783–1784) in Iceland," in P. D. Jones, A. E. J. Ogilvie, T. D. Davies, and K. R. Briffas, *History and Climate: Memories of the Future* (New York: Springer, 2001), 219–246; Charles Q. Choi, "Iceland Volcano Cleared in Case in Extreme Winter of 1783–84," LiveScience, April 13, 2011, https://www.livescience.com/30325-iceland-volcano-laki-eruption-cold-winter.html; Alexandra Witze and Jeff Kanipe, *Island on Fire: The Extraordinary Story of a Forgotten Volcano That Changed the World* (New York: Pegasus Books, 2015).
4. Richard H. Grove, "Global Impact of the 1789–93 El Niño," *Nature* 393 (1998): 318–319; Richard H. Grove, "The Great El Niño of 1789–93 and Its Global Consequences," *Medieval History Journal* 10 (2006); Choi, "Iceland Volcano Cleared in Case in Extreme Winter of 1783–84"; Richard Grove and George Adamson, "The 'Great El Niño,' 1790–1794," in Richard Grove and George Adamson, *El Niño in World History* (London: Palgrave Macmillan, 2018), 81–92.
5. For the extreme cold at the turn of the century, see Lorin Blodget, *Climatology of the United States* (Philadelphia: Lippincott, 1857), 146–148; Vinita Damodaran et al., "The 1780s: Global Climate Anomalies, Floods, Droughts, and Famines," in Sam White, Christian Pfister, and Franz Mauelshagen, eds., *The Palgrave Handbook of Climate History* (London: Palgrave Macmillan, 2018), 517–550.
6. Jonathan I. Israel, *Democratic Enlightenment: Philosophy, Revolution, and Human Rights, 1750–1790* (New York: Oxford University Press, 2011); William Doyle, ed., *The Oxford Handbook of the Ancien Régime* (Oxford: Oxford University Press, 2012).
7. Nathan O. Hatch, *The Democratization of American Christianity* (New Haven, CT: Yale University Press, 1989).
8. Simon Schama, *Citizens: A Chronicle of the French Revolution* (New York: Knopf, 1989); Reynald Secher, *A French Genocide: The Vendée* (Notre Dame, IN: University of Notre Dame Press, 2003).
9. Blodget, *Climatology of the United States*, 146–148; Conevery Bolton Valencius, *The Lost History of the New Madrid Earthquakes* (Chicago: University of Chicago Press, 2013). For the associated revivals, see Walter Brownlow Posey, "The Earthquake of 1811 and Its Influence on Evangelistic Methods in the Churches of the Old South," *Tennessee Historical Magazine* 1.2 (1931): 107–114; Tom Kanon, "Scared from Their

Sins for a Season: The Religious Ramifications of the New Madrid Earthquakes, 1811–1812," *Ohio Valley History* 5.2 (2005): 21–38.

10. John D. Post, *The Last Great Subsistence Crisis in the Western World* (Baltimore: Johns Hopkins University Press, 1977); Patrick Webb, "Emergency Relief During Europe's Famine of 1817," *Journal of Nutrition* 132.7 (2002): 2092S–2095S.
11. Boyd Hilton, *A Mad, Bad, and Dangerous People? England 1783–1846* (Oxford: Oxford University Press, 2006); Shuji Cao, Yushang Li, and Bin Yang, "Mount Tambora, Climatic Changes, and China's Decline in the Nineteenth Century," *Journal of World History* 23.3 (2012): 587–607.
12. Richard J. Evans, *Death in Hamburg: Society and Politics in the Cholera Years, 1830–1910* (Oxford: Oxford University Press, 1987); Charles E. Rosenberg, *The Cholera Years: The United States in 1832, 1849, and 1866* (Chicago: University of Chicago Press, 1962); Steven Johnson, *The Ghost Map: The Story of London's Most Terrifying Epidemic and How It Changed Science, Cities, and the Modern World* (New York: Riverhead Books, 2006).
13. Byron's "Darkness" is quoted from https://poets.org/poem/darkness.
14. Kenneth J. Stewart, *Restoring the Reformation: British Evangelicalism and the Francophone "Réveil," 1816–1849* (Milton Keynes, UK: Paternoster, 2006).
15. The quotations are from Milton V. Backman Jr., "Awakenings in the Burned-Over District," in Samuel Alonzo Dodge and Steven C. Harper, eds., *Exploring the First Vision* (Provo, UT: Religious Studies Center, 2012), 171–197; Whitney R. Cross, *The Burned-Over District* (Ithaca, NY: Cornell University Press, 1950); Marianne Perciaccante, *Calling Down Fire: Charles Grandison Finney and Revivalism in Jefferson County, New York, 1800–1840* (Albany: State University of New York Press, 2003).
16. Book of Mormon: 3 Nephi 8:21–22. Also see, for instance, 1 Nephi 12:5, and many other passages.
17. David L. Rose, *God's Strange Work: William Miller and the End of the World* (Grand Rapids, MI: William B. Eerdmans, 2008).
18. But see Richard Grove and George Adamson, "The Influence of El Niño on World Crises in the Nineteenth Century," in Richard Grove and George Adamson, *El Niño in World History* (London: Palgrave Macmillan, 2018), 93–104.
19. Simon Winchester, *Krakatoa: The Day the World Exploded: August 27, 1883* (New York: HarperCollins, 2003).
20. Alfred Lord Tennyson, "Saint Telemachus," is quoted from https://www.telelib.com/authors/T/TennysonAlfred/verse/deathofoenone/telemachus.html.
21. For the culture and politics of the decade, see Jose Harris, *Private Lives, Public Spirit: Britain, 1870–1914* (Oxford: Oxford University Press, 1993).
22. Patrick L. Abbott, *Natural Disasters*, tenth edition (New York: McGraw-Hill, 2017).
23. Jan Null, "El Niño and La Niña Years and Intensities Based on Oceanic Niño Index (ONI)," Golden Gate Weather Services, 2020, at https://ggweather.com/enso/oni.htm.
24. J. R. McNeill, *Something New Under the Sun: An Environmental History of the Twentieth-Century World* (New York: W. W. Norton, 2000); Stefan Brönnimann, Sam White, and Victoria Slonosky, "Climate from 1800 to 1970 in North America and Europe," in Sam White, Christian Pfister, and Franz Mauelshagen, eds., *The Palgrave Handbook of Climate History* (London: Palgrave Macmillan, 2018).

25. "Agriculture: Occupational Employment and Wages," 2014, *Monthly Labor Review*, Bureau of Labor Statistics, https://www.bls.gov/opub/mlr/2014/article/agriculture-occupational-employment-and-wages.htm.
26. Evan D. G. Fraser and Andrew Rimas, *Empires of Food: Feast, Famine, and the Rise and Fall of Civilizations* (New York: Free Press, 2010).
27. Alexander Mercer, *Infections, Chronic Disease, and the Epidemiological Transition* (Rochester, NY: University of Rochester Press, 2014).
28. Declan Curran, Lubomyr Luciuk, and Andrew G. Newby, eds., *Famines in European Economic History: The Last Great European Famines Reconsidered* (London: Routledge, 2015); Alexander F. More, et al., "The Impact of a Six-Year Climate Anomaly on the Spanish Flu Pandemic and WWI," *GeoHealth* 4(9) (2020).
29. John M. Barry, *The Great Influenza* (New York: Viking, 2004); Simon Winchester, *A Crack in the Edge of the World: America and the Great California Earthquake of 1906* (New York: HarperCollins, 2005); Molly Caldwell Crosby, *The American Plague: The Untold Story of Yellow Fever, the Epidemic That Shaped Our History* (New York: Penguin, 2006); Stephen J. Pyne, *Between Two Fires: A Fire History of Contemporary America* (Tucson: University of Arizona Press, 2015); Stephen Long, *Thirty-Eight: The Hurricane That Transformed New England* (New Haven, CT: Yale University Press, 2016); Joanna L. Dyle, *Seismic City: An Environmental History of San Francisco's 1906 Earthquake* (Seattle: University of Washington Press, 2017); Susan Scott Parrish, *The Flood Year 1927: A Cultural History* (Princeton, NJ: Princeton University Press, 2017); Laura Spinney, *Pale Rider: The Spanish Flu of 1918 and How It Changed the World* (New York: Public Affairs, 2017); Cindy Ermus, ed., *Environmental Disaster in the Gulf South* (Baton Rouge: Louisiana State University Press, 2018); Eric Jay Dolin, *A Furious Sky: The Five-Hundred-Year History of America's Hurricanes* (New York: Liveright, 2020).
30. "A hideous record" is quoted from Mike Davis, *Late Victorian Holocausts: El Niño Famines and the Making of the Third World* (New York: Verso, 2001), 25; Charles Q. Choi, "History's Greatest El Niño May Have Caused Severe 19th-Century Famine," Inside Science, December 18, 2017, at https://www.insidescience.org/news/historys-greatest-el-ni%C3%B1o-may-have-caused-severe-19th-century-famine.
31. Bill Kte'pi, "Chinese Famine (1907)," in K. Bradley Penuel and Matt Statler, eds., *Encyclopedia of Disaster Relief* (Thousand Oaks, CA: Sage, 2010). Compare Chris Courtney, *The Nature of Disaster in China: The 1931 Yangzi River Flood* (New York: Cambridge University Press, 2018).
32. Felix Wemheuer, *A Social History of Maoist China: Conflict and Change, 1949–1976* (Cambridge: Cambridge University Press, 2019).

Chapter 9

1. Philip Shabecoff, "Global Warming Has Begun, Expert Tells Senate," *New York Times*, June 24, 1988, at https://www.nytimes.com/1988/06/24/us/global-warming-has-begun-expert-tells-senate.html.

2. J. R. McNeill and Peter Engelke, *The Great Acceleration: An Environmental History of the Anthropocene Since 1945* (Cambridge, MA: Belknap Press of Harvard University Press, 2016); Jeff Goodell, *The Water Will Come: Rising Seas, Sinking Cities, and the Remaking of the Civilized World* (New York: Little, Brown, 2017); Julian Cribb, *Food or War* (Cambridge: Cambridge University Press, 2019); Christiana Figueres and Tom Rivett-Carnac, *The Future We Choose: Surviving the Climate Crisis* (New York: Alfred A. Knopf, 2020).
3. John Tyndall, *Contributions to Molecular Physics in the Domain of Radiant Heat* (New York: D. Appleton, 1873), 424. For Tyndall, see Joshua P. Howe, ed., *Making Climate Change History: Primary Sources from Global Warming's Past* (Seattle: University of Washington Press, 2017); Hervé Le Treut et al., "Historical Overview of Climate Change Science," in *Climate Change 2007: The Physical Science Basis. Contribution of Working Group I to the Fourth Assessment Report of the Intergovernmental Panel on Climate Change* (Cambridge: Cambridge University Press, 2007), at https://www.ipcc.ch/report/ar4/wg1; Spencer R. Weart, *The Discovery of Global Warming,* revised and updated edition (Cambridge, MA: Harvard University Press, 2008); Syukuro Manabe and Anthony J. Broccoli, *Beyond Global Warming: How Numerical Models Revealed the Secrets of Climate Change* (Princeton, NJ: Princeton University Press, 2020).
4. Wallace S. Broecker, "Climatic Change: Are We on the Brink of a Pronounced Global Warming?," *Science* 189.4201 (1975): 460–463; "Another Ice Age?," *Time,* June 24, 1974.
5. *Summary for Policymakers of IPCC Special Report on Global Warming of 1.5°C Approved by Governments*, October 8, 2018, at https://www.ipcc.ch/2018/10/08/summary-for-policymakers-of-ipcc-special-report-on-global-warming-of-1-5c-approved-by-governments; Intergovernmental Panel on Climate Change, *Special Report on the Ocean and Cryosphere in a Changing Climate* (Geneva: Intergovernmental Panel on Climate Change, 2019), available at https://www.ipcc.ch.
6. Marc Morano, *The Politically Incorrect Guide to Climate Change* (Washington, DC: Regnery, 2018); James Lawrence Powell, *The Inquisition of Climate Science* (New York: Columbia University Press, 2011).
7. "Emissions Gap Report 2017—Executive Summary," A United Nations Environment Synthesis Report, UNEP, Geneva, 2017, at https://wedocs.unep.org/bitstream/handle/20.500.11822/22101/EGR_2017_ES.pdf.
8. Elizabeth Kolbert, "What Will Another Decade of Climate Crisis Bring?," *New Yorker*, January 5, 2020, at https://www.newyorker.com/magazine/2020/01/13/what-will-another-decade-of-climate-crisis-bring.
9. Edmond A. Mathez and Jason E. Smerdon, *Climate Change: The Science of Global Warming and Our Energy Future,* second edition (New York: Columbia University Press, 2018); Nicola Jones, "Redrawing the Map: How the World's Climate Zones Are Shifting," Yale Environment 360, October 23, 2018, at https://e360.yale.edu/features/redrawing-the-map-how-the-worlds-climate-zones-are-shifting; Pamela R. Grothe et al., "Enhanced El Niño–Southern Oscillation Variability in Recent Decades," *Geophysical Research Letters* 47.7 (2020); A. Park Williams et al., "Large Contribution

from Anthropogenic Warming to an Emerging North American Megadrought," *Science* 368 (2020): 314–318. For the loss of soil resources, see David R. Montgomery, *Dirt: The Erosion of Civilizations* (Berkeley: University of California Press, 2007).

10. Goodell, *The Water Will Come*; Vivien Gornitz, *Vanishing Ice: Glaciers, Ice Sheets, and Rising Seas* (New York: Columbia University Press, 2019).
11. For zoonotic diseases, see Ferris Jabr, "How Humanity Unleashed a Flood of New Diseases," *New York Times*, June 17, 2020; David Wallace-Wells, *The Uninhabitable Earth: Life After Warming* (London: Tim Duggan Books/Allen Lane, 2019). For a trenchant critique of "apocalyptic environmentalism," see Michael Shellenberger, *Apocalypse Never: Why Environmental Alarmism Hurts Us All* (New York: HarperCol lins, 2020).
12. "Could Climate Change Make Siberia Habitable for Humans?," Institute of Physics, June 6, 2019, at https://phys.org/news/2019-06-climate-siberia-habitable-humans.html. Greer is quoted from Edward Ksenych and David Liu, eds., *Conflict, Order and Action: Readings in Sociology* (Toronto: Canadian Scholars' Press, 2001), 38.
13. Richard T. Corlett, "Climate Change in the Tropics: The End of the World As We Know It?," *Biological Conservation* 151 (2012): 22–25; Chi Xu et al., "Future of the Human Climate Niche," *Proceedings of the National Academy of Sciences of the United States of America* 117.21 (2020): 11350–11355.
14. Philip Jenkins, *Fertility and Faith* (Waco, TX: Baylor University Press, 2020).
15. Richard Matthew, "Demography, Climate Change, and Conflict," in Jack A. Goldstone, Eric P. Kaufmann, and Monica Duffy Toft, eds., *Political Demography: How Population Changes Are Reshaping International Security and National Politics* (Boulder, CO: Paradigm, 2011), 113–147; Elliott D. Green, "Demographic Change and Conflict in Contemporary Africa," in Goldstone, Kaufmann, and Toft, eds., *Political Demography*, 252–266; John Updike, *Bech at Bay* (New York: Fawcett Books/Ballantine, 1999), 221.
16. Solomon M. Hsiang, Kyle C. Meng, and Mark A. Cane, "Civil Conflicts Are Associated with the Global Climate," *Nature* 476 (2011): 438–441; Jan Selby and Clemens Hoffmann, eds., *Rethinking Climate Change, Conflict and Security* (London: Routledge, 2017); Julian Cribb, *Food or War* (Cambridge: Cambridge University Press, 2019); "Heating Up: How Climate Change Can Fuel Wars," *Economist*, May 23, 2019. For earlier eras, compare Murat Iyigun, Nathan Nunn, and Nancy Qian, *Winter Is Coming: The Long-Run Effects of Climate Change on Conflict, 1400–1900* (Bonn, Germany: Institute of Labor Economics, 2017).
17. Caitlin E. Werrell and Francesco Femia, eds., *The Arab Spring and Climate Change* (Washington, DC: Center for American Progress, 2013); Andrew Freedman, "Global Warming Helped Trigger Syria's Bloody Civil War," Mashable, March 2, 2015, at https://mashable.com/2015/03/02/global-warming-syria-civil-war; Benjamin I. Cook et al., "Spatiotemporal Drought Variability in the Mediterranean over the Last 900 Years," *Journal of Geophysical Research* 121.5 (2016): 2060–2074.
18. Wolfgang Behringer, *Witches and Witch-Hunts: A Global History* (Cambridge: Polity Press, 2004).
19. Eliza Griswold, *The Tenth Parallel* (New York: Farrar, Straus and Giroux, 2010).

20. Sam Hill, "Black China: Africa's First Superpower Is Coming Sooner than You Think," *Newsweek*, January 15, 2020, at https://www.newsweek.com/2020/01/31/nigeria-next-superpower-1481949.html; H. Haider, *Climate Change in Nigeria: Impacts and Responses*, K4D Helpdesk Report 675 (Brighton, UK: Institute of Development Studies, 2019).
21. Ashley Dawson, *Extreme Cities: The Peril and Promise of Urban Life in the Age of Climate Change* (London: Verso, 2017); Andrew Slaughter and Nelson Odume, "It's Only Just Started, Flooding Is Going to Get a Lot Worse in Nigeria," *Quartz*, August 17, 2017, at https://qz.com/africa/1054825/climate-change-in-nigeria-floods-in-lagos-abuja-niger-delta-are-going-to-get-a-lot-worse.
22. *Climate Risk Profile: West Africa Sahel*, 2017, at https://www.climatelinks.org/resources/climate-change-risk-profile-west-africa-sahel; Joe Penney, "West Africa's Sahel Region Is Especially Vulnerable to Climate Change but Also Weak Governance," *Quartz*, October 1, 2019, at https://qz.com/africa/1719442/west-africas-sahel-vulnerable-to-climate-change-bad-governance; Janani Vivekananda et al., *Shoring Up Stability: Addressing Climate and Fragility Risks in the Lake Chad Region* (Berlin: Adelphi, 2019), at https://shoring-up-stability.org. For the larger region, see Ramzi Touchan et al., "Long Term Context for Recent Drought in Northwestern Africa," *Geophysical Research Letters* 35.13 (2008).
23. Lyse Doucet, "The Battle on the Frontline of Climate Change in Mali," BBC, January 22, 2019, at https://www.bbc.com/news/the-reporters-46921487.
24. Rahmane Idrissa, *The Politics of Islam in the Sahel: Between Persuasion and Violence* (New York: Routledge, 2017).
25. Serge Michailof, *Africanistan: Development or Jihad* (New Delhi: Oxford University Press, 2018).
26. Idrissa, *The Politics of Islam in the Sahel.*
27. Salvi Asefi-Najafabady, Karen L. Vandecar, Anton Seimon, Peter Lawrence, and Deborah Lawrence, "Climate Change, Population, and Poverty: Vulnerability and Exposure to Heat Stress in Countries Bordering the Great Lakes of Africa," *Climatic Change* 148 (2018): 561–573.
28. *An Assessment of the Impacts of Climate Change on the Great Lakes* (Chicago: Environmental Law and Policy Center, 2019).
29. Javier Puente, "Making Peru's Sendero Luminoso: The Geography and Ecology of Civil War," Age of Revolutions, March 29, 2017, at https://ageofrevolutions.com/2017/03/29/making-perus-sendero-luminoso-the-geography-ecology-of-civil-war; Shawn William Miller, *An Environmental History of Latin America* (New York: Cambridge University Press, 2007).
30. Philip Jenkins, *The Next Christendom*, third edition (New York: Oxford University Press, 2011).
31. Denise Lu and Christopher Flavelle, "Rising Seas Will Erase More Cities by 2050, New Research Shows," *New York Times*, October 29, 2019, at https://www.nytimes.com/interactive/2019/10/29/climate/coastal-cities-underwater.html.
32. Matt Simon, "Jakarta Is Sinking. Now Indonesia Has to Find a New Capital," Wired, May 2, 2019, at https://www.wired.com/story/jakarta-is-sinking; David Eckstein,

Marie-Lena Hutfils, and Maik Winges, *Global Climate Risk Index 2019: Who Suffers Most from Extreme Weather Events? Weather-Related Loss Events in 2017 and 1998 to 2017* (Bonn: GermanWatch, 2018).

33. Jenkins, *Next Christendom.*
34. Todd Miller, *Storming the Wall: Climate Change, Migration, and Homeland Security* (San Francisco: City Lights Books, 2017); Andrew Lebovich, *Halting Ambition: EU Migration and Security Policy in the Sahel*, European Council on Foreign Relations, September 2018, at https://www.ecfr.eu/publications/summary/halting_ambition_eu_migration_and_security_policy_in_the_sahel; Stephen Smith, *The Scramble for Europe: Young Africa on Its Way to the Old Continent* (Cambridge: Polity, 2019).
35. Dieter Gerten and Sigurd Bergmann, eds., *Religion in Environmental and Climate Change: Suffering, Values, Lifestyles* (London: Continuum, 2012); *Encyclical Letter Laudato Si of the Holy Father Francis on Care for Our Common Home,* https://laudatosi.com/watch.
36. Katharine Hayhoe and Andrew Farley, *A Climate for Change* (New York: FaithWords, 2009); Jim Ball, *Global Warming and the Risen Lord* (Washington, DC: Evangelical Environmental Network, 2010); Katharine Wilkinson, *Between God and Green* (New York: Oxford University Press, 2012); Gerten and Bergmann, eds., *Religion in Environmental and Climate Change*; Celia Deane-Drummond, Sigurd Bergmann, and Markus Vogt, eds., *Religion in the Anthropocene* (Eugene, OR: Wipf and Stock, 2017); Laura Hartman, ed., *That All May Flourish: Comparative Religious Environmental Ethics* (New York: Oxford University Press, 2018); Ernst M. Conradie and Hilda P. Koster, eds., *T&T Clark Handbook of Christian Theology and Climate Change* (London: T&T Clark, 2019). By no means all evangelicals share the new perspective. See Robin Globus Veldman, *The Gospel of Climate Skepticism: Why Evangelical Christians Oppose Action on Climate Change* (Oakland: University of California Press, 2019).
37. I discuss the decline of "cults" and New Age movements in Jenkins, *Fertility and Faith.*
38. Philip Jenkins, *The Great and Holy War* (San Francisco: HarperOne, 2014).
39. Rev 21:1. For distinctive readings of the Bible in the global South, see Philip Jenkins, *The New Faces of Christianity* (New York: Oxford University Press, 2006).

Conclusion

1. J. G. Ballard, *The Drowned World* (first published 1962. 50th anniversary edition, New York, Liveright, 2012), 29–30.

Index

For the benefit of digital users, indexed terms that span two pages (e.g., 52–53) may, on occasion, appear on only one of those pages.